Kabbalah Dictionary
Translation and explanation of terms and concepts of the Kabbalah

Rabbi Raphael Afilalo

From the same author:

The Kabbalah of the Ari Z'al, according to the Ramhal
Kabbalah Editions

La Kabbalah du Ari Z'al, selon le Ramhal
Ramhal Editions

Glossary of Kabbalah
Kabbalah Editions

Kabbalists and their works
Kabbalah Editions

160 Questions on the Kabbalah
Kabbalah Editions

Kabbalah concepts
Kabbalah Editions

www.kabbalah5.com

rav@kabbalah5.com

Publisher's Cataloging-in-Publication
Afilalo, Raphael
    Kabbalah Dictionary: Translation and explanation of terms and concepts of
the   Kabbalah / Raphael Afilalo
p.cm.
Includes bibliographical references and index.
ISBN 2-923241-02-9 (Hard cover)
1.Cabala. 2. Mysticism—Judaism. I. Afilalo, Raphael. II. Title.

BM525. BM723 2005
296.1'6   2005910075

To my wife Simona
and my children,
Miriam, Deborah and David

Approbations

MORDECHAI ELIAHU
FORMER CHIEF RABBI OF ISRAEL & RICHON LEZION

מרדכי אליהו

APPROBATION

[handwritten Hebrew text — largely illegible]

RABBI DAVID HANANIA PINTO
Rehov Bayit Vegan 97
Jerusalem • Israel
Tel: (972-2) 643 3695
Fax: (972-2) 541 2945 • 643 3570

ב"ה

בס"ד יום חמישי לסד "וישב" תשס"ז

שלום וברכה

המלצה

באתי בזאת להמליץ על הספר "*Kabalah Dictionary*"
(מילון הקבלה) שכתב הרב רפאל אפללו שליט"א. בספר הרב
יש הגדרות ומתחים על קבלת הרמח"ל זיע"א הכל מסודר
בצורה טבה תוחה ללימוד ולעיון בו.

לאור ההמלצות הרבות שקיבל הספר, נשאר לי רק להמליץ
עליו בכל לב.

אני מברך בוכת אבותי הקדושים זיע"א את המחבר שליט"א
לברכה והצלחה ושיזכה להוציא מתחת ידי עוד ספרים לזכות
הרבים ושיעלה מעלה בתורה וביראת שמים. אמן

ע"ה דוד חנניה פינטו ס"ט

[signature]

JERUSALEM • ASHDOD • PARIS • LYON • MONTREAL • TORONTO • BUENOS AIRES • MANCHESTER

הרבנות הראשית רמלה
לשכת הרב אבוחצירא רחוב גולומב 25 רמלה טל. 08-9225360
YEHIEL ABEHSSERA
Grand Rabbin de Ramleh
B.P.4 Ramleh
(ISRAEL)
רחוב הרצל 45 ת.ד 4 רמלה טל. בית 08-9221122

בס"ד

ב"ה גוי

[handwritten Hebrew text — largely illegible]

בברכת התורה ולומדיה
יחיאל אבוחצירא
הרב הראשי לרמלה

[signature]

DAVID R. BANON
RABBIN DU CENTRE SÉFARADE DE LAVAL
Membre du Beith Din de Montréal

דוד רפאל באנון
רבון של הקהלה הספרדית בלאוול
וחבר דבית דמונטראל

[handwritten Hebrew text — largely illegible]

4773, Rue Clémenceau – Chomedey Laval – P.Q. H7W 2J5 – Canada Tel.: (450) 681-5412 Fax: (51 4) 341-0694

Table of contents

Introduction	11
The Kabbalah	12
Brief history of the Kabbalah and Kabbalists	15
MAJOR CONCEPTS IN KABBALAH	21
Hishtalshelut - Chain of events	21
CREATION	21
Tsimtsum - retraction	21
Reshimu - imprint	22
Kav - ray	22
SEPHIROT	23
Sephira	23
Sephirot Ha'Igulim - circular	24
Sephirot HaYashar - straight	25
Adam Kadmon - Primordial man	25
Miluyim - spelling	26
Sephirot of BaN (52)	26
Shvirat HaKelim - Breaking of the vessels	27
Rapa'h Nitsutsot - 288 Sparks	27
Sephirot of MaH (45)	28
PARTSUFIM – Configurations	28
Partsuf	28
Partsuf 'Atik Yomin	30
Partsuf Arikh Anpin	30
Partsufim (configurations) Abah and Imah	30

Partsuf Zeir Anpin   30

Partsuf Nukvah   31

Mo'hin - brains   31

Zivugim - Unions   31

THE FOUR WORLDS   32

Atsilut - emanation   32

Beriah - creation   32

Yetsirah - formation   33

'Asiah - action   33

Tikunim - Reparation or action   33

Hanhagua - Guidance   34

Ratson Lehashpia' - Will to bestow   35

Ratson Lekabel - Desire to receive   35

Giluy Yi'hudo - Revelation of his unity   35

Transliteration of the letters   36

DICTIONARY   37

Hebrew / Aramaic – English   37

English – Hebrew / Aramaic   341

Tables   387

8

Introduction

The goal of this dictionary is to provide a genuine picture of the true Kabbalah. In the very rare books that deal seriously with the subject, the concepts of the Zohar and the Kabbalah are often quoted but not explained. The study of Kabbalah involves a good comprehension of its general idea, as well as its details. Unfortunately, there are today numbers of books that use the name "Kabbalah" in their title, yet the great majority does not deal with Kabbalah at all, but rather of often questionable esoteric subjects.

To learn the Kabbalah, it is necessary to be familiar with its usual terms and appellations, because in the language of Kabbalah, particular expressions and metaphors, as well as anthropomorphisms are used. It is of course, well understood, that there is no physical existence at these higher levels. Thus, when terms such as mouth, ears, or other body parts are used, the intention is to describe the esoteric power of these forces, or the position they symbolize.

I have tried to explain the main concepts and expressions used in Hebrew and also in Aramaic, beside each word there is an H for Hebrew or A for Aramaic. For words or concepts hard to understand out of context, I gave examples of their usage in the Zohar or in the texts of the Ari Z'al or the Ram'hal. Since this is a dictionary, I often had to repeat introductions or explanations for better clarification, and to avoid sending the reader to multiple other pages for references. I sincerely do hope, that this work will help to clarify these concepts, and be a good contribution towards an understanding of what Kabbalah truly is.

"Blessed are You G-od, teach me your statutes" (Tehilim, 119, 1

The Kabbalah

The Kabbalah is the mystical and esoteric explanation of the Torah. It teaches the unfolding of the worlds, the various ways of guidance of these worlds, the role of man in the creation, the will of the Creator and more. No other writings explain in details; the creation of this world and the ones above it, the lights or energies that influence its guidance, nor the final goal of everything. These writings are based on ancient Jewish texts and mostly on the Zohar.

The word Kabbalah comes from the verb *Lekabel* (to receive), but to receive it is first necessary to want, and to become a *Keli* (recipient) able to receive and contain this knowledge. When one decides that he wants to know his Creator, in learning this science he realizes his smallness compared to these incredible forces, the perfection of the Lord and His infinite love for His creatures.

The Kabbalah teaches us that the world is guided by an extremely complex system of forces or lights, which through their interactions provoke chain reactions that impact directly on man and the worlds. Each one of these reactions has numerous ramifications, with many details and results. It explains to us the true guidance of the world, so that we may understand the will of G-od. How and why He created the world, in what way He governs it, the provenance of the souls and angels, the purpose of the existence of evil, the reasons for the dualism of reward and punishment, etc.

The Kabbalah also demonstrates to us the importance of man, because only he, by getting closer to the Creator, can influence these incredible forces. For this, one has to elevate to a higher dimension of understanding, and start asking himself some very important questions like; "Why", "What is the purpose of doing this act or this prayer", "What are the outcomes of my actions" etc. The other writings explain in the least details "how" to do, but only the Zohar and the Kabbalah explain to us the exact reasons, and effects of all our prayers and actions.

I believe that most yearn to serve at their best the Creator, but have been accustomed to execute and not seek further, or were kept away from this knowledge. It is now the time to know and learn this magnificent science, as it is written and recommended:

> "From there, you shall seek the Lord your G-od, and you shall find him if you seek him with all your heart, and with all your soul." (Devarim 4-29)

> "The knowledge of the Kabbalah was hidden in those times and concealed for all these *"Talmide 'Hakhamim"* (scholars), except for a few, and even then, discreetly in small groups and not in public as the Gemarah. But as the Ari Z'al wrote; especially now for these last generations, it is allowed and a *"Mitsvah"* (commandment) to reveal this science." (Agarot HaKodesh, 26) - Rabbi Sheniur Zalman Meladi, (Ba'al HaTania)

> "The one, who was able to learn the secrets of the Torah (Kabbalah) and did not make an effort to understand them, will be severely judged" (Even Shelomo 85, 24). - HaGra, HaGaon Rabbi Eliyahu de Vilna

> "Because of this, the spirit of Moshia'h departs and is not coming for the deliverance... When we are not learning this science (Kabbalah) his coming is delayed." (Commentary of Tikune HaZohar, 81, 92) - HaGra, HaGaon Rabbi Eliyahu de Vilna

"What was decreed from above; not to study the Kabbalah openly, was for a limited time only, until the end of the year 5260. From there, and after it was allowed, and from the year 5300 it was decreed that it is a *"Mitsvah"* (commandment) that old and young should study it. For the merit of studying this and for no other merit, the Moshia'h will come.

(Or Ha'Hamah, introduction). Rav Avraham Azulay (grand-father of the 'Hidah)

All the souls in this present world, that will make the effort to know their Creator through His secret writings (Kabbalah), will ascend higher than all the other souls that did not learn and understand, and will be first at the time of the resurrection.

(Zohar, Vayeshev, 182, 2)

The man who learns Kabbalah is above all the others.

(Zohar, Shemini, 42, 1)

The one that learns Kabbalah to understand the secrets of the Torah, and the purpose of the *Mistvot* according to the *Sod* (secret), is called a "Son" of the Lord. (Zohar, Vayera)

And finally, the very clear obligation in the Torah "To know, now", and not just believe:

"וידעת היום והשבת אל-לבבך כי יהו-ה הוא האלה-ים בשמים ממעל ועל-הארץ
מתחת אין עוד"

"Know, today, and consider it in your heart, that the Lord is G-od in heaven above and upon the earth beneath, and there is no other."
(Devarim. 4-39)

14

Brief history of the Kabbalah and Kabbalists

First period – The beginning
Aprox. 1750 B.C.E., Erets Israel
Tradition has that one of the first writing of the Kabbalah called "*Sepher HaYetsira*" (The Book of Formation), was composed by Avraham Avinu. It is the first book that mentions a system of ten lights called *Sephirot*.

Second period – The Zohar
Aprox. 240 C.E, Erets Israel
Rabbi Shim'on Bar Yo'hai lived in Galilee in the second century and was a disciple of Rabbi 'Akiva. To escape the Romans, he went into hiding with his son Rabbi El'azar in a cave for thirteen years. During this time, he composed the Zohar which is the esoteric and mystical explanation of the Torah, and the base of most of the Kabbalah writings.

Third Period – Printing of the Zohar
1270, Spain
After having disappeared for about one thousand years, the book of the Zohar is found and printed by Rabbi Moshe de Leon in Spain. This new printing will be disseminated all over Europe, North Africa and the Middle-East and will allow a wider learning of its writings. It is also the period of the "Prophetic Kabbalah" as taught by Rabbi Abraham Abul'afia.

The three Kabbalah schools in Europe
1200 - 1300
In the cities of Provence in France, Gerona in Spain and Worms in Germany were formed three of the main centers of Kabbalah of that

period. Under prominent Kabbalists as Rabbi Yits'hak the Blind, Rabbi Ezra of Gerona, Rabbi El'azar of Worms, Na'hmanide and others, essential works were published as *"Sepher HaBahir"* *"Sepher Ha'Hesed"* and important commentaries on *"Sepher HaYetsira"*.

In France, was developed a type of contemplative mysticism with meditation on the prayers and *Sephirot*. In Spain, an effort was made to bring the major ideas of the Kabbalah to a wider public. In Germany, Rabbi El'azar of Worms had declared that G-od is even closer to the universe and man, than the soul is to the body.

The Tsfat Kabbalists
1500, Tsfat, Israel
After the expulsion from Spain in 1492, some important Spanish Kabbalists as Rabbi Moshe Kordovero, Rabbi Shlomo Alkabetz and Rabbi Yoseph Karo moved to the city of Tsfat in Israel. There, was founded a school of Kabbalah named "New Kabbalah" or "Kabbalah of Tsfat", it is the golden period of the Kabbalah. After this first generation, Rabbi Yits'hak Luria Ashkenazi; the Ari Z'al, who was born in Jerusalem, became the leading Kabbalist in Tsfat. He explained and clarified all the main concepts of the Kabbalah, and also innovated in the explanation of the *Sephirot* and *Partsufim (configurations)*. He is the author of the corpus *"'Ets 'Haim"* which contains all his works in the style of *Sha'are* (entrances), and is today the major reference in Kabbalah.

***'Hassidic* movement**
1700, east Europe
The *'Hassidic* period started with the Ba'al Shem Tov who was the founder of the *'Hassidic* movement. He declared the whole universe, mind and matter to be a manifestation of G-od, and that whoever maintains that this life is worthless is in error, it is worth a great deal;

only one must know how to use it properly. The Ba'al Shem Tov's teachings were largely based upon the Kabalistic teachings of the Ari Z'al, but his approach made the benefits of these teachings accessible even to the simplest Jew. Some of the other important leaders that founded their own 'Hassidic movement are Rabbi Na'hman of Breslev, great grandson of the Baal Shem Tov, Rabbi Shneur Zalman of Liadi, the "Ba'al HaTanya", founder of the 'Habad Lubavitch movement.

European masters
1700 -, Europe
At the same time, in other parts of Europe there were other important authorities of the Kabbalah as: Rabbi Moshe 'Haim Luzzatto – Ram'hal who lived in Italy and Amsterdam. From an early age, the Ram'hal had showed an exceptional talent for the study of Kabbalah, it is said that when he was only fourteen, he already knew all the Kabbalah of the Ari Z'al by heart, and nobody knew about it, not even his parents. He was a very prolific writer and wrote on the all aspects of the Torah and the Kabbalah, but because of false accusations, he sadly was persecuted for most of his short life.

Rabbi Eliyahu of Vilna - The Gaon of Vilna who was born in Lithuania. He was one of the main leaders of the Mitnagdim (opponents to the 'Hasidic movement). He is considered to be one of the greatest Torah scholar and Kabbalist of the past two centuries.

Sephardic masters
1700 – North and middle Africa
On the other continent the study of the Kabbalah and mostly the Zohar was also widely spread. Some important scholars are:

17

Rabbi Shalom Shar'abi - The Rashash who was born in Yemen in 1720, and died in Israel in 1777. When he arrived in Israel, he joined the *Yeshiva* of the *Mekubalim "Beth El"* in Jerusalem. He is known as the "Master of the *Kavanot*". His *"Siddur HaRashash"* is the *Siddur* used by some Kabbalists in their everyday prayers, and is based on the *Kavanot* of the Ari Z'al.

Rabbi Ya'acov Abe'htsera who was born in Morocco in 1808, and died in Egypt in 1880. He was a Kabbalist renowned for his piety and for performing miracles. He composed works on all facets of the Torah including important commentaries on the Kabbalistic explanations of the Torah.

Rabbi 'Haim Ben 'Atar – Or Ha'Haim, was born in Morocco in 1696, and died in Israel in 1743. The Ba'al Shem Tov was convinced that the Or Ha'Haim was the Moshia'h of that generation. His main work is the commentary on the Torah; "Or Ha'Haim" where he commented the Torah on the four levels of comprehension, from the *Pshat* (simple), to the Kabbalistic meaning.

Rabbi Yosef 'Haim –The Ben Ish 'Hai, was born in Iraq in 1834, and died in Iraq in 1909. He was a prolific author who wrote at incredible speed. It is known that he would finish writing a complete page before the ink at the top of the page had dried. He explained the *Halakhot* (laws) on the Kabbalistic level but in an accessible language.

The latest Kabbalists
1900 - Israel
Since the beginning of this century, Israel is considered to be the main centre of Kabbalah. One of the most important contemporary Kabbalists was Rabbi Yehudah Ashlag who was born in Poland in

1886, and died in Israel in 1955. His main work is the translation of all the Zohar from Aramaic to Hebrew called *"HaSulam"*. Other important Kabbalists are Rabbi Israel Abe'htsera - Baba Sali (1890-1984), Rabbi Yehudah Tzvi Brandwein (1904-1969), Rabbi Avraham Yitzchak HaCohen Kook (1865-1935), Rabbi Yehudah Fatiyah (1859-1942) and others.

Each one of these great Kabbalah scholars brought his own explanations and innovations to this marvelous science. They altogether left a wealth of writings on the Kabbalah which we hope one day, will be more available to the serious learner and seeker of the true Kabbalah.

MAJOR CONCEPTS IN KABBALAH

Hishtalshelut - Chain of events

In the Kabbalah, the *Hishtalshelut* is the chain of events starting from the first act of G-od in this creation which is the "*Tsimtsum*" (retraction), until the complex arrangements that make the guidance of the worlds. Here, are some of the main concepts of the Kabbalah to better understand this chain of events, and the systems of emanation of the lights and *Sephirot*.

CREATION

Tsimtsum - retraction
Contraction

In the beginning, there was no existence except His presence, the Creator was alone, occupying all space with His light. His light without end, borders or limit, filled everything. He was not bestowing His influence, because there was no one to receive it. When He willed to create, He started to influence. His light being of such holiness and intensity, it is not possible for any being to exist in its proximity.

The "*Tsimtsum (retraction)*" is the first act of the *Ein Sof* (infinite) in the creation. It is the retraction of His light from a certain space and encircling it, so as to reduce its intensity and allow created beings to exist. After this contraction, a ray of His light entered this empty space, and formed the first *Sephirot*

By these boundaries, He revealed the concepts of rigor and limit needed by the created beings, and gave a space for all the created to exist.

'Hallal - vacant space

Space – Vacuum

It is the space left by the *Tsimtsum* (retraction) of His light. This space is circular and contains all possibilities of existence for separated entities, given that they are distanced from the intensity of His light.

Reshimu - imprint

Trace

When His light retracted forming the round space, a trace of it, called the *Reshimu* (imprint) remained inside the *'Hallal* (vacant space). This lower intensity light, allowed a space of existence *(Makom)*, for all the created worlds and beings.

The roots of all future existence and events are in the *Reshimu* (imprint). Nothing can come into existence, without having its root in this imprint.

Kav - ray

Line

A straight ray of light called "*Kav*" (ray), emerged from the *Ein Sof* (infinite), and entered on one side of the "'*Hallal*" (vacant space). The combination of the *Kav* (ray) and the *Reshimu* (imprint) is what will give existence to the *Sephirot* with which He governs the worlds.

The *Kav* is the innermost interiority of all this creation.

SEPHIROT

Sephira

The light of G-od is unique and of equal force and quality. A *Sephira* is in a way a "filter" which transforms this light in a particular force or attribute, by which the *Ein Sof* (Infinite) directs the worlds.

Each *Sephira* is composed of a vessel called *Keli* (recipient), which holds its part of light called *Or* (light). There is no difference in the *Or* (light) itself; the difference comes from the particularity, or position of the *Sephira*. There are ten *Sephirot,* their names are:

Keter	Crown	**Tiferet**	Beauty
'Hokhma	Wisdom	**Netsa'h**	Glory
Binah	Understanding	**Hod**	Splendor
'Hesed	Bounty	**Yesod**	Foundation
Gevurah	Rigor	**Malkhut**	Kingship

On the right, the *'Hesed* (kindness*) column: 'Hokhma, 'Hesed, Netsa'h.*
In the middle, the *Ra'hamim* (mercy) *column: Keter, Tiferet, Yesod, Malkhut*
On the left, the *Din* (rigor) column: *Binah, Gevurah, Hod.*

There is one more *Sephira* called *Da'at*, which is counted when *Keter* is not, also in the *Ra'hamim* column. There are also configurations of one or more *Sephirot* acting in coordination, which are called *Partsufim* (configurations).

23

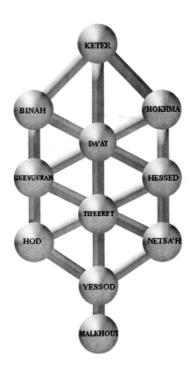

Sephirot Ha'lgulim - circular
Encircling *Sephirot*

After entering the '*Hallal* (vacant space), the *Kav* (ray) made ten circular *Sephirot*, encircling one another, but still maintained a straight shape. These ten *Sephirot* are in charge of the general guidance of the worlds, and are not influenced by the actions of men.

Sephirot HaYashar - straight

Linear *Sephirot*

After making the ten circular *Sephirot*, the *Kav* (ray) maintained his straight shape and made ten other *Sephirot*, but this time in a linear arrangement.

They were later arranged in three columns: right, left and middle, representing the guidance of the world in the manner of *'Hesed, Din* and *Ra'hamim* (Kindness, rigor and mercy). This guidance is dependent on time, and the actions of men.

This first configuration of ten *Sephirot* is called *Adam Kadmon* (Primordial Man).

Adam Kadmon - Primordial man

World on top of *Atsilut* (emanation)

This first configuration, or the first world where the emanated lights were formed into ten *Sephirot* is called *Adam Kadmon* (Primordial Man). It is the union between the *Reshimu* (imprint) and the *Kav* (ray). From this first configuration, all the other worlds came forth into existence.

Adam Kadmon being at such close proximity to the *Ein Sof* (Infinite), we cannot grasp anything of its nature. Our understanding only starts from the emanations that came out of him in the way of his senses, which are called his branches. From *Adam Kadmon* emerged numerous emanations, four of which are called: sight, hearing, smell and speech, and the four worlds of *Atsilut* (emanation), *Beriah* (creation), *Yetsirah* (formation) and *'Asiah* (action).

25

Miluyim - spelling

Letters that are added for the spelling of each individual letter of the Name

י-ה-ו-ה

The creative forces or energies are the different powers in the four letters of the name of G-od י-ה-ו-ה, and the various letters added to make their different spellings. Depending on which letters are used, the numerical value of the name changes, and each one of these possibilities becomes different in its nature and actions.

The four *Miluyim* (spellings) are:

עב ,סג , מה, בן - *'A"V* (72), *SaG* (63), *MaH* (45), *BaN* (52)

יוד הי ויו הי – עב   - *'A"V* = 72
יוד הי ואו הי – סג   - *SaG* = 63
יוד הא ואו הא - מה   - *MaH* = 45
יוד הה וו הה – בן   - *BaN* = 52

Each name can also be divided and subdivided as:
'A"V of 'A"V, SaG of 'A"V, MaH of 'A"V ...
BaN of BaN of SaG, SaG of MaH of 'A"V etc.

Sephirot of BaN (52)

From the eyes of *Adam Kadmon* (Primordial man) came out ten *Sephirot* of the aspect of the name of *BaN (52)*. They correspond to the feminine aspect - rigor, and are the root of deterioration. When they came out, the first three *Sephirot* – KHB *(Keter, 'Hokhma, Binah)*, were able to stand in three columns. The seven lower *Sephirot* could not stand in this order; they formed a single descending line and broke. This imperfect arrangement is the first origin of the *Sitra A'hra* or "evil".

Shvirat HaKelim - Breaking of the vessels

The *Sephirot* of *Keter*, *'Hokhma* and *Binah* of *BaN (52)* that came out from the eyes of *Adam Kadmon* (Primordial man), received and contained their lights because they were in the three-column arrangement. The seven lower *Sephirot* could not contain their lights and broke. Their *Kelim* (recipients) descended to the world of *Beriah* (creation). Their lights also fell, but stayed in *Atsilut* (emanation).

The roots of all the created are in the seven lower *Sephirot*, the three first *Sephirot* are like a crown on them to repair and direct them. In the first three *Sephirot* there is not really a notion of damage, they are above men's deeds, and are not affected by their sins.

This deficient state caused a fall not only of these *Sephirot*, but of all the worlds also.

Rapa'h Nitsutsot - 288 Sparks

To sustain the *Kelim* (recipients) after they broke, 288 sparks of the lights came down as well, because a connection to their original lights was needed to keep them alive. The fall of the *Kelim* (recipients), is also called their death. It is important to understand that all that happens in our world is similar to what occurred in this fall.

The goal of all the works, deeds and prayers of men in this existence, is to help and participate in the ascent of these sparks to their origin. At the completion of this *Tikun* of unification between the fallen sparks and their *Keli* (recipient), it will be the time of the resurrection of the dead and the arrival of *Moshia'h*.

Sephirot of MaH (45)

After the breaking of the *Kelim* (recipients) and the separation from their lights, it was necessary for the guidance of the world that reparation be done. From the forehead of *Adam Kadmon* (Primordial man) came out ten *Sephirot* of the aspect of the name of *MaH (45);* corresponding to the masculine - reparation. In contrast to the *Sephirot* of *BaN (52) which* correspond to the feminine aspect - rigor, and are the root of deterioration.

The *Tikun* (rectification) was done by the union of the *Sephirot* of *MaH (45)* (mercy) and *BaN (52)* (rigor) in complex arrangements, as to allow the feminine *BaN* to be repaired by the masculine *MaH,* and for the *Sephirot* to stand in the three-column arrangement of kindness, rigor and mercy. With the proper order of the *Sephirot* in place, various configurations that are called *Partsufim* completed the creation.

PARTSUFIM – Configurations

Partsuf

A *Partsuf* is a configuration of one or more *Sephirot* acting in coordination.

There are five main *Partsufim* (configurations):

- *Arikh Anpin*
- *Abah*
- *Imah*
- *Zeir Anpin*
- *Nukvah*

And one on top of them; *'Atik Yomin* (clothed inside *Arikh Anpin*).

From these five *Partsufim* (configurations); emerge seven more. They emanate from the ten *Sephirot* as follows:

From *Keter:*
- *'Atik Yomin* and his *Nukvah*
- *Arikh Anpin* and his *Nukvah*

From *'Hokhma:* - *Abah*
- From *Malkhut* of *Abah* - *Israel Saba*
- From *Malkhut* of *Israel Saba* - *Israel Saba* 2

From *Binah:* - *Imah*
- From *Malkhut* of *Imah* -*Tevunah*
- From *Malkhut* of *Tevunah* - *Tevunah* 2

Israel Saba and *Tevunah* are also called by their initials *ISOT* or *ISOT* 2.

From *'Hesed, Gevurah, Tiferet, Netsa'h, Hod,* and *Yesod:* - *Zeir Anpin.*

From *Zeir Anpin:* - *Ya'acov, Israel.*

From *Malkhut:* - *Nukvah*, divided in two *Partsufim* (configurations): *Ra'hel* and *Leah*

The *Partsufim Zeir Anpin* and *Nukvah* are the root of all the created. It is by their *Tikunim* (actions) that the guidance of justice is manifested. Here, the "*Tikun*" is a description of the actions, illuminations and inter-relations of the *Sephirot* and *Partsufim*. These *Tikunim* will result in various illuminations of different intensities, for the guidance of the worlds.

Partsuf 'Atik Yomin

The *Partsuf 'Atik* is superior to all the *Partsufim* (configurations). His *Nukvah* (feminine) is never separated from him, her back attached to his back. *Partsuf 'Atik* makes the connection between each world.

Partsuf Arikh Anpin

The innermost of all the other *Partsufim* (configurations) is *Arikh Anpin* and his *Nukvah*, they make one *Partsuf;* the masculine on the right, and the feminine on the left. *Arikh Anpin* is the first *Partsuf* in *Atsilut* (emanation), and the root of all the others which are his branches.

Partsufim (configurations) Abah and Imah

These two *Partsufim* are the link between the superior *Partsuf Arikh Anpin* and *Z'uN* (*Zeir Anpin* and *Nukvah*). *Abah* is the *Sephira 'Hokhma, Imah* is the *Sephira Binah*.

Partsuf Zeir Anpin

Zeir Anpin (*Z"A*) is composed of the six lower *Sephirot*: *'Hesed, Gevurah, Tiferet, Netsa'h, Hod, Yesod*.

The abundance comes down to the world when *Zeir Anpin* and *Nukvah* (*Z"uN*) unite. It is given to *Nukvah*, and from her, to the lower worlds. All this abundance that comes down to the world, proceeds from the various *Zivugim* (unions) of *Z"uN*. Each new day, is of a new emanation that governs it. For each day, there are new *Zivugim* of different aspects of *Z"uN*.

The guidance of the world is dependent on the different positioning and interaction, of *Z"A* and *Nukvah*, since they have a direct effect on the measures and balance of the factors of kindness, rigor and mercy.

The goal of the service of the creatures, is to help prepare the *Partsufim* (configurations) *Z"A* and *Nukvah* for the *Zivug* (union), and this by the elevation and adhesion of the worlds by way of the *Tefilot* (prayers) and *Mitsvot* (commandments).

Partsuf Nukvah

The *Partsuf Nukvah* represents the feminine – the principle of receiving. It comprises of two distinct *Partsufim: Ra'hel and Leah*.

The *Partsufim* (configurations) of *Zeir Anpin* and *Nukvah* are the root of all the created. It is by them, that the guidance of justice is manifested. There is perfection for the masculine only when it completes itself with its feminine.

Mo'hin - brains

The *Mo'hin* (brains) are the directive force given to the *Partsuf*. There are interior and encircling *Mo'hin*.

Zivugim - Unions

The *Zivug* is the union of the masculine with its feminine. All the outcomes of the higher emanations are a result of the different unions of the masculine and feminine lights.

There are different kinds of *Zivugim*:
-   the ones for the construction of the worlds
-   for the building of the *Partsufim* (configurations),
-   for the guidance of the worlds.

For the abundance to come down to the world, *Zeir Anpin* needs to unite with *Nukvah*. There can be abundance only when the masculine and the feminine are in harmony. Each day, according to the actions of man, the *Tefilot* (prayers) during the week, *Shabbat* or holidays, and depending on time, various configurations allow different *Zivugim*, and therefore outflows of abundance of variable intensities.

The guidance of the world is dependent on the different positioning and interaction, of these masculine and feminine *Partsufim*. The results of these unions vary, and produce different emanations of kindness, rigor and mercy.

The goal of the service of the creatures, is to help prepare the *Partsufim* (configurations) *Z"A* and *Nukvah* for the *Zivug* (union), and this, by the elevation and adhesion of the worlds by way of the *Tefilot* and *Mitsvot*.

THE FOUR WORLDS

Atsilut - emanation
First world
There are four worlds. The first to unfold from *Adam Kadmon* (Primordial man) is called *Atsilut;* the world of emanation, where there is no existence of the separated, and no *Sitra A'hra* (negative force) even at its lowest levels. It is the first of the four worlds, on top of *Beriah* (creation), *Yetsirah* (formation) and *'Asiah* (action). From *Atsilut* (emanation) unfolded all the lower worlds, which are the source of existence for the physical worlds, and the possibility of reward, punishment and evil.

Beriah - creation
World of the souls
The second world is *Beriah* (creation); the world of the *Neshamot;* of the souls.

Yetsirah - formation

World of the angels

The third world is *Yetsirah* (formation); the world of formation, the world of the angels.

'Asiah - action

World of physical existence

'Asiah (action) is the fourth world; the world of action, the world of physical existence. The three superior worlds of *Atsilut* (emanation), *Beriah* (creation) and *Yetsirah* (formation), are interior to the fourth world of *'Asiah* (action).

From the last level of the *Sephirot* of *'Asiah* - *Malkhut* of *'Asiah*, the *Sitra A'hra* came out.

Tikunim - Reparation or action

In Hebrew, the word "*Tikun*" has different meanings. It can be understood as reparation or rectification, and also as function, relation or action.

There are different types of *Tikunim:*
- *Tikunim* that took place in the first emanations to repair the worlds
- *Tikunim* for the construction and inter-relations of the *Sephirot* and *Partsufim* (configurations)
- *Tikunim* of certain *Partsufim* (function or action) for the guidance of the worlds
- *Tikunim* (rectifications) for the *Neshamot*.

For the guidance, the *Tikunim* of the *Partsufim* (configurations) are the actions, illuminations and inter-relations of the *Sephirot* and *Partsufim,* and their influence on the worlds. These *Tikunim* result in

33

various illuminations of different intensities, depending on time and the actions of man.

The *Tikun* of the soul is realized by the *Gilgul* (reincarnation), and by the *'Ibur* (attachment).

By giving man a role in the general *Tikun (Tikun 'Olam),* it is now up to him to restore, and make the necessary reparations to the world. However, if man does not act accordingly, the *Tikun* will still be realized, but in the time set by the Creator.

Hanhagua - Guidance

The Kabbalah is the only science that explains to us in the least details, the true guidance of the world, so that we may understand His will. It teaches us that the world is guided by an extremely complex system of forces or lights, which through their interactions provoke chain reactions that impact directly on man and the guidance of the worlds. Each one of these reactions has numerous ramifications with many details and results.

The guidance of the worlds is done through the influence of the different *Sephirot* and *Partsufim* (configurations).

There are two main kinds of guidance:
- The general guidance, which is for the subsistence of the worlds, and is not influenced by the actions of men. This guidance is by the encircling *Sephirot.*

- The variable guidance, which is on the basis of justice, reward and punishment, and is dependant on the actions of men. This guidance is by the linear *Sephirot.*

The guidance of the world is dependent on the different positioning and interactions of the masculine and feminine *Partsufim*, since they have a direct effect on the measure and balance of the factors of kindness, rigor and mercy. The masculine *Partsufim* bestow kindness, the feminine bestow rigor. By their unions, different equilibriums of the two forces of kindness and rigor make the guidance.

Ratson Lehashpia' - Will to bestow
The will of the Creator is to bestow goodness on His creatures, all the levels of creation were put in place so His kindness could emanate to them, yet in such a way that they would be able to receive it.

Ratson Lekabel - Desire to receive
By his nature man is himself a *Keli* (recipient) with a will to receive without limits, and containing a spiritual light; his soul. A guidance based on this desire will permit anything without restriction, and not allow man to have merit.

The perfect goal for man is to elevate his bodily desires by sanctifying his ways, and resemble his Creator by becoming a giver with a will to bestow goodness to all.

Giluy Yi'hudo - Revelation of his unity
The goal of all these possibilities of guidance have only one purpose: to allow man to merit by his own efforts, to get closer to his Creator, receive His goodness, and live the *Dvekut* – the adhesion with G-od. In this way, man will attain perfection and be directly involved in the ultimate goal of the creation, which is the revelation of G-od's Sovereignty – *Giluy Ye'hudo.*

Transliteration of the letters

Letter	Name	Equivalent	Transliteration
א	Aleph	A, O, E, I	A, O, E, I
ב	Beit	B, V	B, V
ג	Gimel	G	G
ד	Dalet	D	D
ה	He	H	H
ו	Vav	V	V
ז	Zain	Z	Z
ח	'het		'h
ט	Tet	T	T
י	Yud	Y	Y
כ	Khaf	C, K, KH	C, K, KH
ל	Lamed	L	L
מ	Mem	M	M
נ	Nun	N	N
ס	Samekh	S	S
ע	'ain		'
פ	Pey	P, F	P, F
צ	Tsadey	TS	TS
ק	Kuf	C, K	C, K
ר	Resh	R	R
ש	Shin	S, SH	S, SH
ת	Tav	T	T

DICTIONARY

Hebrew –
Aramaic / English

Hebrew / Aramaic Phonetic	L	Dictionary
א"א A"A	H	***Partsuf Arikh Anpin*** *Initials*
א"ס E"S	H	***Ein Sof, The without end or limit - Infinite*** *Initials*
א"ק A"K	A	***Adam Kadmon*** *Initials*

אבא   H   ***Partsuf Abah***
Abah

One of the five main *Partsufim* (configurations). It is the *Sephira 'Hokhma*. He dresses the right arm (*'Hesed*) of *Partsuf Arikh Anpin*. His three lower *Sephirot (NHY (Netsa'h, Hod, Yesod))* dress inside the *NHY* of *Partsuf Imah*, together they make the *Mo'hin* (brains) of *Partsuf Z"A*. His *Zivug* (union) with *Partsuf Imah* is constant.

Partsuf Abah had two aspects of the name of *MaH* (45). From the first aspect, he was made, and from the second, another *Partsuf, Israel Saba*.

See Abah ve Imah, Partsuf, Zivug

אבא ואמא   H   ***Partsufim Abah and Imah***
Abah ve
Imah

These two *Partsufim (configurations)* are essential in the guidance of the worlds, they are the link between *Partsuf Arikh Anpin* which is the highest configuration, and *Partsuf Zeir Anpin* who communicates these emanations to the worlds by his *Zivug* (union) with the *Partsuf Nukvah*. *Abah* is the *Sephira 'Hokhma*, *Imah* the *Sephira Binah*.

Hebrew / Aramaic L *Phonetic*	Dictionary

They were arranged by the *Zivug (union)* of *Partsuf Arikh Anpin* with his *Nukvah* (feminine), *Abah* is the masculine aspect, and *Imah* the feminine. They are constructed from the aspects of the names of *MaH* (45) and *BaN* (52), and are influenced and built by the lights of *Partsuf Arikh*.

From the arms (*Sephirot 'Hesed* and *Gevurah*) of *Arikh Anpin*, lights build their *HBD* ('Hokhma, Binah, Da'at), and from his *Tiferet* lights build their bodies. This is a first emanation to build them together.

There is a second emanation to build them as separate *Partsufim*. From the first parts of *Sephirot 'Hesed* and *Gevurah* of *Arikh*, will be constituted the *HBD* ('Hokhma, Binah, Da'at) of *Abah* and *Imah*, from the second parts their *HGT* ('Hesed, Gevurah, Tiferet), and from the third parts their *NHY* (Netsa'h, Hod, Yesod).

Abah has two aspects of the name of *MaH* (45): the first and the second. From the first aspect of *MaH* (45), *Abah* was made and from the second, another *Partsuf; Israel Saba*. Similarly, from the first *BaN* (52) *Imah* was made and from the second, another *Partsuf; Tevunah*.

To communicate their emanations, there are for *Abah* and *Imah* two types of *Zivug* (unions): the constant *Zivug* is called exterior and is for the subsistence of

Hebrew / Aramaic Phonetic	L	Dictionary

the worlds, the other is called interior and is for the renewing of the *Mo'hin (brains)* of *Z"uN (Zeir Anpin and Nukvah)*.

There are different states of growth for the *Partsuf Z"A*, in its first growth he receives his *Mo'hin* from the *Partsufim ISOT (Israel Saba* and *Tevunah)*, in his second more important growth, he receives them directly from *Abah* and *Imah*.

See Partsuf, Zivug

אבולעפיה
Abul'afia

Rabbi Abraham Abul'afia

Born in 1240 at Saragossa, in Aragon; died in Greece after 1291.

He is the precursor of what is called the "Prophetical Kabbalah" where combinations and permutations of *Autiot* (letters), numerals and *Nikud* (vowels) are symbols which explain and disclose the deepest esoteric meanings. Some of his best known works are: "*Sefer ha-Ot*" and "*Imre Shefer*".

אבחנה
Av'hana

H **Distinction – Insight**

Understanding of the deeper meaning or Kabbalistic interpretation.

אבי"ע
ABYA

H **Atsilut, Beriah, Yetsirah and Asiah**

Initials of the four worlds.

אביחצירא
Ab'htsera

Rabbi Ya'acov Ab'htsera

Born in Morocco in 1808, died in Dimanhur, Egypt, 1880.

41

Hebrew / Aramaic Phonetic	L	Dictionary
		Rabbi Ya'acov was a Kabbalist renowned for his piety and for performing miracles. He composed works on all facets of the Torah including important commentaries on the Kabbalistic explanation of the Torah. Some of his main works are "*Makhsof HaLavan*", "*Pitu'he 'Hotam*".
אבן אבנים *Even* *Avanim*	H	***Stone of stone*** Term used for the hardheaded, or the one not willing or ready, to listen and learn.
אבר *Ever*	H	***Organ – Limb (Anthropomorphism)*** In the language of Kabbalah, anthropomorphisms are used only to illustrate the esoteric power of these forces. It is well understood, that there is no physical existence at these higher levels. Thus, when terms such as mouth, ears, or other body parts are used, the intention is to describe the metaphor, or the position they symbolize.
אברהם *Avraham*	H	***Avraham*** First patriarch, one of the first books on the Kabbalah "*Sepher HaYetsira*" the "Book of Formation" is attributed to him. He is represented by the *Sephira 'Hesed*.
אברים *Evarim*	H	***Organs – Limbs*** See Ever
אגדה *Agadah*	H	***Legend*** Also used as a name for Kabbalah.

Hebrew / Aramaic Phonetic	L	Dictionary
אדם *Adam*	H	**Man – Human** A microcosm of the higher lights and configurations.
אדם **הראשון** *Adam* *Harishon*	H	**The First Man** Representation of the *Partsuf* (configuration) *Zeir Anpin* in the book of *Bereshit*. In the beginning, all the souls were inside *Adam HaRishon*, when he sinned, some fell down to the *Klipot* (negative world) and some remained in him.
אדם **קדמון** *Adam* *Kadmon*	H	**Primordial man - World on top of Atsilut** After entering the *'Hallal* (vacant space) and making the ten circular *Sephirot*, the *Kav* (ray) maintained his straight shape and made ten other *Sephirot*, but this time in a linear arrangement. They were arranged in three columns: right, left and middle, representing the guidance of the world in the manner of *'Hesed, Din and Ra'hamim* (Kindness, rigor and mercy). This first emanation is the origin of all future emanations. This first configuration, or the first world where the emanated lights were formed into ten *Sephirot,* is called *Adam Kadmon (Primordial Man)*. It is the union between the *Reshimu* (imprint) and the *Kav* (ray). From this first configuration, all the other worlds came forth into existence. *Adam Kadmon* being at such close proximity to the *Ein Sof*, we cannot grasp anything of its nature. Our

Hebrew / Aramaic Phonetic	L	Dictionary

understanding only starts from the emanations that came out of him in the way of his senses, which are called his branches. These four branches are called: sight, hearing, smell and speech. They spread out from his eyes, ears, nose, and mouth. In the language of Kabbalah we use names of body parts solely to illustrate the esoteric powers of these forces. It is understood, of course, that there is no physical existence at these level. When we say ears, mouth, or any other physical expression, the goal is to describe the inner sense, or the position they represent.

From the ears, came out lights of the aspect of the name *SaG* (63); ten linear *Sephirot* from the left ear, and ten encircling *Sephirot* from the right ear.
From the nose, came out lights also of the aspect of the name of *SaG* (63); ten encircling *Sephirot* from the right nostril and ten linear from the left nostril. The lights of the encircling *Sephirot* are of a finer aspect, which is why they came out of the right side; the side of *'Hesed* (kindness), as opposed to the left; which is of the side of *Gevurah* (rigor). In the emanations (lights) of the ears and nose, there is not yet a concept of *Keli* (vessel).

From the mouth, came out lights also of the aspect of the name of *SaG* (63); ten internal *Sephirot*, and ten encircling *Sephirot*.

Hebrew / Aramaic Phonetic	L	Dictionary
		From the eyes, came out lights of the aspect of the name *BaN (52)*. These feminine lights caused the *Shvirat HaKelim* (breaking of the vessels). From the forehead, came out lights of the aspect of the name of *MaH (45)*, these masculine lights will make the *Tikun* (rectification) of the broken *Sephirot*, and together with *BaN* make all the *Partsufim* (configurations) for the guidance of the worlds. From all these emanations, the other four worlds of *Atsilut* (emanation), *Beriah* (creation), *Yetsirah* (formation) and *'Asiah* (action) will unfold.
אדמה *Adamah*	H	**Earth** Made from the words Adam (man) and the letter ה (5) as the five levels of the soul.
אדן *Adon*	H	**Lord** One of the names of G-od, He is the Lord on all His creation.
אדנ-י *Adona-y*	H	**Adona-y** One of the names of G-od, represented by the *Sephira Malkhut*.
אהבה *Ahavah*	H	**Ahavah (Love)** Name of a *Hekhal* (portal). Fifth of seven *Hekhalot*, corresponding to the *Sephira 'Hesed*. Each world (*Atsilut, Beriah, Yetsirah, 'Asiah*) is built from four aspects: *Partsuf* (configuration), *Levush*

Hebrew / Aramaic Phonetic	L	Dictionary

(garment), *Or Makif* (encircling lights), and *Hekhalot*.

In each *Partsuf* there are interiority and exteriority, the exteriority is always of the aspect of the *Sephira Malkhut*, and the *Hekhalot* are the ramifications of the *Malkhuts* of the *Partsufim*.

The *Hekhalot* are also the different levels of ascension of the *Tefilot* (prayers) before reaching the final seventh *Hekhal* (portal); *Kodesh Hakodashim*. Their principal function is to allow the adhesion and attachment, in various and particular ways during the *Tefilot*, until the world of *Atsilut* (at the 'Amidah).

The *Neshamot* and the angels have their root in the *Hekhalot*, each one depending on its respective level.

אהי-ה דאלפין *EHY-H de Alphin*	H	***Name of*** אהי-ה ***spelled using the letter*** א אלף הא יוד הא It is the *Miluy* (spelling) of the name אהי-ה with the letter *Aleph*. It corresponds to the *Sephira Keter*. It is the *Miluy* of the exteriority of the third head (*Avirah*) of *Partsuf Arikh Anpin*. *See Tikun, Arikh Anpin*
אהי-ה *AHY-H*	H	***AHY-H*** One of the names of G-od, represented by the *Sephira Keter*.
או"א *Av"I*	A	***Partsufim Abah and Imah*** *Initials*

46

Hebrew / Aramaic Phonetic	L	Dictionary
אודנין Udnin	A	**Ears** See Orot HaOzen
אוזן Ozen	H	**Ear** See Orot HaOzen
אוזן חוטם פה Ozen, 'Hotem, Pey	H	**Ear, nose, mouth**

After entering the 'Hallal (vacant space) and making the ten circular Sephirot, the Kav (ray) maintained his straight shape and made ten other Sephirot, but this time in a linear arrangement. They were arranged in three columns: right, left and middle, representing the guidance of the world in the manner of 'Hesed, Din and Ra'hamim (Kindness, rigor and mercy).

This first configuration, or the first world where the emanated lights were formed into ten Sephirot, is called Adam Kadmon (Primordial Man). It is the union between the Reshimu (imprint) and the Kav (ray). From this first configuration, all the other worlds came forth into existence.

Adam Kadmon being at such close proximity to the Ein Sof (infinite), we cannot grasp anything of its nature. Our understanding only starts from the emanations that came out of him in the way of his senses, which are called his branches. These four branches are called: sight, hearing, smell and speech. They spread out from his eyes, ears, nose, and mouth. In the language of Kabbalah we use

Hebrew / Aramaic *Phonetic*	L	Dictionary

names of body parts solely to describe the inner sense, or the position they represent. It is understood, of course, that there is no physical existence at these level.

From the ears, came out lights of the aspect of the name *SaG* (63); ten linear *Sephirot* from the left ear, and ten encircling *Sephirot* from the right ear.

From the nose, came out lights also of the aspect of the name of *SaG* (63); ten encircling *Sephirot* from the right nostril and ten linear from the left nostril. The lights of the encircling *Sephirot* are of a finer aspect, which is why they came out of the right side; the side of *'Hesed* (kindness), as opposed to the left; which is of the side of *Gevurah* (rigor). In the emanations (lights) of the ears and nose, there is not yet a concept of *Keli* (vessel).

From the mouth, came out lights also of the aspect of the name of *SaG* (63); ten internal *Sephirot*, and ten encircling *Sephirot*.

These lights in conjunction with other emanations, will make the four worlds of *Atsilut* (emanation), *Beriah* (creation), *Yetsirah* (formation) and *'Asiah* (action).

See Orot Ha'Enayim, Orot HaOzen, Orot HaOzen, Orot HaPeh.

אויר   H   *Air – Space*

Avir   In the space between the *Sephirot Keter* and

Hebrew / Aramaic Phonetic	L	Dictionary

'Hokhma of Partsuf (configuration) Arikh Anpin, there is Sephira Da'at of Partsuf 'Atik.

אווירא   A   ***Second of the three heads of Partsuf Arikh Anpin***

Avirah   Avirah is in the space between the *Sephirot Keter* and *'Hokhma* of *Partsuf* (configuration) *Arikh Anpin*. *Sephira Da'at* of *Partsuf 'Atik* is clothed Inside it.

These three heads are the roots of the direction of kindness, rigor and mercy. They emanate from *Arikh Anpin* to *Abah* and *Imah,* and from there, to the *Mo'hin (brains)* of *Z"A.*

These three heads are the first *Tikun* (action) of *Partsuf Arikh Anpin* they are:
1- *Gulgolta - Keter* of *Arikh Anpin*
2- *Avirah* - In the space between *Keter* and *'Hokhma* of *Arikh Anpin,* there is *Da'at* of *'Atik*
3- *Mo'ha - 'Hokhma* of *Arikh Anpin*

For each head there are three levels of lights: Interior, encircling (*Makif*), and encircling of the encircling (*Makif* le *Makif*). The name ה-ו-ה-י represents the interiority. The name א-ה-י-ה the encircling. Depending on their vowels they correspond to one of the three heads.
When the first letters have the vowels as pronounced, and (vowel) *Segol* instead of *Tsere*.
The *Miluy* (spelling) has vowels as pronounced.

Hebrew / Aramaic *Phonetic*	L	Dictionary
		The *Miluy* has *Kamatz* as a vowel. This is the second head –*Avirah*.
אור *Or*	H	**Light** Term used to describe an emanation, a force or energy.
אור חוזר *Or 'hozer*	H	***Returning light*** The emanations that came out from the mouth of *Adam Kadmon,* were ten interior and ten encircling *Sephirot* of the aspect of the lower *Ta'amim* (cantillation). After coming out, they returned inside the mouth to be completed and came out again, they are called "returning lights".

When they ascended to their origin, each one of these lights left its own trace. These traces, which did not return thickened, and together with the sparks of the returning higher lights made the *Kelim* (recipients).

From the upper realms the lights are emanated to the lower beings in two different ways; with mercy, when they are "facing" toward the receivers and transmitting the light to them in a linear fashion, these are called "linear lights". When the *Sephirot* draw the lights "facing" higher, and transmit the lights by their rear, they are of the aspect of rigor and are called "returning lights".

Hebrew / Aramaic *Phonetic*	L	Dictionary

אור ישר H **Straight, linear light**
Or
Yashar

The *Sephirot* draw the lights from the upper realms to the lower beings in two different ways: with mercy, when they are "facing" toward the receivers and transmitting the light to them in a linear fashion, these are linear lights. With rigor, when they are "facing" higher and transmitting the light by their rear, these are returning lights.

For the *Sephirot* there are two types of encircling lights: linear and returning. The linear light, which did not enter in the *Keli* (recipient), encircles its *Sephira* and all those under it. The returning light, which entered and came out from the *Keli*, only encircles its *Sephira*. Therefore, each *Sephira* has one interior and two encircling lights.

אור מקיף H **Encircling light**
Or
Makif

In the first emanations from *Adam Kadmon,* the lights of the encircling *Sephirot* which are of a finer aspect, came out from the right side; the side of *'Hesed* (kindness), as opposed to the left, which is of the side of *Gevurah* (rigor).

For each *Sephira* and *Partsuf* there are interior and encircling lights. When a *Partsuf* receives his *Mo'hin* (brains) from a superior *Partsuf*, a part of its light (*NHY* (Netsa'h, Hod, Yesod)) enter him, while the other parts (*HGT* ('Hesed, Gevurah, Tiferet) and *HBD* ('Hokhma, Binah,

Hebrew / Aramaic *Phonetic*	L	Dictionary

Da'at)) do not enter, but surround him.

As for *Z"A*, when his *Mo'hin* are given to him from *Abah* and *Imah* or *ISOT*, they do not enter completely in him; only the *Sephirot NHY* do, the *HGT* and *HBD* stay on top of him, encircling his head. His *Mo'hin* are called his צ ל מ. The *NHY* which are composed of nine parts corresponding to צ, spread in the nine *Sephirot* of *Z"A*. The encircling ל מ, do not need to spread in him, and stand on his exterior in the three-column arrangement of kindness, rigor and mercy. *HGT* make his first encircling; this corresponds to the ל, *KHBD* (Keter, 'Hokhma, Binah, Da'at) make his second encircling; this corresponds to the מ.

For the *Sephira*, there are two types of encircling lights: linear and returning. The linear light, which did not enter in the *Keli* (recipient), encircles its *Sephira* and all those under it. The returning light, which entered and came out from the *Keli*, only encircles its *Sephira*. Therefore, each *Sephira* has one interior and two encircling lights.

The difference between the encircling light and the *Levush* (garment) is that the encircling light sustains the *Keli*, while the *Levush* is like a curtain that protects him from the exterior or negative lights.

Hebrew / Aramaic *Phonetic*	L	Dictionary
אור עליון *Or* *'Elyon*	H	**Upper Light** The original light which left its *Reshimu* (imprint) in the *'Hallal* (vacant space) after the *Tsimtsum* (retraction). *See Reshimu, 'Hallal, Kav, Tsimtsum*
אור פנימי *Or* *Pnimi*	H	**Inner Light** The light that enters and makes the inner light of a *Partsuf* are the *NHY (Netsa'h, Hod, Yesod)* of the superior *Partsuf*. The *HBD ('Hokhma, Binah, Da'at)* and *HGT ('Hesed, Gevurah, Tiferet)* of the superior *Partsuf* that do not enter, surround him, and are called encircling lights.
אורות *Orot*	H	**Lights** *See Or*
אורות האוזן *Orot HaOzen*	H	**Lights of the ears** From the ears of *Adam Kadmon* came out ten linear *Sephirot* from the left ear, and ten encircling *Sephirot* from the right ear, they went down until the beard on the chin. They are of the aspect of the higher *Ta'amim* (cantillations) and of the name of *SaG* (63).
אורות החוטם *Orot Ha'Hotem*	H	**Lights of the Nose** From the nose of *Adam Kadmon* came out ten linear *Sephirot* from the left nostril, and ten encircling *Sephirot* from the right nostril, they went down until the chest, closer than the ones of the ears but still separated.

Hebrew / Aramaic Phonetic	L	Dictionary

They are of the aspect of the middle *Ta'amim* (cantillations) and of the name of *SaG* (63).

אורות המצח *Orot* *HaMetsa'h*	H	**Lights of the forehead**

After the breaking of the *Kelim* (recipients) and the separation from their lights, it was necessary for the guidance of the world that reparation be done. From the forehead of *Adam Kadmon* came out ten *Sephirot* of the aspect of the name of *MaH (45)*; corresponding to the masculine - reparation. In contrast, the *Sephirot* of *BaN (52)* correspond to the feminine aspect - rigor, and are the root of deterioration. These two aspects (*MaH (45)* and *BaN (52)*) are necessary for the guidance of justice, and to give man the possibility of free choice.

The union between the lights of *MaH (45)*; which represent mercy, with the ones of *BaN (52)*, which represent rigor, made the *Tikun* of the broken *Sephirot*.

See Tikun

אורות העינים *Orot* *Ha'Enayim*	H	**Lights of the eyes**

Other lights, of the aspect of the name of *BaN (52)*, emerged from the eyes of *Adam Kadmon*. When they came out, they found *Kelim (recipients)* to contain them.

These lights of *BaN (52)*, which are of the aspect of the *Nekudim (vowels)*, came out with the general *BaN (52)* through the eyes; ten encircling *Sephirot*

Hebrew / Aramaic Phonetic	L	Dictionary

from the right eye, and ten interior from the left eye, they descended lower than the navel. These lights are not visible above the navel because the lights of the ears, nose and mouth extend to that point.

Each one of these *Sephirot* had its own *Keli,* but only the three first ones: *Keter, 'Hokhma* and *Binah,* were structured in the three-column order. However, the seven lower *Sephirot* were aligned one under the other in a straight line, and not ready for the guidance of kindness, rigor and mercy. Therefore, they could not contain their lights and broke. This caused an important damage called *Shvirat HaKelim – the breaking of the vessels.* See Shvirat HaKelim.

אורות H **Lights of the mouth**

הפה

Orot

HaPeh

When the emanations came out from the mouth of *Adam Kadmon,* they did not find an individual *Keli* (recipient) and returned to their origin in the mouth. They did not return completely, only the most tenuous part did, each one leaving its trace. The parts that remained thickened, but were still illuminated by their own parts that ascended.

When the light of the *Sephira Keter* went back up, it did not come out again, *Sephira 'Hokhma* came out and took its place, *Sephira Binah* took the place of *'Hokhma,* and so on, until *Sephira Malkhut* was left with no light,

These lights came out from the same conduit,

Hebrew / Aramaic Phonetic	L	Dictionary

intermingled, and this is how the concept of *Keli* (recipient) came to be. They spread down until the navel, but in one unique *Keli.*

אורח תחות חוטמא *Ora'h* *Ta'hot* *'Hotma*	A	**Vacant space under the nose** *Ora'h Ta'hot 'Hotma* is the third *Tikun* (action) of the *Dikna* (beard) of *Arikh Anpin,* it corresponds to the vacant space under the nose. There are hairs (lights) that come out from the face of *'Hokhma Stimaah* of *Arikh Anpin,* and spread downward. They divide in thirteen, and are called the thirteen *Tikunim* of the *Dikna* of *Arikh Anpin.* אל רחום .. מי אל כמוך. . נושא עון... Each one of these *Tikunim* has its particular function or action for the general guidance. The *Dikna* reveals the guidance of kindness, rigor and mercy, which was concealed in *'Hokhma Stimaah*, by bringing it down to *Z"A* through the two *Mazalot; Notser* and *Nake,* which are the eighth and thirteenth *Tikun.*
אורח תחות פומא *Orot* *Ta'hot* *Puma*	A	**Space under the mouth** *Orot Ta'hot Puma* is the fifth *Tikun* (action) of the *Dikna* (beard) of *Arikh Anpin,* it corresponds to the space under the mouth There are hairs (lights) that come out from the face of *'Hokhma Stimaah* of *Arikh Anpin,* and spread downward. They divide in thirteen,

56

Hebrew / Aramaic Phonetic	L	Dictionary

and are called the thirteen *Tikunim* of the *Dikna* of *Arikh Anpin*.

אל רחום ..

מי אל כמוך . . נושא עון...

Each one of these *Tikunim* has its particular function or action for the general guidance.

The *Dikna* reveals the guidance of kindness, rigor and mercy, which was concealed in *'Hokhma Stimaah*, by bringing it down to *Z"A* through the two *Mazalot; Notser* and *Nake,* which are the eighth and thirteenth *Tikun*.

אוריתא *Auraita*	A	**Torah**

The Kabbalah is the mystical and esoteric explanation of the Torah.

The Torah contains four levels of comprehension, of which the highest is the *Sod (secret)*. At this level, we understand that our *Tefilot* (prayers) and the accomplishment of each one of the *Mitsvot* (commandments) has a direct influence on the superior worlds and on their guidance. Only man, by praying and the accomplishment of the *Mitsvot* can influence these incredible forces.

As there are 613 veins and bones to man, similarly, there are 613 parts to the soul and 613 *Mitsvot* in the Torah, this number is not arbitrary as there are important interrelations and interactions between them.

Hebrew / Aramaic *Phonetic*	L	Dictionary
אות *Ot*		**Sign** Alliance as the *Brit* (circumcision), *Tefilin* etc.
אותות *Otot*	H	**Signs** *See Ot*
אותיות *Autiot*	H	**Letters** The *Autiot* are the expression of the *Ma'hshava* (thought). In combination with the *Ta'amim (cantillation)*, *Nekudot* (vowels), *Tagin* (crowns), or with other letters, they transform the higher lights into action. There are twenty two letters and five ending letters. The five ending letters correspond to the *Gevurot* (rigors).

The creative forces or energies are the different powers in the four letters of the name of G-od י-ה-ו-ה, and the various letters added to make their different spellings. All the emanations are in the order of this name and all the configurations are drawn from these four letters and their different spellings, which are called *Miluyim* (spelling of the letters). Depending on the *Miluyim* of these letters, we obtain different names as: *'A"V* (72), *SaG* (63), *MaH* (45) and *BaN* (52).

Each name can also be subdivided, as: *'A"V* of *'A"V*, *SaG* of *"A"V*, *MaH* of *'A"V* ...*BaN* of *BaN* etc. When these names act in combination with each other, more interrelations and different actions occur.

Hebrew / Aramaic Phonetic	L	Dictionary

The lights or forces that are clothed in these letters or their combinations, emanate masculine or feminine configurations that make the guidance of the worlds.

The construction of a *Partsuf* is done by the twenty two letters. For the construction of *Nukvah;* twenty two letters are given to her by *Partsuf Z"A*, once they build her, they end in her *Sephira Yesod* and make a *Keli (recipient)*. The five ending letters: מנצפך are her five *Gevurot* (rigors) and also contain the *Mayin Nukvin* (feminine waters). After the *Nesirah* (her separation from *Z"A*), when *Abah* and *Imah* have built her, they also give her twenty two letters, מנצפך and *Mayin Nukvin*.

The reading of the Torah is incomplete without the *Ta'amim, Nekudot, Tagin,* and *Autiot*. The *Ta'amim* (cantillation marks) are the highest level and subdivide in three: Higher, middle and lower. The *Nekudot* (vowels) are second, also in three levels: Higher, middle and lower. The *Tagin* (crowns) are third, and appear on top of some letters only. The *Autiot* (letters) are fourth.

The *Autiot* correspond to the name of *BaN (52)*, and to the world of *'Asiah*.

Hebrew / Aramaic *Phonetic*	L	Dictionary
אח"פ *A'Ha'P*	H	***Ozen (ears), 'Hotem (nose), Pey (mouth)*** *Initials*
אחד *E'had*	H	**One – Unique** One of the qualities of the Creator. Until the world was created, He and His Name were one. The light of G-od is unique, of equal force, quality and beyond all description. Since the concept of limitlessness is above our human comprehension, we therefore have to use terms accessible to our understanding. In the Kabbalah, the term 'quality' is used, to differentiate the various transformations of this "unique light", and to help us understand its effects upon the guidance of the worlds. The *Sephirot* or *Partsufim* are called the attributes or qualities of G-od. A *Sephira* is in a way a "filter" which transforms this unique light in a particular force or quality, by which the Creator guides the worlds. *See Sephirot, Partsufim*
אחור *A'hor*	H	**Backside – Behind** In general it represents rigor.
אחור **באחור** *A'hor* *Be* *A'hor*	H	**Back to Back** There is a notion of closeness and interaction, depending on whether the *Partsufim* (configurations) face or turn their back to each other. The three possibilities are: face to face, face to back, or back to back.

Hebrew / Aramaic *Phonetic*	L	Dictionary
		Back to back is the lowest level, and corresponds to dissimulation and rigor.
אחור בפנים *A'hor B Panim*	H	**Back to Face** There is a notion of closeness and interaction, depending on whether the *Partsufim* face or turn their back to each other. The three possibilities are: face to face, back to face, or back to back. Back to face is the second level, between the face to face which is the ideal level and corresponds to the bestowing of abundance, and back to back which corresponds to dissimulation and rigor. Back to face denotes a readiness to get close from one side only. It is a position of waiting or longing for the ideal face to face situation.
אחוריים *A'horaim*	H	**Rears** *Sephirot Netsa'h, Hod* and *Yesod (NHY)* of a *Sephira* or *Partsuf*. The *Klipot* (husks) can only attach to the rears *(NHY)* of the *Sephirot* or *Partsufim*.
אחיזה *A'hizah*	H	**To hold – Attach** The *Klipot* (husks) nourish themselves by attaching to the exteriority of the *Sephirot*. They get their livelihood from the higher lights and gain more power to act negatively. These negative forces can only get strength when men sin, and are not doing G-od's will. *See Sitra A'hra*

61

Hebrew / Aramaic *Phonetic*	L	Dictionary
אחר *A'her*	H	**Other** Name also used for the other side or negative force.
אילן *Ilan*	A	**Tree** The disposition of the *Sephirot* in the three pillars arrangement is called the *Sephirotic* tree.
אילנה דחיי *Ilana* *De'Haye*	A	**Tree of life** *See 'Ets Ha'Haim*
אילנה דמותא *Ilana de* *Motah*	A	**Tree of Death** During the night the "Tree of Life" ascends higher and the "Tree of death" governs. It is only in the morning that the governance is given back to the Tree of Life and that all the souls return in men's bodies. *(Zohar, Bamidbar)*
אין *Ein*	H	**Without - Nothing** *See Yesh Meein*
אין סוף *Ein Sof*	H	**The without end or limit - Infinite** One of the names of G-od. The Name of G-od that is the most used in the Kabbalah. His light is perfect, and cannot be measured by any definition or limiting terms. If we think about definitions, we introduce a notion of limit, or absence of its opposite. Being ourselves distinct separate beings, we cannot grasp the concept of the "non-distinct".

Hebrew / Aramaic Phonetic	L	Dictionary
		Everything we know is finite, by having a measure or an opposite. We therefore use the name "*Ein Sof*" (without limit) since we know and admit that G-od and the concept of limitlessness or without end is beyond our human comprehension.
אל El	H	***El*** One of the names of G-od, represented by the *Sephiran 'Hesed.*
אל חי El 'Hay	H	***El 'Hay*** One of the names of G-od, represented by the *Sephira Yesod.*
אלוה-ים Elohi-m	H	***Elohi-m*** One of the names of G-od, represented by the *Sephira Gevurah.* In general it denotes rigor in the actions of G-od.
אלוה-ים צבאות Elohi-m Tsebaot	H	***Elohi-m Tsebaot*** One of the names of G-od, represented by the *Sephira Hod.*
אלכסון Alakhson	H	***Diagonal*** There are lights or *Partsufim* (configurations) that are diagonal to a more important *Partsuf.* In diagonal on the two sides of *Partsuf Z"A*: "The Clouds of Glory" on his right, and "*Manna*" on his left.

Hebrew / Aramaic *Phonetic*	L	Dictionary

In diagonal on the two sides of *Partsuf Leah D'hM*: "*The Scepter of Elokim*", and "*The Scepter of Moshe*".

In diagonal on the two sides of *Partsuf Ya'acov*: "'*Erev Rav*" on his right, and "'*Essav*" on his left.

These other lights, or *Partsufim* are not considered as complete *Partsufim*; their actions are temporary and at particular times only.

| אלפין
Alphin | A | **Plural of the letter Aleph** |

One of the emanations that came out of *Adam Kadmon* is called the lower *Ta'amim* (cantillation), it came out from his mouth in the form of ten internal and ten encircling *Sephirot,* and four *Alphin* א א א א were revealed.

Another emanation came out from the nose of *Adam Kadmon* called the middle *Ta'amim (cantillation),* it came out in the form of ten internal and ten encircling *Sephirot,* and six *Alphin* א א א א א א were revealed.

| אמא
Imah | A | **Partsuf Imah** |

One of the five main configurations. It is the *Sephira Binah*. She dresses the left arm (*Gevurah*) of *Partsuf Arikh Anpin*. Her three lower *Sephirot* (*NHY* (Netsa'h, Hod, Yesod)) dress on the *NHY* of *Partsuf Abah, together* they make the *Mo'hin (brains)* of *Partsuf Z"A*. Her *Zivug (union)* with *Partsuf Abah* is constant.

Partsuf Imah had two aspects of the name of *BaN*

Hebrew / Aramaic *Phonetic*	L	Dictionary
		(52). From the first, *Imah* was made, and from the second, another *Partsuf*; *Tevunah*.
		See Abah ve Imah
אמה *Amah*	H	**Measurement** Equal to 50 cm.
אמצע *Emtsa'h*	H	**Middle** Some *Sephirot* as *'Hesed, Gevurah, Tiferet, Netsa'h and Hod* have three parts: first, middle and third. These parts emanate their lights or actions independently.
אספקלרי א דלא נהרא *Aspaklari a de lo Nehara*	A	**Non luminous mirror** From *Adam Kadmon,* different emanations spread out as a preparation for the future worlds. One of these first emanations came out from its mouth; these lights did not find an individual *Keli* (recipient) and returned to their origin in the mouth. They did not return completely, only the most tenuous part did, each one leaving its trace. The parts that remained thickened, but were still illuminated by their own parts that ascended. When the light of the *Sephira Keter* went back up, it did not come out again, *Sephira 'Hokhma* came out and took its place, *Sephira Binah* took the place of *'Hokhma*, and so on, until *Sephira Malkhut* was left with no light, like a "non luminous mirror.

Hebrew / Aramaic *Phonetic*	L	Dictionary
אצילות *Atsilut*	H	*World of Emanation*

World of Emanation

From the first configuration; *Adam Kadmon,* four worlds unfolded.

The first world to unfold is called *Atsilut;* the world of emanation, where there is no existence of the separated and no *Sitra A'hra* (evil), even at its lowest levels. It is the highest of the four worlds, on top of *Beriah, Yetsirah* and *'Asiah.*

It consists of five main *Partsufim: Arikh Anpin, Abah, Imah, Zeir Anpin* and *Nukvah.* One more *Partsuf, 'Atik Yomin,* is on top of them, his three first *Sephirot* are in the superior world (above *Atsilut*), his seven lower *Sephirot* are inside the ten *Sephirot* of *Arikh Anpin* and make the link with the superior world; *Adam Kadmon. Arikh Anpin* reaches from the top to the bottom of *Atsilut.*

In the emanation of the lights from the eyes of *Adam Kadmon,* first the individual *Keli* (recipient) for each *Sephira* came out, and then the lights. The *Kelim* could not contain their lights and broke. The seven lower broken *Sephirot,* which did not contain their lights, descended to the world of *Beriah,* the lights also fell, but stayed in *Atsilut.* The breaking of the *Kelim* caused a descent of the world of *Atsilut.* However, *KHB (Keter, 'Hokhma, Binah)* remained in what is called the "first *Atsilut".* The seven lower *Sephirot* fell in the higher parts of *Beriah,* which became the *Atsilut* of today.

Hebrew / Aramaic *Phonetic*	L	Dictionary

From *Atsilut* unfolded all the lower worlds, which are the source of existence for the physical worlds, the possibility of reward, punishment and evil.

At the bottom of *Atsilut,* the lights of its *Malkhut* collided, and a curtain was made between *Atsilut* and *Beriah* from the striking of these lights. From there, other *Partsufim* similar to the ones in *Atsilut* were formed in the lower worlds, but of a lower force since the lights were dimmed by the curtain. It is because of the diminution of these light's intensities, that existence for separated entities became possible.

The world of *Atsilut* is of the aspect of the name of 'A"V and *Partsuf Abah.*

אצילות H **Atsilut, Beriah, Yetsirah and 'Asiah**

בריאה
יצירה
עשייה
Atsilut
Beriah
Yetsirah
'Asiah

From the first configuration; *Adam Kadmon* (*Primordial man*) emanations made the four lower worlds. There is a screen (divider) that separates one world from another, and from this screen the ten *Sephirot* of the lower world came out from the ten *Sephirot* of the higher world.

The first world is *Atsilut* – the world of emanation. Under the divider of *Atsilut* is the world of *Beriah* (creation) - the world of the *Neshamot* (souls). Under the divider of *Beriah* is the world of *Yetsirah* (formation) - the world of the angels. Under the divider of *Yetsirah* is the world of *'Asiah* (action) - the

Hebrew / Aramaic *Phonetic*	L	Dictionary
		physical world.

Atsilut is of the aspect of *Partsuf Abah*, *Beriah* of *Imah*, *Yetsirah* of *Z"A*, and *'Asiah* of *Nukvah*.
All the worlds are similar (they all contain 10 *Sephirot* and five *Partsufim*), but the quintessence of the higher is superior.
See Atsilut, Beriah, Yetsirah, Asiah

אר"י
Ari

H **Ari**

See Ari Z'al

ארוך
Arokh

H **Long**

Some *Sephirot* are longer and reach higher or lower than others. The masculine *Yesod* of *Israel Saba* is longer than the feminine *Yesod* of *Tevunah;* he reaches lower and ends in *Tiferet* of *Z"A*.

ארי ז"ל
Ari Z'al

H **Rabbi Its'hak Luria Ashkenazi**

Born in Jerusalem in 1534, died in 1572 in Tsfat, Israel.
He was the leading Kabbalist in Tsfat; he explained and clarified all the main concepts of the Kabbalah. He also innovated in the explanation of the *Sephirot* and *Partsufim* (configurations). He is the author of the corpus "*Kitve HaAri*" which contains all his works in the style of *Sha'are* (entrances). His main work is the "*Ets 'Haim*".

Hebrew / Aramaic *Phonetic*	L	Dictionary

A **Partsuf – Long countenance**

The main *Partsuf* (configuration) in each world. All the other *Partsufim* are his "branches". He is called *Arikh Anpin* and his *Nukvah*, together they make one *Partsuf;* the masculine on the right and the feminine on the left.

It is by the *Zivug* (union) of *Partsuf 'Atik* that *Arikh Anpin* and his *Nukvah* were built. *Arikh Anpin* is the first *Partsuf* in *Atsilut,* and the root of all the others.
Arikh Anpin reaches from the top to the bottom of *a world*, *Abah* and *Imah* dress his right and left arm, their *Keter* reach his *Sephira Binah* and their *Malkhut* his *SephiraTiferet.*
Arikh Anpin is different from the other *Partsufim*, his *Sephira Binah* is under *Keter* and *'Hokhma,* which are in a straight line.
Partsuf 'Atik Yomin is clothed inside of *Arikh Anpin.* The *G"aR* (three first *Sephirot*) of *'Atik Yomin* are in the world above, his *Za"T* (seven lower *Sephirot*) are inside the ten *Sephirot* of *Arikh Anpin.*
The emanations and actions of *Partsuf Arikh Anpin* are called his *Tikunim* :

its three heads are the roots of the direction of kindness, rigor and mercy. They emanate from *Arikh Anpin* to *Abah* and *Imah,* and from there, to the *Mo'hin* of *Z"A.*

Hebrew / Aramaic *Phonetic*	L	Dictionary

These three heads are the first *Tikun* (action) of *Partsuf Arikh Anpin* they are:

1- *Gulgolta* - *Keter* of *Arikh Anpin*

2- *Avirah* - In the space between *Keter* and *'Hokhma* of *Arikh Anpin,* there is *Da'at* of *'Atik*

3- *Mo'ha* - *'Hokhma* of *Arikh Anpin*

The second *Tikun* is of the head of *Arikh Anpin*. It is achieved by the passing of the seven lower *Sephirot* of *'Atik* into the head of *Arikh Anpin* before they are clothed in him.

There are more *Tikunim* of *Arikh Anpin,* they are called:

'Hivarti (חיורתי) - from his *Sephira Keter*

Nimin (נימין) - from *Avirah* (*Sephira Da'at* of *'Atik;* between *Keter* and *'Hokhma*)

Dikna (דיקנא) - from his *Sephira 'Hokhma* called *'Hokhma Stimaah*

These emanations; *'Hivarti, Nimin* and *Dikna* are called hair and beard because they spread out in individual conduits.

The hairs (lights) that come out from the face of *Sephira 'Hokhma Stimaah* of *Arikh Anpin* and spread downward, divide in thirteen and are called the thirteen *Tikunim* of the *Dikna* of *Arikh Anpin*.

The other *Tikunim* are lights needed for the

Hebrew / Aramaic Phonetic	L	Dictionary
		attainment and abundance. However, the guidance itself is from the *Dikna*, and it is through it that the abundance flows. *See Tikunim, Partsuf*
אש *Esh*	H	**Fire** One of the four main levels of *Klipot* (negative husks) corresponding to the four lower worlds is called "*Eish Mitlaka'hat*" - *A dividing fire.*
אש מתלקחת *Eish* *Mitlaka'hat*	H	**Eish Mitlaka'hat - A dividing fire** One of the four main levels of *Klipot* corresponding to the four lower worlds. *See Klipot*
אשלג *Ashlag*		**Rabbi Yehudah Ashlag** Born in Poland 1886, died in Israel in 1955. One of the main contemporary Kabbalists. His main work is the translation of all the Zohar from Aramaic to Hebrew called "*HaSulam*" and "*Talmud 'Eser HaSephirot*".
אשת-חיל עטרת בעלה *Eshet* *Hail* *Ateret* *Ba'la*	H	**A virtuous woman is a crown of her husband** There can be abundance only when the masculine and the feminine are in harmony. For the abundance to come down to the world, *Partsuf Zeir Anpin* needs to unite with *Partsuf Nukvah*. He has to build her and wait until she comes from the back to back to the front-to-front position for the *Zivug* (union).

71

Hebrew / Aramaic *Phonetic*	L	Dictionary
אתב"ש *ATBaSH*	H	**ATBaSH** Permutation of letters to understand hidden meanings of words. First letter replaced by the last, second by the before last etc.
אתערותא דלעילא *Eta'arut a de La'ila*	A	***Awakening from above*** The descent of the *Mayin Dukhrin* (masculine waters of the aspect of *MaH (45)*) from *Partsuf Z"A*, happens when *Nukvah* is ready, and has brought up her *Mayin Nukvin* (feminine waters of the aspect of *BaN (52)*). It is only after the awakening from below that there is the awakening from above.
אתערותא דלתתא *Eta'arut a de Letata*	A	***Awakening from below*** There are two conditions needed for the *Zivug* (union) to be possible: The *Partsufim* have to be constructed, and the feminine has to stimulate a reaction from the masculine. This stimulation happens when she brings up her *Mayin Nukvin* (of the aspect of *BaN (52)*). It is only after the awakening from below that there is the awakening from above.

Hebrew / Aramaic Phonetic	L	Dictionary
ב"ן BaN	H	*BaN (52)* *Miluy (spelling) of the name ה-ו-ה-י with a total of 52*

The creative forces or energies are the different powers in the four letters of the name of G-od ה -ו-ה-י, and the various
letters added to make their different spellings. Depending on which letters are used, the numerical value of the name changes, and each one of these possibilities becomes different in its nature and actions.

The letters that are added for the different spellings of the letters are: י ה ו א ד
The different spellings of the letters are:
The letter י *(Yud)* can only be spelled one way: יוד
The letter ה *(He)* can be spelled with a י *(Yud)* or an א *(Aleph)* or a ה *(He):* הא הה הי
The Letter ו *(Vav)* can be spelled with a וי *(Yud and Vav)* or with או *(Aleph and Vav)* or
With a ו *(Vav):* ואו ויו וו

The four *Miluyim* (spellings) are:
עב ,סג , מה, בן - *'A"V, SaG, MaH, BaN*

יוד הי ויו הי – עב	- *'A"V* = 72
יוד הי ואו הי – סג	- *SaG* = 63
יוד הא ואו הא - מה	- *MaH* = 45
יוד הה וו הה – בן	- *BaN* = 52

Hebrew / Aramaic *Phonetic*	L	Dictionary

Each name can also be divided and subdivided as:
'A"V of 'A"V, SaG of 'A"V, MaH of 'A"V …
BaN of BaN of SaG, SaG of MaH of 'A"V etc.

The name *BaN* (52) is the *Miluy* (spelling) of the name
ה-ו-ה-י with the letter ה.
יוד הה וו הה – בן - *BaN* = 52

It corresponds to the feminine aspect - rigor, and is the root of deterioration. When it came out through the eyes of *Adam Kadmon*, the first three *Sephirot* – *KHB (Keter, 'Hokhma, Binah)* were able to stand in three columns, the seven lower *Sephirot* who only took from the lights of the mouth, could not stand in this order and broke.

The *Tikun* (rectification) is the union of the *Sephirot* of *MaH (45)* (mercy) and *BaN (52)* (rigor) in complex arrangements, as to allow the feminine *BaN (52)* to be repaired by the masculine *MaH (45),* and for the *Sephirot* to stand in the three-column arrangement of kindness, rigor and mercy

All the emanations and *Sephirot* that came out of *Adam Kadmon (Primordial man)* by way of his apertures were of the various aspects of these four names. They have different actions and *Tikunim,* and all the *Partsufim (configurations)* will be constructed by their union.

See Orot Ha'Enayim, Sephirot Shel BaN

74

Hebrew / Aramaic *Phonetic*	L	Dictionary
באר *Beer*	H	**Well** Partsuf Leah is called the higher well, Partsuf Ra'hel the lower well.
בוהו *Bohu*	H	**Void** The world of Shvirat HaKelim (breaking of the vessels).
בוצינא *Butsina*	A	**Light** See Or
בוצינא קדישא *Butsina Kadisha*	A	**The saintly light or lamp** Name given to Rabbi Shim'on Bar Yo'hai, author of the Zohar.
בורא *Boreh*	H	**The Creator** One of the names of G-od.
בחינה *Be'hina*	H	**Aspect - Feature – Quality** The light of G-od is unique, of equal force, quality and beyond all description. Since the concept of limitlessness is above our human comprehension, we therefore have to use terms accessible to our understanding. In Kabbalah the term 'quality' is used, to differentiate the various transformations of this "unique light", and to help us understand its effects upon the guidance of the worlds.

The Sephirot or Partsufim are called the attributes or |

Hebrew / Aramaic Phonetic	L	Dictionary

qualities of G-od. A *Sephira* is in a way a "filter" which transforms this light in a particular force or quality, by which the Creator guides the worlds.

See Sephirot, Partsufim

בחינות H **Aspects - Features – Qualities**
Be'hinot   *See Be'hinah*

בחירה H **Choice**
Be'hirah

Since the intention of the Creator is to bestow goodness on His creatures, all the levels of creation were put in place so His kindness could emanate to them, yet in such a way that they would be able to receive it. Complete rigor will be the destruction of anything not perfect, while complete kindness will permit everything without restriction. However, these two aspects are necessary to make the guidance of kindness and justice and to give man the possibility of serving the Creator by their free will.

After the *Shvirat HaKelim* (breaking of the vessels) with the emanation of the lights of the name *MaH (45)* and *BaN (52)*, He could have done the *Tikun* (repair) of all the worlds, but then, there would not have been a reason for the participation of man in this *Tikun*. For man to have a possibility to act and repair the creation, G-od restrained in a way, his outflow of kindness to this world, to give men the merit of doing the *Tikun* with their free will. The root of

Hebrew / Aramaic Phonetic	L	Dictionary

the *Sitra A'hra* (negative force) is in the lack, or absence of the *Kedushah* (holiness). Its existence was willed by the Creator to give man free choice.

The good deeds of man have an effect on the four higher worlds, his bad deeds; on the four lower worlds. It is only when man sins, that the negative side can grow in strength. His negative aspect (his *Yetser Hara')* grows inside him, cuts him off from the higher worlds, and uproots him from the *Kedushah.* It almost constantly tries to seduce him and make him stumble, while the *Yetser Hatov* (positive aspect)*,* on the other side, tries to attract him to *Torah* and *Mitsvot* and to help him do the *Tikun* of his *Neshama.*

The two aspects of *Yetser Tov* and *Yetser Hara'* are also necessary for the guidance of justice, and to give man the possibility of free choice.

בטן H **Abdomen**

Beten

After the diffusion of the lights of the name *"A"V* of *SaG* from the ears, nose and mouth, the other lights of the name *SaG* needed to come out also. Inside of *Adam Kadmon (in his abdomen), SaG* gathered its own aspects of *MaH (45)* and *BaN (52)* together with the general *MaH (45)* and *BaN (52)* of *Adam Kadmon.* It brought them up above the navel and put a veil as a separation.

Hebrew / Aramaic Phonetic	L	Dictionary
בי"ע *BYA'*	H	***Beriah, Yetsirah, Asiah*** Initials
ביאה קדמאה *Bia* *Kadma'*	A	***First intercourse*** The *Partsuf Nukvah* cannot receive from *Partsuf Z"A*, until she becomes a *Keli (recipient)*; this is the goal of the first union. On this first union, it is said: "A woman is an unfinished vessel, and binds a covenant only with who makes her a *Keli*." (Sanhedrin 22.b)
ביאור *Biur*	H	***Explanation*** Clarifications and explanations are needed to understand the sometimes complex concepts of the Kabbalah.
ביטול *Bitul*	H	***Nullification*** There is sometimes nullification of an inferior force or emanation, when a higher one intervenes.
בינה *Binah*	H	***Sephira (understanding)*** Third of the *Sephirot*. Quality: Kindness to all, even to the less deserving (but from her, the rigors start). Column: Left – *Din* (rigor) Position: Top – left Other *Sephirot* on the same column: *Gevurah, Hod.*

Hebrew / Aramaic *Phonetic*	L	Dictionary
		Partsufim made from this *Sephira:* - *Imah* - From *Malkhut* of *Binah -Tevunah* - From *Malkhut* of *Tevunah* - *Tevunah* 2 Corresponding name: YHV-H י-ה-ו-ה *(but with the vowels of Elokim)* Corresponding *Miluy* of name: *SaG* - סג (63) Corresponding vowel: *Tsere* Physical correspondence: Left brain Level of the soul: *Neshama*. See Sephira, Partsuf
בירא *Bira*	A	**Well** See Beer
בירור *Birur*	H	**Selection or clarification** Act of separation between the positive and negative.
בית *Bayit*	H	**House** A *Hekhal (portal)* is sometimes called a house. See Hekhal
בית המקדש *Beit hamikdash*		**The Temple** When the Temple was built, the guidance of 'Hesed – Kindness was prevailing.
בית קבול *Beit Kibul*	H	**Receptacle – Container** To hold the *Tumah* (impurity), a receptacle has to be in a shape able to contain a substance.

Hebrew / Aramaic Phonetic	L	Dictionary
ביתא Beita	A	**Home** See Bayit
בעל שם טוב Ba'al Shem tov		**Ba'al Shem Tov** *Rabbi Israel Ben Eliezer* Born in 1698 in Russia, died in Ukraine in 1760 The founder of the 'Hassidic movement. He declared the whole universe, mind and matter, to be a manifestation of G-od, and that whoever maintains that this life is worthless is in error, it is worth a great deal; only one must know how to use it properly. Being a living legend, the *Ba'al Shem Tov* spent most of his time in worship, serving G-od, teaching his disciples, and giving blessings to the thousands that came to see him. One of his favorite sayings was that no man has sunk too low to be able to raise himself to God.
בציור Betsiur	H	**In the form of** Similar. In the same way as.
בקיעה Beki'ah	H	**Cleaving** Emanations or lights can cleave out from an inside to the outside. From the forehead of *Partsuf* (configuration) *Z"A*, emerged and cleaved out four emanations which are his four *Mo'hin* (brains), these are the four *Parashiot* of the head *Tefilin*. The four compartments are their garments.

Hebrew / Aramaic Phonetic	L	Dictionary

From the *Sephira Yesod* of *Imah* cleaved out an emanation which is one of the aspects of *Partsuf Leah*, but this time outside of *Partsuf Z"A,* and made the main *Leah.*

בר יוחאי
Bar Yo'hay

Rabbi Shim'on Bar Yo'hay

Born in Galilee and died in Meron, Israel during the 2nd century.

He was a disciple of *Rabbi Akiva.* To escape the Romans he went into hiding with his son *Rabbi El'azar* in a cave for thirteen years. During this time he composed the *Zohar* which is the esoteric and mystical explanation of the Torah, and the base for most of the Kabbalah writings.

ברודים H
Berudim

Berudim

See *'Olam HaBerudim*

ברוך הוא H
Barukh Hu

Blessed He is

Used after the pronunciation or writing of G-od's names.

בריאה H
Beriah

World of creation – of the souls

From the first configuration of *Adam Kadmon,* four worlds unfolded.

On these four worlds, the four letters of the Name (ה-ו-ה-י) *B'H*, govern.

י in *Atsilut;* by it, all the repaired levels are put in order.

Hebrew / Aramaic Phonetic	L	Dictionary

ה descends from it (*Atsilut*) to *Beriah,* and guides it.
ו to *Yetsirah,* and ה to *'Asiah.*
The second world to unfold is called *Beriah*; the world
of creation. It is the world of the *Neshamot* (souls). It
is under *Atsilut* and on top of *Yetsirah* and *'Asiah.*

It consists of five main *Partsufim: Arikh Anpin, Abah,
Imah, Zeir Anpin* and *Nukvah.* One more *Partsuf,
'Atik Yomin,* is on top of them, his three first *Sephirot*
are in the superior world (*Atsilut*), his seven lower
Sephirot are inside the ten *Sephirot* of *Arikh Anpin*
and make the link with the superior world; *Atsilut .
Arikh Anpin* reaches from the top to the bottom of
Beriah.
In the emanation of the lights from the eyes of *Adam
Kadmon,* first the individual *Keli* (recipient) for each
Sephira came out, and then the lights. The *Kelim*
could not contain their lights and broke. The seven
lower broken *Sephirot*, which did not contain their
lights, descended to the world of *Beriah*, the lights
also fell, but stayed in *Atsilut.* The breaking of the
Kelim caused a descent of all the worlds, *SaG (63),
MaH (45)* and *BaN (52)* descended to the lower
worlds, *SaG* descended in *Beriah (creation)* and
Beriah fell lower to become the *Atsilut (emanation)* of
today.
At the bottom of *Beriah,* the lights of its *Malkhut*
collided, and a curtain was made between *Beriah*

Hebrew / Aramaic Phonetic	L	Dictionary

and *Yetsirah* from the striking of these lights. From there, other *Partsufim* similar to the ones in *Beriah* were formed in the lower worlds, but of a lower force since the lights were dimmed by the curtain. It is because of the diminution of these light's intensities, that existence became possible for even more separated entities as angels and man.

In parallel to the four worlds (*ABYA*), there are four types of existence in our world; mineral corresponding to *'Asiah (action)*, vegetal corresponding to *Yetsirah (formation)*, animal corresponding to *Beriah (creation)*, and man corresponding to *Atsilut (emanation)*.
The world of *Beriah (creation)* is of the aspect of *SaG (63)*. Thus, *Beriah* is of the aspect of *Partsuf Imah – Sephira Binah*.

ברייה H **Creature**
Briah Of the four worlds, three contain separate creatures. *Neshamot* (souls) in *Beriah* (creation), angels in *Yetsirah* (formation), physical beings in *'Asiah* (action).

ברית H **Covenant – Circumcision**
Brit Represented by the *Sephira Yesod*.

ברכה H **Blessing**
Berakha When saying the blessing with the Kabbalistic

Hebrew / Aramaic Phonetic	L	Dictionary

meditation on the appropriate words or names, we act and participate directly on the *Tikun* (repair) of the thing being blessed.

See Kavanot

ברסלב
Breslev

Rabbi Na'hman of Breslev
Born in Russia in 1772, died in Uman, Russia in 1811
Rabbi Na'hman was the great grandson of the Ba'al Shem Tov. He gave great importance to "*Dvekut*" (attachment to G-od) and pure joy. Some of his main works are "*Likutey Moharan*", "*Tikun HaKlali*" and his well known stories and fables.

בשר H *Flesh*
Bassar

Used as a metaphoric description of an emanation of *Partsuf Imah*. When *NHY (Netsa'h, Hod, Yesod)* of *Imah* entered in *Partsuf Z"A*, her skin, flesh, bones and veins included with his. A *Levush (garment)* was made for *Z"uN (Z"A and Nukvah),* from the exteriors of *NHY (Tevunah)* of *Imah*. In *NHY* there are three aspects of *Kelim (recipients)*: flesh, bones and veins, and one more aspect of *Keli* from *Malkhut*, which is the skin in surplus of *Imah*.

Hebrew / Aramaic Phonetic	L	Dictionary

ג'
ראשונות
Shalosh Rishonot

H **The three first Sephirot**

Keter, 'Hokhma, Binah

The roots of all the created are in the seven lower *Sephirot* (*Za"T*), the three first *Sephirot* are like a crown on the *Za"T* to repair and direct them. In the three first *Sephirot* there is not really a notion of damage, they are above men's deeds, and are not affected by their sins.

In the *Shvirat HaKelim* (breaking of the vessels), the inferior part of *'Hokhma* and *Binah* did not contain their lights, they fell but did not break. These lower parts correspond to what is needed for the guidance of the seven lower *Sephirot*, if it had contained their lights, these *Sephirot* would not have broken, and the notions of *Kilkul* (damage) and *Tikun* (repair) not existed.

ג"ר
G"aR

H **The three first Sephirot**

Keter, 'Hokhma, Binah

גבול
Gevul

H **Boundary – Limit**

By putting boundaries to His light, the Creator revealed the concepts of rigor and limit needed by the created beings, and gave a space for all the created to exist.

See Tsimtsum

Hebrew / Aramaic *Phonetic*	L	Dictionary

גבורה H **Rigor**
Gevurah

The light of G-od is unique, of equal force, quality and beyond all description. In Kabbalah the term 'quality' is used, to differentiate the various transformations of this "unique light", and to help us understand its effects upon the guidance of the worlds.

The *Sephirot* or *Partsufim* (configurations) are called the attributes or qualities of G-od. A *Sephira* is in a way a "filter" which transforms this light in a particular force or quality, by which the Creator guides the worlds. One of these manifestations of this light once filtered by the *Sephira Gevurah* emanates rigor.

The *Sephirot* are arranged in three columns: right, left and middle, representing the guidance of the world in the manner of *'Hesed, Din* and *Ra'hamim* - Kindness, rigor and mercy. In the attribute of rigor, the guidance is from the left pillar – the pillar of rigor, it contains the *Sephirot: Binah, Gevurah, Hod.* The corresponding name to this attribute is: *Elohi-m* - אלהי-ם

Some *Partsufim* are masculine and bestow kindness, others are feminine and bestow rigor. By their union, different equilibriums of these two forces (Kindness and rigor), make the guidance. Complete rigor will be the destruction of anything not perfect, while complete kindness will permit everything without restriction. Thus we see that everything that is, and happens, is always composed of a variable measure and balance of these two forces.

Hebrew / Aramaic Phonetic	L	Dictionary

Rigor is mostly manifested by all the feminine aspects as: the name of *BaN (52)*, the *Sephira Gevurah* and by all the concealments of the masculine aspects which represent bounty.

There are particular moments, or days of rigor during the year. This is dependent on the different position of the *Partsufim.* In the absence of *Zivug* (union) when the masculine and feminine *Partsuf* are back to back, it corresponds to dissimulation and rigor.

גבורה *Gevurah*	H	**Sephira (Rigor)** Fifth of the *Sephirot.* Quality: Full rigor to who is deserving. Column: Left – *Din* (rigor) Position: Left – Middle Other *Sephirot* on the same column: *Binah, Hod.*

Partsufim made from this *Sephira:*
One of the *Sephirot* that make the *Partsuf Z"A.*
Corresponding name: *Elohi-m* אלהי-ם
Corresponding *Miluy* of name: *MaH* (מה) 45
Corresponding vowel: *Sheva*
Physical correspondence: Left arm
Level of the soul: *Rua'h*
See Gevurah, Sephira, Partsuf

גבורות *Gevurot*	H	**Rigors** For the guidance five emanations of the aspect of *'Hesed* (kindness) and five emanations of the aspect of *Gevurah* (rigors), are given by the *Sephira Da'at* to

Hebrew / Aramaic Phonetic	L	Dictionary

the *Partsufim* (configurations) *Z"A* and *Nukvah*. *Partsuf Z"A* receives the five *'Hasadim* and *Nukvah* receives the five *Gevurot*.

The five *Gevurot* come down afterwards and are appeased in *Yesod* of *Partsuf Z"A*, two and a half in the descent, and two and a half by the *'Hasadim* returning upwards. From the *Sephira Yesod* of *Z"A*, the *Gevurot* are given to the *Sephira Da'at* of *Nukvah*, they go down until her *Yesod* and then ascend to her *Sephira Keter*.

Rigor is also manifested by the five ending letters: מנצפך, they are called the five *Gevurot,* and also contain the *Mayin Nukvin* (feminine waters).

See Gevurah, Mayin Nukvin

גג
Gag

H **Roof**

See Ma'akeh

גדול
Gadol

H **Big – Adult**

A *Partsuf* (configuration) is called big or adult when it has received all his *Mo'hin* (brains), and is in *Gadlut* (growth) 1 or *Gadlut* 2. *See Gadlut, Zeir Anpin*

גדלות
Gadlut

H **Adulthood – Growth**

The *Gadlut* of a *Partsuf* (configuration) is its final stage of growth, when it is able to act with all its strength. There are two stages of *Gadlut*: *Gadlut* 1 and *Gadlut* 2.

At first, during the gestation in the upper *Nukvah* (the

Hebrew / Aramaic Phonetic	L	Dictionary

Nukvah above), the lights of *MaH* *(45)* needed for the *Tikun* (repair) are drawn to the lights of *BaN* *(52)*, and are kept in the upper *Nukvah* to give birth to the *Partsuf.*

Inside of *Nukvah*, the *Partsuf* is arranged and completed until there is nothing more to add. When it is totally repaired, the *Partsuf* is revealed, this is the birth.

Once on the outside there is a period of suckling, first infancy and growth. Afterwards, there is a second period of infancy and growth. It is only after the second growth that a *Partsuf* is considered fully grown. *See Mo'hin, Partsuf, Z"A*

| גדלות ראשון של ז"א Gadlut rishon shel Z"A | H | **First growth of Z"A** |

The *Gadlut* of a *Partsuf* (configuration) is its final stage of growth, when it is able to act with all its strength. At first, *Partsuf Z"A* is in a state of *Dormita* (somnolence), to act it needs to get his *Mo'hin* (brains) from *Partsuf ISOT* or *Partsuf Abah* and *Imah*, and to get to a stage of growth.

Inside of *Partsuf Imah, Z"A* goes through a period of gestation, followed by a first period of infancy and a first growth. In the first growth his *Mo'hin* are from *NHY (Netsa'h, Hod, Yesod)* of *Partsuf Tevunah.* During the time of the gestation, *Z"A* is not really acting as it is being built, at the time of suckling it starts to act, and at the growth it is ready to act.

Hebrew / Aramaic Phonetic	L	Dictionary

The *Mo'hin* that are given to *Z"A*, do not enter completely in him; only the *NHY* (Netsa'h, Hod, Yesod) do, the rest stays on top of him, encircling his head.

The *NHY* which are composed of nine parts, correspond to the צ, and spread in the nine *Sephirot* of *Z"A*. The encircling *Mo'hin* are ל מ, they do not need to spread in him, and stand on his exterior in the three-column arrangement of kindness, rigor and mercy. This is *Gadlut* 1.

גדלות שני
של ז"א
Gadlut
sheni
shel
Z"A

H **Second growth of Z"A**

The *Gadlut* of a *Partsuf* (configuration) is its final stage of growth, when it is able to act with all its strength. After its first growth, *Z"A* goes through a second period of gestation, followed by a second period of infancy and a second of growth. In the second growth, his *Mo'hin* are directly from *Abah* and *Imah* and enter in the same way as in the first growth. During the time of the second gestation, *Z"A* is not really acting as it is being built, at the time of suckling it starts to act, and at the growth it is ready to act with its full strength.

It is only after the second growth, that *Z"A* has reached its full potential. This is *Gadlut* 2.

גוף
Guf

H **Body**

A *Partsuf* or *Sephira* has two parts; its head which are the three first *Sephirot* of *Keter*, *'Hokhma*, *Binah*, and its body which are the seven other *Sephirot*.

See Sephira, Partsuf

Hebrew / Aramaic Phonetic	L	Dictionary
גופא Gufa	A	**Body** *See Guf*
גזר Gazar	H	**To decree** An outcome that has been decided. *See Gezera*
גזרה Gezera	H	**Decree – Edict** One of the important decrees, and for reasons only known to Him, the Creator decreed that man should not be able to see the truth and the finality of everything without much effort.
גידים Gidim	H	**Sinews** There are 613 parts to the soul, similarly, there are 613 *Mitsvot*, and 613 sinews and bones to man, this number is not arbitrary, as there are important interrelations and interactions between them.
גילוי Giluy	H	**Revelation – Clarity** There are periods of more or less revelation depending on time and the positions of the *Partsufim*.
גילוי יחודו Giluy Yi'hudo	H	**Revelation of his unity** The goal of all the complex inter-relations and possibilities of guidance have only one purpose: to allow man to merit by his own efforts, to get closer to his Creator, and live the *Dvekut* – the adhesion with G-od. In this way, man will attain perfection and be directly involved in the ultimate goal of the creation, which is the revelation of *Giluy Ye'hudo* –G-od's sovereignty.

Hebrew / Aramaic *Phonetic*	L	Dictionary
גימטריה *Gematria*	H	**Numerical values of the letters**

Numerical values of the letters

Each letter has its own numerical value. The fact that some words have the same numerical value is not just coincidence, but denotes a similarity or complementarity.

There are seven main types of *Gematriot*:

Ragil, Katan, HaKlali, Kolel, HaKadmi, HaPerati, Miluy

1 - *Ragil*: the numbers of the letters are as follows:

From	To	Value
א	ט	1 - 9
י	צ	10 -90
ק	ת	100 - 400
ך	ץ	500 -900

Ex :   הארץ   = 1106

2 – *Katan*: tens and hundreds are reduced to one digit.

From	To	Value
א	ט	1 - 9
י	צ	1 - 9
ק	ת	1 - 4
ך	ץ	5 -9

Ex :   הארץ   = 17

3 – *HaKlali*: the *Ragil* value of the word squared.
Ex : הארץ = 1106 * 1106 = 1 223 236

4 – *Kolel*: the *Ragil* value of the word + the numbers of letters, or + 1 for the word.
Ex :   הארץ   = 1106 + 4 = 1110 or 1106 + 1 = 1107

Hebrew / Aramaic Phonetic	L	Dictionary

5 – *HaKadmi* : each letter has its *Ragil* value plus the total of all the ones preceding it.

From	To	Value
א	ט	1 - 45
י	צ	55 – 495
ק	ת	595 –1495
ך	ץ	1995 – 4995

Ex : הארץ = 15+1+795+4995 = 5806

6 – *HaPerati* : each letter is squared.
Ex : הארץ = 5 * 5 = 25, 1 * 1 = 1
200 * 200 = 40 000, 900 * 900 = 810 000 Total = 850 026

7 – *Miluy:* the sum of the spelling of each letter.

Letter	Miluy	Value
ה	הא	6
א	אלף	111
ר	ריש	510
ץ	צדי	104

Ex : הארץ = 731 *See Miluy*

גימל בגימל *Gimel* *Be* *Gimel*	H	**Three on three** After the *Shvirat HaKelim* (breaking of the vessels), when the lights were separated from their *Kelim*, the first act of reparation for this damage was to reunite again these fallen lights and *Kelim*. To repair them *Partsuf Arikh Anpin* folded his legs (*NHY* (Netsa'h, Hod, Yesod)) and drew them upwards.

Hebrew / Aramaic Phonetic	L	Dictionary

Partsuf Arikh brought up his three lower *Sephirot* – *NHY* (legs) and the lower third of his *Tiferet,* on to clothe his *HGT* (*'Hesed, Gevurah, Tiferet*), this is called the folding of the legs; three *(NHY)* on three (*HGT*). This folding made an attraction that drew the *Kelim* of *Z"A* upward on the *Sephirot* of *HGT* and *NHY* of *Arikh Anpin* that were folded on themselves in *Atsilut.*

This folding of the legs of *Partsuf Arikh Anpin* was the first force given to the broken *Kelim* of the seven *Sephirot* to ascend to *Atsilut.*

See Kipul Reglaim shel Arikh Anpin

גלגול
Gilgul
H **Reincarnation**

The soul has five names: *Nefesh, Rua'h, Neshama, 'Hayah* and *Ye'hidah,* which correspond to its five levels. The soul is the spiritual entity inside the body, the latter being only his outer garment.

Each level of the soul is subdivided in five levels. As for the level of *Nefesh;* there are *Nefesh* of *Nefesh, Rua'h* of *Nefesh, Neshama* of *Nefesh, 'Hayah* of *Nefesh* and *Ye'hidah* of *Nefesh.*
As there are for each of the five worlds; ten *Sephirot* and five *Partsufim.* Each soul has its origin corresponding to one of these levels. Therefore, a soul could be from the level of *Nefesh* of *Malkhut* of *Nukvah* of *'Asiah,* or *Rua'h* of *'Hesed* of *Abah* of *'Yetsirah,* or *Neshama* of *Abah* of *Z"A* of *Yetsirah* etc.

The higher levels of the soul cannot be acquired at once. Most men only have the level of *Nefesh,* and if they merit, they will acquire the next levels - but one by one.

To reach the next higher level of his soul, man must do the *Tikun* of the preceding level. The *Tikun (rectification)* of the soul is realized by the *Gilgul* (reincarnation), and by the *'Ibur* (attachment). The *Gilgul* is the reincarnation of a soul from the time of birth until death, the *'Ibur* is an attachment of another soul to his, which could come and leave anytime.

There is a *Levush* (garment) or envelope, which is necessary for the soul to attach to the body of man (*Gilgul*), and when another soul attaches to him (*'Ibur*), it could use the same *Levush* to remain in him.

By accomplishing what he did not accomplish of the 613 *Mitsvot,* man makes the necessary *Tikun* of his soul, which can now elevate to the higher realms and rejoin its source. But if man does not do the *Tikun* of the level of his soul for which he came, he comes back and reincarnates. It is not all of the soul that comes back, but only the parts that need to be repaired (by doing the missing *Mitsva*), that come again.

For the *Mitsvot* that it was obligated to accomplish, it accomplishes them by the *Gilgul*, for the ones it did

Hebrew / Aramaic Phonetic	L	Dictionary

not have to accomplish, it accomplishes them by the *'Ibur,* which departs afterwards.

To help him accomplish the missing *Mitsvot,* another soul could attach to his soul (*'Ibur*), until he accomplishes it, and then departs. The missing *Mitsva* could be one he chose not to do, or one he could not do in his previous life.

As long as one undertakes the *Tikun* of his soul in three reincarnations, he will come back again as needed to complete his *Tikun.* However, if he maintains his wrong behaviour, he will not come back after the third reincarnation.

The goal of all these complex systems of reincarnation has only one purpose: to allow man to merit by his own efforts, to get closer to his Creator, by perfecting his ways and doing the *Tikun* of his soul.

See Tikun, Neshama

גלגל H ***Wheel***
Galgal

See Sephirot Ha'Igulim

גלגלתא A ***First of the three heads of Arikh Anpin***
Gulgolta

The three heads of *Arikh Anpin* are the roots of the direction of kindness, rigor and mercy. They emanate from *Arikh Anpin* to *Abah* and *Imah,* and from there, to the *Mo'hin* (brains) of *Z"A.*

These three heads are the first *Tikun* (action) of *Partsuf Arikh Anpin* they are:

96

Hebrew / Aramaic Phonetic	L	Dictionary

1- *Gulgolta* - *Keter* of *Arikh Anpin*

2- *Avirah* - In the space between *Keter* and *'Hokhma* of *Arikh Anpin,* there is *Da'at* of *'Atik*

3- *Mo'ha* - *'Hokhma* of *Arikh Anpin*

For each head there are three levels of lights: Interior, encircling (*Makif*), and encircling of the encircling (*Makif* le *Makif*). The name י-ה-ו-ה represents the interiority, the name א-ה-י-ה the encircling. Depending on their vowels they correspond to one of the three heads.

They differentiate by their *Nekudot* (vowels).

When the first letters have the vowels as pronounced – interiority

The *Miluy* has vowels as pronounced – encircling

The *Miluy* has *Kamatz* as a vowel, and the first letters have vowels as

pronounced – encircling of encircling. This is the first head – *Gulgolta.*

גלגלתא לבנה *Gulgolta Levanah*	A	**Gulgolta Levanah**

From the head of *Partsuf* (configuration) *Arikh Anpin,* seven emanations come out to act and influence on the guidance, called the *Tikunim* of *Arikh Anpin.*

The second *Tikun* (action) of *Arikh Anpin* is achieved by the passing of the seven lower *Sephirot* of *'Atik* into its head before they are clothed in him. These seven *Tikunim* of the head of *Arikh Anpin* are revealed from the seven lower *Sephirot* of *'Atik*

The first *Tikun* - גולגלתא לבנה (*Gulgolta Levanah*) is

Hebrew / Aramaic Phonetic	L	Dictionary
		realized by *'Hesed* of *'Atik*; this is the root of all the *'Hasadim*.
גמור **Gamur**	H	**Complete - Finish** *(masculine)* A *Partsuf* is *Gamur* after the stages of *'Ibur, Yenikah, Leida, Katnut* (gestation, suckling, birth, and infancy) , has received all his *Mo'hin* (brains), and is in *Gadlut* (growth) 1 or *Gadlut* 2.
גמורה **Gmurah**	H	**Complete - Finish** *(feminine)* See Gamur
גן עדן **Gan 'Eden**	H	**The Garden of Eden** The place of rest for the *Neshamot* (souls) after their separation with their former physical bodies. There is a lower and a higher *Gan 'Eden*.
גן עדן עליון **Gan 'Eden 'Elyon**	H	**The upper Garden of Eden** In the higher *Gan 'Eden*, the *Neshamot* (souls) are enjoying pure spiritual pleasures, and do not have any spiritual image resembling their former bodies.
גן עדן תחתון **Gan 'Eden Takhton**	H	**The lower Garden of Eden** In the lower *Gan 'Eden*, the *Neshamot* (souls) are enjoying spiritual pleasures but still have a spiritual body resembling their former bodies.
גנוז **Ganuz**	H	**Concealed - Hidden** Some emanations or *Sephirot* are hidden. Like *Sephira Da'at* of *Partsuf 'Atik Yomin* which is hidden

Hebrew / Aramaic Phonetic	L	Dictionary
		in *Avirah;* one of the three heads of *Arikh Anpin.*
גס Gass	H	**Coarse** The *Klipot* (husks) are by definition of a coarse nature. They get their strength by attaching to the lower *Sephirot* and nourish from the lights of the *Kedushah* (holiness).
גרון Garon	H	**Throat** Of the thirteen *Tikunim* (rectification) of the *Dikna* (beard) of *Partsuf Arikh Anpin;* the eleventh *Tikun* is the hair on the throat.
גשמיות Gashmiut	H	**Corporeality** The possibilities of existence for separated entities became possible, only once distanced from the intensity of His light. The greater the distance more is the corporality possible. Under each world there is a divider, which further diminishes the intensity of the light. Under the divider of *Atsilut,* is the world of *Beriah;* the world of creation, the beginning of existence for the separated; it is the world of the souls. Under the divider of *Beriah,* is the world of *Yetsirah;* the world of formation, the world of the angels. Under the divider of *Yetsirah,* is the world of *'Asiah;* the world of action, the world of corporeality - physical existence.

Hebrew / Aramaic Phonetic	L	Dictionary
דבוק *Davuk*	H	**Attached - Joined to** Even if they are two distinct *Partsufim* (configurations) and have their own *Tikunim* (actions), all the time that *Partsuf Z"A* is being built, *Partsuf Nukvah* is attached to him. For the abundance to come down to the world, *Partsuf Zeir Anpin* needs to unite with *Nukvah*. There can be abundance only when the masculine and the feminine are not joined back to back and come to a face to face position.
דבקות *Dvekut*	H	**Adhesion – Adherence** The goal of all the complex inter-relations and possibilities of guidance, have only one purpose: to allow man to merit by his own efforts, to get closer to his Creator, and live the *Dvekut* – the adhesion with G-od. In this way, man will attain perfection and be directly involved in the ultimate goal of the creation, which is the revelation of *Giluy Ye'hudo* – G-od's Sovereignty.
דו"ן *D"uN*	A	**Masculine and feminine** Initials
דוחה *Do'heh*	H	**Rejects - To push** *Partsuf Z"A* pushes out by his rear his *Gevurot* (rigors) to *Nukvah*.
דוכרין *Dukhrin*	A	**Masculine** See *Mayin Dukhrin*

Hebrew / Aramaic Phonetic	L	Dictionary
דוכרין ונוקבין Dukhrin VeNukvin	A	**Masculine and feminine** *See Mayin Dukhrin, Mayin Nukvin*
דומם Domem	H	**Inanimate** In parallel to the four worlds of *Atsilut, Beriah, Yetsirah* and *'Asiah,* there are four types of existence in our world: mineral (דומם), vegetal (צומח), animal (חי), and the speaking (מדבר). Mineral corresponds to the world of *'Asiah.*
דומם, צומח, חי, מדבר Domem, Tsomeah 'Hay, Medaber	H	**Mineral, vegetal, animal and the spoken** In parallel to the four worlds of *Atsilut, Beriah, Yetsirah* and *'Asiah,* there are four types of existence in our world: mineral (דומם), vegetal (צומח), animal (חי), and the speaking (מדבר). Mineral corresponding to *'Asiah*, vegetal corresponding to *Yetsirah*, animal corresponding to *Beriah,* and the speaking corresponding to *Atsilut.*
דורמיטא Dormita	A	**Sleep – Somnolence** At first *Partsuf Z"A* is in a state of *Dormita* (somnolence), to act it needs to get his *Mo'hin (brains)* from *Partsuf ISOT* or from *Partsuf Abah* and *Imah,* and to get to a stage of growth. Inside of *Partsuf Imah, Partsuf Z"A* goes through a period of gestation, followed by a first period of infancy and a first growth. In the first growth his *Mo'hin* are from *NHY (Netsa'h, Hod, Yesod)* of *Partsuf Tevunah.* During

Hebrew / Aramaic *Phonetic*	L	Dictionary

the time of the gestation, *Z"A* is not really acting as it is being built, at the time of suckling it starts to act, and at the growth it is ready to act.

דיבור H *Speech*

Dibur From the lights that were invested inside of *Adam Kadmon* emerged numerous worlds in the way of his senses; which are called his branches.

These "branches" are the lights that spread forth from *Adam Kadmon,* by way of its apertures in the head, four of which are called: Sight, hearing, smell and speech. They spread out from his eyes, ears, nose, and mouth.

In the language of Kabbalah, we use names of body parts solely to illustrate the esoteric powers of these forces. It is understood, of course, that there is no physical existence at these level. When we say ears, mouth, or any other physical expression, the goal is to describe the inner sense, or the position they represent.

These emanations and configurations are drawn from the four letters of the Name of G-od. *B'H*, and their different spellings, which are called *Miluyim (spelling)*. From the mouth came out lights of the aspect of *SaG* (lower *Ta'amim*).

See Orot HaPeh

Hebrew / Aramaic Phonetic	L	Dictionary

דין H **Rigor – Judgment**
Din

At first, the *Ein Sof* (without end) retracted His light from a certain space, and encircled it, so that it would not emanate with its full force. By putting boundaries to his light, He revealed the concepts of rigor and limit needed by the created beings, and gave a space for all the created to exist.

From the *Kav* (ray), ten *Sephirot* were formed in a linear arrangement, and later in three columns: right, left and middle, representing the guidance of the world in the manner of *'Hesed*, *Din* and *Ra'hamim* (Kindness, rigor and mercy).
On the left, the *Din* (rigor) column contains the *Sephirot: Binah, Gevurah, Hod.*
Some *Partsufim* are masculine and bestow kindness, others are feminine and bestow rigor. By their union, different equilibriums of these two forces (Kindness and rigor), make the guidance. Complete rigor will be the destruction of anything not perfect, while complete kindness will permit everything without restriction. Thus we see that everything that is, and happens, is always composed of a variable measure and balance of these two forces.

Rigor is manifested by all the feminine aspects as: The name of *BaN (52)*, the *Sephira Gevurah* and by all the concealments of the masculine aspects which represent bounty.

Hebrew / Aramaic *Phonetic*	L	Dictionary

| דיקנא
Dikna | A | **Beard (illuminations of the face)** |

Beard (illuminations of the face)

There are hairs (lights) that come out from the face of *Partsuf Arikh Anpin* and *Partsuf Z"A*. They are called *Dikna* (beard), because they spread out in individual conduits.

The ones of *Arikh Anpin* come out from his *'Hokhma Stimaah* and spread downward. They divide in thirteen, and are the thirteen *Tikunim* (actions) of the *Dikna* of *Arikh Anpin*.

The other *Tikunim* are lights needed for the attainment and abundance. However, the guidance itself is from the *Dikna*, it is through it that the abundance flows. The hairs of the *Dikna* are short and stiff, being of the aspect of rigor. They are also divided in two aspects: masculine; which includes the first twelve *Tikunim,* and feminine, which comprise the thirteenth *Tikun*. Each one of these *Tikunim* has its particular function or action for the general guidance.

The *Dikna* reveals the guidance of kindness, rigor and mercy, which was concealed in *'Hokhma Stimaah*, by bringing it down to *Z"A* through the two *Mazalot;* *Notser* and *Nake,* which are the eighth and thirteenth *Tikun*.

The *Dikna* will have a supreme function at the end of times: To reveal the *Yi'hud* – the divine sovereignty.

Hebrew / Aramaic Phonetic	L	Dictionary

The second *Tikun* of *Z"A* is expressed by the lights that come out of him, as the hair on his head, and on his face. These *Tikunim* are similar to the ones of *Arikh Anpin,* but with some differences. From *Arikh Anpin* all the hair come out from *'Hokhma Stimaah,* from *Z"A*; they come out from his *HBD* ('Hokhma, Binah, Da'at). The hairs of *Z"A* are black and intermingled; being more of the aspect of *Gevurah,* the hairs of *Arikh Anpin* are white, and express bounty.

The *Tikunim* of the *Dikna* of *Z"A,* are similar to the ones of *Arikh Anpin,* even if they are nine. However, with an illumination from *Arikh Anpin,* they become thirteen, and act as a principle of kindness for the guidance of justice.

דכיא A **Pure – Clean**
Dakhya Without any attachments of negative forces.
See Kedushah

דם H **Blood**
Dam Blood is of the aspect of the *Gevurot (rigors),* and also contains the *Nefesh (soul).* This is in part why we are not allowed to eat it.

דמות H **Resemblance – Image**
Demut Man was created to the image of the *Sephirot* and *Partsufim.*
See Partsuf

Hebrew / Aramaic Phonetic	L	Dictionary
דעת Da'at	H	**Sephira (Knowledge)** Fourth of the *Sephirot*. *Da'at* is counted when *Keter* is not. Quality: Guidance that makes the equilibrium between *'Hokhma and Binah*. Column: Middle – *'Ra'hamim* (mercy) Position: Middle – center Other *Sephirot* on the same column: *Keter, Tiferet, Yesod, Malkhut* *Partsufim* made from this *Sephira: none, but from it come out the five 'Hasadim and five Gevurot*. Its role is mainly to make the *Mo'hin* for *Z"A* and *Nukvah*. Corresponding name: *AHV-H* – אהו-ה *See Sephira, Partsuf*
דעת Da'at	H	**Knowledge** The essential knowledge is the one of the will of the Creator and His ways of guidance in this existence, as explained in the Kabbalah. *See Torah, Kabbalah*
דק Dak	H	**Thin - Fine – Tenuous** When the *Sephirot* came out the first time from the mouth of *Adam Kadmon,* only the most tenuous part of the lights returned to their origin in the mouth. *See Orot HaPeh*
דרך Derekh		**Way** Direction. In the manner of.

106

Hebrew / Aramaic *Phonetic*	L	Dictionary
ה' אלעה Hey Ela'a	A	**Higher (ה) Hey** First H (ה) of the Tetragamon (י-ה-ו-ה) *B'H.* Corresponds to *Partsuf Imah*.
ה' תתאה Hey Tataa	A	**Lower (ה) Hey** Second H (ה) of the Tetragamon (י-ה-ו-ה) *B'H,* Corresponds to *Sephira Malkhut*.
הארה Hearah	H	**Illumination** Special outburst of a light for a specific purpose.
הבדל Hevdel	H	**Difference – Change** There are differences in the emanations of the lights depending on their importance or position. Each *Sephira* is composed of a vessel called *Keli*, which holds its part of light called *Or*. There is no difference in the *Or* itself, which is a unique emanation form G-od; the difference comes from the particularity, or quality of the *Sephira*.
הבטה Habtah	H	**Looking** *See Histaklut*
הבל Hevel	H	**Breath – Vapor – Utterance** From the different emanations that came out from *Adam Kadmon*, ten internal *Sephirot* and ten encircling *Sephirot*, of the aspect of the lower *Ta'amim* (cantillation), came out from his mouth. They are described as two vapors from the right side of the mouth, two utterances from the left side and rooted in the two jaws; upper and lower. These

Hebrew / Aramaic Phonetic	L	Dictionary
		emanations descended until the navel of *Adam Kadmon.*
הבלא דגרמי Habela Degarmi	A	**Habela Degarmi** The *Or* (light) that gives life to the *Keli* (recipient) is comparable to the soul that keeps the body alive. When a man dies and his soul separates from his body, the latter will remain with the "*Habela Degarmi*" (הבלא דגרמי) which like the 288 sparks, will allow the conservation of the body from the time the soul has left him, until the resurrection. *See Rapa'h Netsutsot*
ההין HaHin	M	**Of ה (H)** When the letter ה is used to make the *Miluy* (spelling).
הוד Hod	H	**Sephira – Glory** Eighth of the *Sephirot.* Quality: Diminished rigor to who is deserving. Column: Left – *Din* (rigor) Position: Left – bottom Other *Sephirot* on the same column: *Binah, Gevurah.* *Partsufim* made from this *Sephira:* One of the *Sephirot* that make the *Partsuf Z"A.* Corresponding name: *Elohi-m Tsebaot* אלהי-ם -צבאות Corresponding *Miluy* of name: *MaH (45)* (מה) Corresponding vowel: *Kubutz* Physical correspondance: Left leg Level of the soul: *Rua'h* *See Sephira, Partsuf*

Hebrew / Aramaic Phonetic	L	Dictionary
הוי"ה HaVaYaH	H	**HaVaYaH** One of the ways of mentioning the Tetragamon ‫יְ-ה-ו-ה‬ without pronouncing it.
הולדה Olada	H	**Giving birth** One of the steps in the *Tikun* (repair – rectification) of a *Partsuf* (configuration). After the gestation inside the superior feminine *Partsuf Nukvah*, the *Partsuf* comes out and continues his growth process.
היכלות Hekhalot	H	**Portals – Levels** See Hekhal
היכל Hekhal	H	**Portal – Level** Each world (*ABYA*) is built from four aspects: *Partsuf (configuration)*, *Levush* (garment), *Or Makif* (encircling lights), and *Hekhalot* (portals). In each *Partsuf*, there are interiority and exteriority, the exteriority is always of the aspect of *Malkhut*, and the *Hekhalot* are the ramifications of the *Malkhuts* of the *Partsufim (configurations)*. The principal function of the *Hekhalot* is to allow the adhesion and attachment, to ascend in various ways, until the seventh highest *Hekhal (portal) Kodesh Hakodashim*. The *Neshamot* and the angels have their root in the *Hekhalot*, each one depending on its respective level. The *Hekhalot* are also the different levels of ascension of the *Tefilot* before reaching the *'Olam Atsilut* during the *Amidah*.

Hebrew / Aramaic Phonetic	L	Dictionary

Hekhal / Portal   **Corresponding to**

First   לבנת הספיר   *Yesod* and *Malkhut*

(*Livnat Hasapir*)

Second   עצם השמים   *Hod*

(*'Etsem Hashamayim*)

Third   נוגה (*Nogah*)   *Netsa'h*

Fourth   זכות (*Zekhut*)   *Gevurah*

Fifth   אהבה (*Ahavah*)   *'Hesed*

Sixth   רצון (*Ratson*)   *Tiferet*

Seventh   קדש קדשים   *Keter, 'Hokhma,*

(*Kodesh Kodashim*)   *Binah*

The goal of the service of the creatures, is to help prepare the *Partsufim Z"A* and *Nukvah* for the *Zivug (union),* and this, by the elevation and adhesion of the worlds of *Beriah, Yetsirah* and *'Asiah* to the *Hekhalot* of *Nukvah* of *Atsilut. See Kavanah*

הכאה	H	**Colliding**
Hakaah		

The lights that came out from the mouth of *Adam Kadmom* did not find an individual *Keli* (recipient). The most tenuous parts of these lights went back up and collided with the trace of the lower lights that remained. From this colliding, sparks made the *Keli.* This is *'Olam Ha'Akudim* (world of the Attached), where there was one unique *Keli* for all the *Sephirot.*

At the bottom of *Atsilut,* the lights of *Malkhut* collided, and a curtain was made from the striking of the lights, between *Atsilut* and *Beriah* (creation) and for each of the lower worlds. *See Ma'akeh*

Hebrew / Aramaic Phonetic	L	Dictionary
הכללי HaKlali	H	**HaKlali** One of the seven main types of *Gematriot*. The *Ragil* value of the word squared. Ex : הארץ = 296 * 296 = 87616 *See Gematria*
הכנה Hakhana	H	**Preparation** The word Kabbalah comes from the verb *Lekabel* (to receive), but to receive it is first necessary to be prepared, and to be a *Keli (recipient)* able to receive and contain this knowledge. There is a preparation needed for the *Partsufim Z"A* and *Nukvah* for the *Zivug (union)*. This is done by the elevation of the worlds when men are doing the *Tefilot* (prayers) and *Mitsvot*. *See Tefilah, Mitsvot*
הכפלה Hakhpalah	H	**Increase** There are increases in the size of the *Sephirot* or *Partsufim* (configurations) *Z"A* and *Nukvah*, depending on their growth stage. There are also increases in numbers. When *Partsuf Z"A* receives five 'Hasadim from *Sephira Da'at* for the guidance, they go down and return upward from *Sephira Yesod* of *Z"A* to *Sephira 'Hesed* and *Gevurah* (of *Z"A*). They increase and double from three thirds each, to six thirds. Each one becoming now six thirds. *See Gadlut*

111

Hebrew / Aramaic Phonetic	L	Dictionary
המשכה Hamsha-khah	H	**Drawing – Extension** For the *Tikun* (rectification), the lower feminine lights ascend and draw to them the masculine higher lights. During the *Zivug* (union), the masculine lights of *MaH* (45) needed for the *Tikun*, are drawn to the feminine lights of *BaN* (52) and are kept in the upper *Nukvah*.
המתקה Hamtakah	H	**Mitigation – Sweetening** A mitigation or sweetening of the *Gevurot* (rigors) occurs when they are in direct contact with the *'Hasadim*. For the guidance, *Partsuf* (configuration) *Z"A* receives five *'Hasadim* and five *Gevurot* from *Sephira Da'at*, they go down and return upward from the *Sephira Yesod* of *Z"A*. When the five *Gevurot* come down from *Da'at* of *Z"A*, they are sweetened (appeased) in *Yesod* of *Z"A*.
הנהגה Hanhagah	H	**Guidance** The Kabbalah is the only science that explains to us in the least details, the true guidance of the world, so that we may understand G-od's will. It teaches us that the world is guided by an extremely complex system of forces or lights, which through their interactions provoke chain reactions that impact directly on man and the guidance of the worlds. Each one of these reactions has numerous ramifications with many details and results. The guidance of the worlds is done through the influence of the different *Sephirot* and *Partsufim*.

Hebrew / Aramaic *Phonetic*	L	Dictionary

There are two main kinds of guidance:
The general guidance, which is for the subsistence of the worlds, and is not influenced by the actions of men. This guidance is by the encircling *Sephirot.*

The variable guidance, which is on the basis of justice, reward and punishment, is dependant on the actions of man. This guidance is by the linear *Sephirot.*

The linear *Sephirot* are arranged in three columns: right, left and middle, representing the guidance of the world in the manner of *'Hesed, Din* and *Ra'hamim* - Kindness, rigor and mercy.

The guidance of the world is dependent on the different positioning and interaction of the masculine and feminine *Partsufim (configuration)*, since they have a direct effect on the measure and balance of the factors of kindness, rigor and mercy.

The masculine *Partsufim (configurations)* bestow kindness, the feminine bestow rigor. By their union, different equilibriums of the two forces of kindness and rigor make the guidance. Complete rigor will be the destruction of anything not perfect, while complete kindness will permit everything without restriction. However, these two aspects are necessary for the guidance of justice, and to give man the possibility of free choice

See Sephirot, Partsuf, Tikun, Sephira

Hebrew / Aramaic Phonetic	L	Dictionary

הסתכלות
Histaklut

H **Looking – Observation**

To look is a readiness to come closer, avoiding to look or turning, creates distance.

In the *Shvirat HaKelim (breaking of the vessels)*, *Sephira 'Hokhma* and *Binah* were face to face. When *Sephira Da'at* broke, the *'Hasadim* and *Gevurot* (rigors) of *'Hokhma* and *Binah* fell into their body, they turned back to back; so as not to look at each other.

In the positions of the *Partsufim (configurations)*, sometimes, *Partsuf Ra'hel* is face to face with *Partsuf Z"A,* who is in the middle having her and *Partsuf Ya'acov* on his sides - the three of them looking at each other.

הפרעות
Hafra'ot

H **Disturbance**

Disturbance is caused by the increase of the *Klipot* (husks) or in the absence of *Kedushah* (Holiness).

הפרתי
HaPerati

H **HaPerati**

One of the seven main types of *Gematriot.*
Each letter is squared.
Ex : הארץ = 5 * 5 = 25, 1 * 1 = 1,
200 * 200 = 40 000, 900 * 900 = 810 000
Total = 850 026
See Gematria

הקדמי
HaKadmi

H **HaKadmi**

One of the seven main types of *Gematriot.*
Each letter has its *Ragil* value plus the total of all the ones preceding it.

Hebrew / Aramaic Phonetic	L	Dictionary

From To Value

א ט 1 - 45

י צ 55 – 495

ק ת 595 – 1495

ך ץ 1995 – 4995

Ex : הארץ = 15 + 1 + 795 + 4995 = 5806

See Gematria

הרחקה H *Distancing*

Har'hakah

Distance denotes a contrary or a non compatibility.

The possibilities of existence for separated entities became possible, only once distanced from the intensity of His light.

See Tsimtsum, A'hor Be A'hor

הריון H *Pregnancy- Gestation*

Herayon See 'Ibur

השגה H *Attainment - Comprehension*

Hasagah

The *Tikunim* (actions) of the *Partsufim* are lights needed for the attainment and abundance. To reach a higher level of understanding or comprehension, one has to make the effort of studying the *Sod* (secret) of the Torah which is the Kabbalah.

See Kabbalah, Torah

השוואה H *Equivalence*

Hashavah

Depending on time, the masculine and feminine *Partsufim* (configurations) vary in size. The ideal is when the *Zivug* (union) is done when these *Partsufim* are equivalent in size.

Hebrew / Aramaic Phonetic	L	Dictionary
השפעה Hashpa'ah	H	**Bestowal**

Bestowal

At first, the Creator was alone, occupying all space with His light. His light without end, borders or limit, filled everything. He was not bestowing His influence, because there was no one to receive it. When He willed to create, He started to influence.

Since the intention of the Creator is to bestow goodness on His creatures, all the levels of creation were put in place so His kindness could emanate to them, yet in such a way that they would be able to receive it.

Some *Partsufim* (configurations) are masculine and bestow kindness, others are feminine and bestow rigor. By their union, different equilibriums of the two forces of Kindness and rigor make the guidance. When the masculine and feminine *Partsuf* are face to face, it is the ideal level and corresponds to the bestowing of abundance. Back to face is the second level, and back to back corresponds to dissimulation and rigor.

All and everything is sustained by one and only one source; the light of G-od, which is bestowed through these *Partsufim* and *Sephirot*. *See Ratson Lehashpia'*

Evolution - Chain of events

השתלשלות *Hishtal-shelut* H

In the Kabbalah the *Hishtalshelut* is the chain of events starting from the first act of G-od in creation which is the "*Tsimtsum*" *(retraction)*, until the complex arrangements that make the guidance of the worlds.

Hebrew / Aramaic Phonetic	L	Dictionary

התעבות H **Thickening**

Hit'abot

From *Adam Kadmon,* different emanations spread out as a preparation for the future worlds. One of these first emanations came out from its mouth; these lights did not find an individual *Keli* (recipient) and returned to their origin in the mouth. They did not return completely, only the most tenuous part did, each one leaving its trace. The parts that remained thickened, but were still illuminated by their own parts that ascended.

התפשטות H **Spreading**

Hitpashtut

After entering, the different lights spread down.

For *Adam Kadmon,* the "branches" are the lights that spread forth from him by way of its apertures in the head.

When the *Mo'hin* (brains) enter *Partsuf Z"A, Sephira Da'at* needs to spread down more than the rest of the *Mo'hin,* and spreads in all the sides of *Partsuf Z"A* and *Nukvah.* After the complete spreading of the *'Hasadim* in *Partsuf Z"A* and their rise until *Keter, Partsuf Z"A* has attained the growth level.

Hebrew / Aramaic Phonetic	L	Dictionary
ו' קצוות *Vav* *Ktsavot*	H	***Six edges*** Six edges are all the possible directions; front, back, right, left, up and down. The six edges of *Partsuf Z"A* are the *Sephirot HGT* and *NHY)*. During the gestation of *Z"A*, his six edges are three on three; *NHY* fold on *HGT*, and *Sephira Malkhut* is fourth after them on *Sephira Yesod* of *Z"A*. When it is said that *Z"A* integrates the six edges of the world of *Atsilut*, and *Nukvah* is its *Malkhut*, it means that *Z"A* is in a way the body of *'Olam Atsilut* and his *Malkhut* is the *Malkhut* of *Atsilut*.
ויהוא"ל *Vihue"l*		***Vihue"l*** Name of one of the three great princes of the Angels.
ויטאל *Vital*	H	***Rabbi 'Haim Vital*** Born in Tsfat in 1543, died in Damascus in 1620. Main student of the Ari Z'al. During the two years that the Ari lived in Tsfat, he studied with him the Kabbalah. After the passing of the Ari, he put all of his teachings in writing in what is called the *"Kitve HaAri"* (the Writings of the Ari).
וילנא *Vilna*		***Rabbi Eliyahu of Vilna - The Gaon of Vilna*** Born in Vilna, Lithuania, 1720, died in 1797. One of the main leaders of the *Mitnagdim* (opponents to the *'Hasidim*). Very important Torah scholar and Kabbalist of the past two centuries. Some of his works on the Kabbalah are: *"Kitvei HaGra Be'eniene Kabbalah"*

Hebrew / Aramaic Phonetic	L	Dictionary

ולד
Valad

H **Child - Infant – Fetus**

All the *Tikunim* of the masculine and feminine *Partsufim (configurations)* are achieved by way of *Zivug* (union), gestation and birth. During the *Zivug*, the lights of *MaH (45)* needed for the *Tikun* are drawn to the lights of *BaN (52)*, and are kept in the upper *Nukvah*. During the gestation, inside of *Nukvah*, they are arranged and completed until there is nothing more to add. When it is totally repaired, the *Partsuf* is born or revealed, and this is the birth.

Hebrew / Aramaic Phonetic	L	Dictionary
ז' מלכים *Sheva'* *Malkhin*	H	**Seven kings** The seven kings of Edom that died (Bereshit, 36, 31), correspond to the seven lower *Sephirot* that broke during the *Shvirat HaKelim* (breaking of the vessels). *See Shvirat HaKelim*
ז"א *Z"A*	A	***Zeir Anpin (Small countenance)*** Initials of *Partsuf Zeir Anpin*, used more often than the full name. *See Zeir Anpin*
ז"ת *Za"T*	A	***Zain Takhtonot*** Initials of the seven lower *Sephirot*
זו"ן *Z"UN*	A	***Zeir Anpin and Nukvah*** Initials of *Partsuf Zeir Anpin and Nukvah*, used more often than the full names.
זוהמא *Zohama*	H	***Filth – Foulness*** State of distance from the *Kedushah* and closeness to the *Sitra A'hra (negative force).* See *Sitra A'hra*
זוהר *Zohar*	A	***Zohar*** The book of splendor, written by Rabbi Shim'on Bar Yo'hay. The *Zohar* is the esoteric and mystical explanation of the Torah, and the base for most of the Kabbalah writings. *See Bar Yo'hay*
זווג **דנשיקין** *Zivug De* *Neshikin*	A	***Union of the kisses*** There are two types of unions for the *Zivug* (unions): the kissing and the *Yesodot* (by the *Sephira Yesod*). The kissing is to attach the interiority of the masculine

Hebrew / Aramaic Phonetic	L	Dictionary

with the one of the feminine. The *Yesodot* is to attach the exteriority of the masculine with the one of the feminine.

The first of the two steps for the *Zivug* is realized in the heads of the *Partsufim;* it is the kissing (the *Zivug* of the mouths), this attachment is afterwards extended to the rest of the *Partsuf.* The kissing is in the heads, their *Zivug* is double; the *Rua'h* of the masculine is in the mouth of the feminine, and the *Rua'h* of the feminine is in the mouth of the masculine. There are then two *Ru'hot* unified as one.

See Zivug, Tikun

זווג של **יסודות** **Zivug shel Yesodot**   H   *Union of the Yesodot*

There are two types of unions for the *Zivug* (unions): the kissing and the *Yesodot* (by the *Sephira Yesod*). The kissing is to attach the interiority of the masculine with the one of the feminine. The *Yesodot* is to attach the exteriority of the masculine with the one of the feminine.

The second of the two steps for the *Zivug*, is the *Zivug* of the *Yesodot* (by the two *Sephirot Yesod*), it completes the *Zivug,* and it is from this *Zivug* that emanations are spread to the worlds.

See Zivug, Tikun

זיו **Ziv**   H   *Radiance – Illumination*

A superior light will illuminate to a lower one to influence it, or to create a new emanation.

Hebrew / Aramaic Phonetic	L	Dictionary
זיווג Zivug	H	**Union**

Union

The *Zivug* is the union of the masculine with its feminine. All the outcomes of the higher emanations are a result of the different unions of the masculine and feminine lights.

There are different kinds of *Zivugim*; the ones for the construction of the worlds, for the building of the *Partsufim*, and for the guidance of the worlds.

After the *Shvirat HaKelim (breaking of the vessels)*, the first *Tikun (rectification)* was the *Zivug* of the *Sephirot* of *MaH (45)* and *BaN (52)* in complex arrangements, as to allow the feminine *BaN (52)* to be repaired by the masculine *MaH (45)*, and for the *Sephirot* to stand in the three-column arrangement of kindness, rigor and mercy.

All the *Tikunim* of the *Partsufim* (masculine and feminine) are achieved by way of *Zivug* (union), gestation and birth. During the *Zivug*, the lights of *MaH (45)* needed for the *Tikun* are drawn to the lights of *BaN (52)*, and are kept in the upper *Nukvah*. During the gestation, inside of *Nukvah*, they are arranged and completed until there is nothing more to add. When it is totally repaired, the *Partsuf* is revealed, and this is the birth. There is afterwards the suckling, and finally the growth so that the *Partsuf* will be fully independent

Hebrew / Aramaic L Phonetic	Dictionary

Partsuf 'Atik was constructed by the *Zivug* of *"A"V* and *SaG* of *Adam Kadmon*. His *MaH* (45) corresponds to the masculine principle, his *BaN* (52) to the feminine; he is called *'Atik* and his *Nukvah*. His *Nukvah* is never separated from him, her back attached to his back, *'Atik* is thus all face; the face of *BaN* (52) corresponding to his back, the face of *MaH* (45) to his front. By the *Zivug* of *'Atik*, *Arikh* and his *Nukvah* were built, and from their *Zivug Abah* and *Imah* were built. By the *Zivug* of *Abah* and *Imah Z"A* and *Nukvah* were built.

For *Abah* and *Imah* there are two types of *Zivug:* the constant *Zivug* is called exterior, and is for the subsistence of the worlds and no more, the other is called interior, and is for the renewing of the *Mo'hin* (brains) of *Z"uN*.

For the abundance to come down to the world, *Zeir Anpin* needs to unite with *Nukvah*. There can be abundance only when the masculine and the feminine are in harmony. Each day, according to the actions of man, the *Tefilot* during the week, *Shabbat* or holidays and depending on time, various configurations allow different *Zivugim*, and therefore outflows of abundance of variable intensities.

The *Tikun* is only possible by the *Zivug* (union) of the masculine and the feminine. The masculine

Hebrew / Aramaic *Phonetic*	L	Dictionary

corresponds to *'Hesed* and *MaH (45)*, the feminine to *Gevurah* and *BaN (52)*. Two conditions are needed for the *Zivug* to be possible: the *Partsufim* have to be constructed, and the feminine has to stimulate a reaction from the masculine. This stimulation happens when she brings up her *Mayin Nukvin* (feminine waters of the aspect of *BaN (52)*), which then provokes the descent of the *Mayin Dukhrin* (masculine waters of the aspect of *MaH (45)* from the masculine.

All the abundance that comes down to the world, proceeds from these various *Zivugim* of *Z"uN*. There are five different *Zivugim*:

- The *Zivugim* with *Ra'hel* are of the highest level; being of the aspect of kindness.
- The ones with *Leah* are more of the aspect of rigor.
- The one of *Israel* and *Ra'hel* is the most superior. *Israel* represents all of *Z"A*, *Ra'hel* is the essential of *Nukvah*. The abundance that is bestowed by this *Zivug* is the most complete.
- The other *Zivugim* of *Z"uN* are of different levels, in various times, and of lesser plenitude.

Each new day, is of a new emanation that governs it. For each day, there are new *Zivugim* of different aspects of *Z"uN*.

124

Hebrew / Aramaic *Phonetic*	L	Dictionary

- In the *Tefilah* of *Sha'hrit*, there is the *Zivug* of *Ya'acov* and *Ra'hel*
- In the *Tefilah* of *Min'ha*, there is the *Zivug* of *Israel* and *Leah*.
- In the *Tefilah* of *'Arvit*, there is the *Zivug* of *Ya'acov* and *Leah* (from the chest up).
- In *Tikun 'Hatsot*, there is the *Zivug* of *Ya'acov* and *Leah* (from the chest down).

There are two steps for the *Zivug*, the first is realized in the heads of the *Partsufim;* it is the kissing (the *Zivug* of the mouths); by them the interiors of both *Partsufim* attach, this attachment is afterwards extended to the rest of the *Partsuf.* The second, is the *Zivug* of the *Yesodot* (by the two *Sephirot Yesod*), it is from this *Zivug* that emanations are spread to the worlds.

The guidance of the world is dependent on the different positioning and interaction, of these masculine and feminine *Partsufim*, since they have a direct effect on the measure and balance of the factors of kindness, rigor and mercy.

The goal of the service of the creatures, is to help prepare the *Partsufim Z"A* and *Nukvah* for the *Zivug*, and this, by the elevation and adhesion of the worlds by way of the *Tefilot* and *Mitsvot*.

Hebrew / Aramaic Phonetic	L	Dictionary
זיווגים Zivugim	H	**Unions** See Zivug
זין תחתונות Zayin Takhtonot	H	**Seven lower** The seven lower *Sephirot:* *'Hesed, Gevurah, Tiferet, Netsa'h, Hod, Yesod, Malkhut.* See Partsuf Zeir Anpin
זך Zakh	H	**Tenuous - Refined** In general when a light needs to ascend, its most tenuous part will go up, and the remaining will "thicken" being now separated from its more tenuous part. In the world of *Ha'Akudim* (the attached), when the *Sephirot* came out the first time from the mouth of *Adam Kadmon*, each one had its own place, but in one unique *Keli.* The most tenuous part of the lights returned to their origin in the mouth but not completely, each one leaving its trace. The parts of the lights that remained thickened, but were still illuminated by their own parts that ascended. The lights strike each other and produced sparks which formed the *Kelim* (recipients) for the more tenuous lights that returned a second time.
זכות Zakhut	H	**Purity** See Zakh

Hebrew / Aramaic Phonetic	L	Dictionary

זכות
Zekhut

H **Zekhut**

Name of a *Hekhal (portal)*.

Fourth of seven *Hekhalot*, corresponding to *Gevurah*. Each world (*ABYA*) is built from four aspects: *Partsuf*, *Levush* (garment), *Or Makif* (encircling lights), and *Hekhalot*.

In each *Partsuf*, there are interiority and exteriority, the exteriority is always of the aspect of *Malkhut*, and the *Hekhalot* are the ramifications of the *Malkhuts* of the *Partsufim*.

The *Hekhalot* are also the different levels of ascension of the *Tefilot* before reaching the seventh *Hekhal (portal)*, *Kodesh Hakodashim*.

Their principal function is to allow the adhesion and attachment, in various and particular ways during the *Tefilot*, until the *'Olam Atsilut* (during the *Amidah*)

The *Neshamot* and the angels have their root in the *Hekhalot*, each one depending on its respective level.

זכר
Zakhar

H **Masculine**

There are masculine *Partsufim* that bestow kindness, and feminine *Partsufim* that bestow rigor. By their union, different equilibriums of these two forces (kindness and rigor), make the guidance. Kindness is manifested by all the masculine aspects which represent bounty, and by the concealment of the

Hebrew / Aramaic *Phonetic*	L	Dictionary

feminine aspects, which represent rigor.

The *Zivug* is the union of the masculine with its feminine. All the outcomes of the higher emanations are a result of the different unions of the masculine and feminine lights.

The masculine corresponds to *'Hesed* and *MaH (45)*, the feminine to *Gevurah* and *BaN (52)*. The *Tikun* is only possible by the *Zivug* (union) of the masculine and the feminine.

The guidance of the world is dependent on the different positioning and interaction, of the masculine and feminine *Partsufim*, since they have a direct effect on the measure and balance of the factors of kindness, rigor and mercy.

See Zivug, Tikun, Zeir Anpin

| זמן | H | **Time** |

Zman

Each day, according to the actions of man, the *Tefilot* during the week, *Shabbat* or holidays, and depending on time, various configurations allow different *Zivugim*, and therefore outflows of abundance of variable intensities.

Each moment can also be described in term of permutation of the names of G-od, and by the various *Sephirot and Partsufim*.

Hebrew / Aramaic *Phonetic*	L	Dictionary

זמנים   H   *Times*
Zmanim

            See Zman

זעיר אנפין   A   *Partsuf Zeir Anpin (Small countenance)*

Zeir
Anpin

Zeir Anpin (Z"A) is composed of the seven lower *Sephirot*: *'Hesed, Gevurah, Tiferet, Netsa'h, Hod, Yesod* and *Malkhut* of a world.

At first *Z"A* is in a state of *Tardema* (somnolence), to act he needs to get his *Mo'hin (brains,)* which are his first three *Sephirot* of *"Hokhma, Binah* and *Da'at* from *ISOT* or *Abah* and *Imah*, and to get to a stage of growth.

Inside of *Imah*, *Z"A* goes through a period of gestation, followed by a first period of infancy and a first growth. In the first growth his *Mo'hin (brains)* are from *NHY* of *Tevunah*. During the time of the gestation, *Z"A* is not really acting as it is being built, at the time of suckling it starts to act, and at the growth it is ready to act.

When *NHY* of *ISOT* 2 are clothed in *Z"A* as his *Mo'hin (brains)*; it is the first growth. But when *NHY* of *ISOT* 1 are clothed in him, it is considered as if *Abah* and *Imah* were clothed in him directly as *Mo'hin (brains)*; and this is the second growth. It is only after the second growth, that *Z"A* has reached its full potential. This is *Gadlut* 2.

For the abundance to come down to the world, *Zeir Anpin* needs to unite with *Nukvah*. There can be abundance only when the masculine and the feminine

Hebrew / Aramaic Phonetic	L	Dictionary

are in harmony. Each day, according to the actions of man, the *Tefilot* during the week, *Shabbat* or holidays and depending on time, various configurations allow different *Zivugim*, and therefore outflows of abundance of variable intensities. The abundance first comes to *Z"A*, then to *Nukvah,* and from her, to the lower worlds.

The masculine corresponds to *'Hesed* and *MaH (45),* the feminine to *Gevurah* and *BaN (52).* The *Tikun* is only possible by the *Zivug (union)* of the masculine and the feminine. There are two conditions needed for the *Zivug (union)* to be possible: the *Partsufim (configurations)* have to be constructed, and the feminine has to stimulate a reaction from the masculine. This stimulation happens when she brings up her *Mayin Nukvin (Feminine waters)* of the aspect of *BaN (52),* which then provokes the descent of the *Mayin Dukhrin* (Masculine waters) from the masculine of the aspect of *MaH (45).*

All the abundance that comes down to the world, proceeds from the various *Zivugim* of *Z"uN.* There are five different *Zivugim,* the *Zivugim* with *Ra'hel* are of the highest level; being of the aspect of kindness, the ones with Leah are more of the aspect of rigor. The one of *Israel* and *Ra'hel* is the most superior. *Israel* represents all of *Z"A, Ra'hel* is the essential of *Nukvah.* The abundance that is bestowed by this *Zivug (union)* is the most complete. The other *Zivugim* of *Z"uN* are of different levels, in various times, and of

130

Hebrew / Aramaic *Phonetic*	L	Dictionary

lesser plenitude.

Each new day, is of a new emanation that governs it. For each day, there are new *Zivugim* of different aspects of *Z"uN*.

The guidance of the world is dependent on the different positioning and interaction, of *Z"A* and *Nukvah*, since they have a direct effect on the measure and balance of the factors of kindness, rigor and mercy.

The goal of the service of the creatures, is to help prepare the *Partsufim (configurations) Z"A* and *Nukvah* for the *Zivug (union),* and this by the elevation and adhesion of the worlds by way of the *Tefilot* and *Mitsvot. See Partsuf, Tikun, Zivug, Sephira*

זקוף
Zakuf

H **Upright**

See straight Sephirot

זקן
Zakan

H **Beard**

The beard *(Zakan)* is also called *Dikna* and is the illuminations that come out from the face.

There are hairs (lights) that come out from the face of *Sephira 'Hokhma Stimaah* of *Partsuf Arikh Anpin* and spread downward. They divide in thirteen, and are called the thirteen *Tikunim* (action – rectification) of the *Dikna* of *Arikh Anpin*. They are called *Dikna* (beard), because they spread out in individual conduits.

The other *Tikunim* are lights needed for the attainment and abundance. However, the guidance

itself is from the *Dikna*, it is through it that the
abundance flows. The hairs of the *Dikna* are short
and stiff, being of the aspect of rigor. They are also
divided in two aspects: masculine; which includes the
first twelve *Tikunim,* and feminine, which comprise the
thirteen *Tikun.* Each one of these *Tikunim* has its
particular function or action for the general guidance.

The *Dikna* reveals the guidance of kindness, rigor and
mercy, which was concealed in *'Hokhma Stimaah,* by
bringing it down to *Z"A* through the two *Mazalot;*
Notser and *Nake,* which are the eighth and thirteenth
Tikun.

The *Dikna* will have a supreme function at the end of
times: To reveal the *Yi'hud* – the divine sovereignty.

The second *Tikun* of *Z"A* is expressed by the lights
that come out of him, as the hair on his head, and on
his face. These *Tikunim* are similar to the ones of
Arikh Anpin, but with some differences. From *Arikh*
Anpin all the hair come out from *'Hokhma Stimaah,*
from *Z"A*; they come out from his *HBD* (*'Hokhma, Binah,*
Da'at). The hairs of *Z"A* are black and intermingled;
being more of the aspect of *Gevurah*, the hairs of
Arikh Anpin are white, and express bounty.

The *Tikunim* of the *Dikna* of *Z"A*, are similar to the
ones of *Arikh Anpin,* even if they are nine. However,
with an illumination from *Arikh Anpin*, they become
thirteen, and act as a principle of kindness for the
guidance of justice

Hebrew / Aramaic *Phonetic*	L	Dictionary
חבד 'HaBaD	H	**'Hokhma, Binah and Da'at** Initials of the first triplet of: 'Hokhma, Binah and Da'at. They act together as Mo'hin (brains) for a lower Partsuf and are called the Mo'hin of Gadlut (growth).
חגת 'HaGaT	H	**'Hesed, Gevurah and Tiferet** Initials of the second triplet of the Sephirot: 'Hesed, Gevurah and Tiferet. They mostly act together as Mo'hin (brains) for a lower Partsuf.
חוורתי 'Hivarti	A	***The white on the scalp between the hair*** From the Partsuf (configuration) Arikh Anpin there are emanations that come out from its head to act and influence on the guidance called the Tikunim of Arikh Anpin. One of these Tikunim of Arikh Anpin is from his Keter; thirteen חיורתי ('Hivarti) from the three (הוי"ה), they are the white parts between each hair. Their place is between the thirteen נימין (Nimin) they are extremities of the hairs on the head. They are four on the right side, four on the left, four on the back, and one containing all. The four on the back, spread down to the Dikna (beard) of Z"A. They are called hair because they spread out in individual conduits.
חוזר 'Hozer	H	***Returning*** See Or 'Hozer
חוטם 'Hotem	H	***Nose*** See Orot Ha'Hotem

Hebrew / Aramaic Phonetic	L	Dictionary
חולם 'Holam	H	**'Holam – Vowel O** The vowel that represents the Sephira Tiferet.
חומר 'Homer	H	**Material – Physical** Materiality is only found in the lower world of 'Asiah – action.
חוץ 'Huts	H	**Outside** Denotes a position of non compatibility or a contrary.
חושך 'Hoshekh	H	**Darkness** State of distance from the Kedushah and closeness to the Sitra A'hra (negative side).
חותם 'Hotam	H	**Seal** Represented by the Name Shada-y - שד-י
חותמא 'Hotma	A	**Seventh of seven Tikunim of the head of Arikh Anpin** From the head of Partsuf (configuration) Arikh Anpin, seven emanations come out to act and influence on the guidance, called the Tikunim of Arikh Anpin. The second Tikun (action) of Arikh Anpin is achieved by the passing of the seven lower Sephirot of 'Atik into its head before they are clothed in him. These seven Tikunim of the head of Arikh Anpin are revealed from the seven lower Sephirot of 'Atik The seventh Tikun – חותמא ('Hotma), is realized by the Malkhut of 'Atik; it also splits in two: - שני נחירים - (Shene Ne'hirin), corresponding to the two parts of Nukvah – Ra'hel and Leah.

Hebrew / Aramaic Phonetic	L	Dictionary

חזה   H   ***Chest***

'Hazeh

The chest corresponds to the first third of the *Sephira Tiferet*. In general the lights will enter until the chest, or lower to the level of the navel.

In the first emanations from the nose of *Adam Kadmon*, the ten encircling *Sephirot* from the right nostril and the ten linear from the left nostril, went down until the chest.

The rears (*NHY (Netsa'h, Hod, Yesod)*) of *Imah*, extend from the chest of *Z"A* upwards. *Z"A* starts from the chests of *ISOT*, and extends down. *Ra'hel* starts from the chest of *Z"A* and extends down.

In the *Tefilot* the *Zivugim (unions)* of *'Arvit* and *Tikun 'Hatsot* start from the chest:

Arvit – *Ya'acov* and *Leah* - from the chest up.

Tikun 'Hatsot – *Ya'acov* and *Leah* - from the chest down.

חיבוק   H   ***Embrace***

'Hibuk

Before the *Zivug* (union) of the *Yesodot*.

חיבור   H   ***Attachment***

'Hibur

One of the first world to unfold was the *'Olam Ha'Akudim* (world of the attached), where there was one unique *Keli* for all the *Sephirot*.

All the *Sephirot* and *Partsufim* have a certain degree of attachment between them. Even if they are two distinct *Partsufim* (configurations) and have their own *Tikunim* (actions), all the time that *Partsuf Z"A* is being built, *Partsuf Nukvah* is attached to him.

135

Hebrew / Aramaic Phonetic	L	Dictionary

For their livelihood, the negative forces get strength by attaching to the exteriority of the *Sephirot*. They nourish from their lights and gain more power to act negatively.

There are also other temporary attachments as body and soul, interiority and exteriority etc.

See Partsufim

חידוש H *Innovation*
'Hidush

New interpretation or new understanding.

חיה H *Fourth level of the soul*
'Hayah

The soul has five names: *Nefesh, Rua'h, Neshama, 'Hayah* and *Ye'hidah*, which correspond to its five levels. The soul is the spiritual entity inside the body, the latter being only his outer garment.

Since it is men that provoke the union of the four worlds, it is necessary for their souls to have their origin from them, and from the five *Partsufim*:

Soul / Level	Partsuf	World
Nefesh	Nukvah	'Asiah
Rua'h	Zeir Anpin	Yetsirah
Neshama	Imah	Beriah
'Hayah	Abah	Atsilut
Ye'hidah	Arikh Anpin	Atsilut

Each level of the soul is subdivided in five levels. As for the level of *Nefesh;* there are *Nefesh* of *Nefesh, Rua'h* of *Nefesh, Neshama* of *Nefesh, 'Hayah* of *Nefesh* and *Ye'hidah* of *Nefesh.*

Hebrew / Aramaic *Phonetic*	L	Dictionary

Each one of these levels of the soul subdivides for each level of *Partsuf* and for each world. Therefore, there are five levels of the souls for *Partsuf Nukvah* and there are five levels of *Partsufim* for the world of *'Asiah* etc. Also, as there are in each world ten *Sephirot*, each soul has its origin corresponding to one of them.

Therefore, a soul could be from the level of *Nefesh* of *Malkhut* of *Nukvah* of *'Asiah,* or *Rua'h* of *'Hesed* of *Abah* of *'Yetsirah*, or *Neshama* of *Abah* of *Z"A* of *Yetsirah* etc.

'Hayah is the fourth level and can only be acquired after the preceding levels.

The higher levels of the soul cannot be acquired at once. Most men only have the level of *Nefesh,* and if they merit, they will acquire the next levels - but one by one. To reach the next higher level of his soul, man must do the *Tikun* of the preceding level. If he needs to acquire the level of *Imah* of *'Asiah*, he must first do the *Tikun* of *Malkhut* of *'Asiah* and *Z"A* of *'Asiah,* and so on. To acquire his level of *Neshama*, he must do the *Tikun* of all the levels of the *Sephirot* and *Partsufim* of his *Nefesh* and *Rua'h* etc.

חיות   H   ***Livelihood***

'Hayut

The livelihood of everything, whether positive or negative has only one origin; G-od the Creator and sustainer of all.

Hebrew / Aramaic Phonetic	L	Dictionary
חיצון *'Hitson*	H	**Exterior** As there are interior aspects, there are also exterior aspects. All the lights subdivide among themselves in interiority and exteriority aspects. Depending on the context, the exterior aspect could be superior or opposite to the interior aspect. For the *Mo'hin* the interior aspect are the *NHY* (Netsa'h, Hod, Yesod), and the exterior aspects are the *HGT* ('Hesed, Gevurah, Tiferet) and *HBD* ('Hokhma, Binah, Da'at), which are superior. Concerning the *Kedushah* the term exterior means opposite or negative.
חיצוניות *'Hitsoniut*	H	**Exteriority (The)** There are different types of exteriority. The exteriority of a world is its inferior aspect. The exteriority could also be a contrary or opposite, and is in general inferior to the interiority. As the *Neshama* is the interiority, and the body exteriority, so is also the *Kav* interiority and *Reshimu* exteriority etc. The *Malkhuts* of the *Sephirot,* which are their lower level, are called their exteriority. The external or negative force – *Sitra A'hra* is also called the exteriority. *See Sitra A'hra*
חיריק *'Hirik*	H	**'Hirik – Vowel I** The vowel that represents the *Sephira Netsa'h*

138

Hebrew / Aramaic Phonetic	L	Dictionary
חכמה 'Hokhma	H	**Sephira – Wisdom** Second of the *Sephirot.* Quality: Kindness to all, even to the not deserving (but less than *Keter,* and not always). Column: Right – *'Hesed* (Kindness) Position: Top – right Other *Sephirot* on the same column: *'Hesed, Netsa'h.* *Partsufim* made from this *Sephira:* - *Abah* - From *Malkhut* of *Abah* - *Israel Saba* - From *Malkhut* of *Israel Saba* - *Israel Saba* 2 Corresponding name: *YH* י-ה Corresponding *Miluy* of name: *''A"V* -עב *(72)* Corresponding vowel: *Pata'h* Physical correspondence: Right brain Level of the soul: *'Hayah.* See Sephira, Partsuf
חכמה 'Hokhma	H	**Wisdom – Intelligence – Knowledge** "The beginning of wisdom is to awe (venerate) G-od."*(Tehilim 111, 10)*
חכמת האמת 'Hokhmat HaEmet	H	**Knowledge of the truth** One of the names of the Kabbalah.
חלון 'Halon	H	**Window** Sephira Yesod of Arikh Anpin ('Ets 'Haim)

139

Hebrew / Aramaic *Phonetic*	L	Dictionary
חלונות *'Halonot*	H	**Windows** Name given to the seven openings from where the lights came out of *Adam Kadmon*: eyes, ears, nose (nostrils) and mouth.
חלל *'Hallal*	H	**Space – Vacuum** The space left by the *Tsimtsum* (retraction) of His light. This space is circular and contains all possibilities of existence for separated entities, since they are distanced from the intensity of His light. *See Tsimtsum, Kav, Reshimu*
חסד *'Hesed*	H	**Bounty - Kindness** Since the intention of the Creator is to bestow goodness on His creatures, all the levels of creation were put in place so His kindness could emanate to them, yet in such a way that they would be able to receive it. From the *Kav (ray of His light),* ten *Sephirot* were formed in a linear arrangement, and later in three columns: right, left and middle, representing the guidance of the world in the manner of *'Hesed, Din* and *Ra'hamim* (Kindness, rigor and mercy). This guidance is dependent on time, and the actions of men. For the emanation of Kindness, there are various *Tikunim* (actions) of the *Sephirot* and *Partsufim.* Some *Partsufim* are masculine and bestow kindness, others are feminine and bestow rigor. By their union, different equilibriums of the two forces of Kindness

Hebrew / Aramaic Phonetic	L	Dictionary

and rigor make the guidance. Complete rigor will be the destruction of anything not perfect, while complete kindness will permit everything without restriction.

Kindness is manifested by the different positioning and interaction of these masculine and feminine *Partsufim*, since they have a direct effect on the measure and balance of the factors of kindness, rigor and mercy. *See Partsufim*

חסד

'Hesed

Sephira (Bounty)

Fourth of the *Sephirot*.

Quality: Complete kindness to who is deserving.

Column: Right – *'Hesed* (kindness)

Position: Right – Middle

Other *Sephirot* on the same column: *'Hokhma, Netsa'h.*

Partsufim made from this *Sephira:*

One of the *Sephirot* that make the *Partsuf Z"A.*

Corresponding name: *El –* אל

Corresponding *Miluy* of name *MaH (45)* (מה)

Corresponding vowel: *Segol*

Physical correspondence: Right arm

Level of the soul: *Rua'h. See Sephira, Partsuf*

חסד,

גבורה,

תפארת

'Hesed,

Gevurah

Tiferet

'Hesed, Gevurah and Tiferet

Second triplet of the *Sephirot,* they correspond to the right and left arm and the body. They mostly act together as *Mo'hin* (brains) for a lower *Partsuf.*

141

Hebrew / Aramaic Phonetic	L	Dictionary
חסדים 'Hasadim	H	**Kindnesses** For the guidance five emanations of the aspect of 'Hesed (kindness) and five emanations of the aspect of Gevurah (rigors), are given by the Sephira Da'at to the Partsufim (configurations) Z"A and Nukvah. Partsuf Z"A receives the five 'Hasadim and Nukvah receives the five Gevurot. The five 'Hasadim come down to group in Sephira Yesod of Partsuf Z"A, and return upwards on their columns (Netsa'h and Hod), until they ascend in all the six edges of Partsuf Z"A. The five Gevurot come down afterwards and are appeased in Yesod of Partsuf Z"A, two and a half in the descent, and two and a half by the 'Hasadim returning upwards.After the complete spreading of the 'Hasadim in Partsuf Z"A, and their rise until Keter, Partsuf Z"A has attained the growth level.
חסדים מכוסים 'Hasadim Mekhusim	H	**Hidden Kindnesses** When Partsuf 'Atik entered Partsuf Arikh Anpin, two and a half 'Hasadim came out from Sephira Yesod of 'Atik and pushed out all the Gevurot. Two and a half of the 'Hasadim stayed in Yesod of 'Atik but remained covered. Therefore, there are two and a half 'Hasadim revealed and two and a half covered.
חסרון 'Hisaron	H	**Lack – deficiency** State of distance from the Kedushah and closeness to the Sitra A'hra (negative force).

Hebrew / Aramaic *Phonetic*	L	Dictionary

חפירה
'Hafirah

H *Digging – Deepening*

Term used as analyzing and deepening the first levels of understanding.

חקיקה
'Hakika

H *Carving*

Carving of the letters (*Sepher Yetsirah*).

חשוב
'Hashuv

H *Important*

See *'Hashivut*

חשיבות
'Hashivut

H *Importance*

All the worlds are similar; they all contain ten *Sephirot* and five *Partsufim*, but the higher is more complete and important than the one under it.

There is also a difference of importance in the position and the various emanations of the lights, *Sephirot* and *Partsufim*. See *Sephirot, Partsufim*

חשמל
'Hashma"l

H *Name of a Levush (garment)*

The *Levush* (garment) is an emanation given to a *Partsuf* to protect it from the negative forces.

The difference between the *Levush* and the encircling light is that the encircling light sustains the *Keli*, while the *Levush* is like a curtain that protects him from the negative forces.

'Hashma"l is a Levush made by the *NHY* (Netsa'h, Hod, Yesod) (*Tevunah*) of *Imah* and clothes the *Partsufim Zeir Anpin* and *Nukvah*. It encircles *Z"uN* underneath its legs all the way down, and makes a curtain between *Atsilut* and *Beriah*.

143

Hebrew / Aramaic Phonetic	L	Dictionary
חתך	H	**Cutting**
'Hatakh		When *Imah* and *Tevunah* are joined as one, there are three levels of *Yesod* in them: *Yesod* of *Imah*, *Yesod* of *Tevunah,* and the place of the cutting when they are separated and cut from each other.
		The *Kelim* (recipients) of *Partsuf Z"A* are repaired by *Yesod* of *Tevunah*, his sparks, at the place of the cutting, and his lights, by *Yesod* of *Binah* (*Imah*).

Hebrew / Aramaic Phonetic	L	Dictionary
ט ראשונות *Tet Rishonot*	H	**First Nine** First nine *Sephirot: Keter,* to *Yesod.*
טבור *Tabur*	H	**Navel** The navel corresponds to the second third of *Tiferet.* In general the lights will enter until the chest, or lower to the level of the navel. As for the lights of *BaN (52),* they came out through the eyes of *Adam Kadmon* and descended lower than the navel. They were not visible above the navel because the lights of the ears, nose and mouth extended to that point.
טיפה *Tipah*	H	**Drop** From the *Zivug* (union) of *Partsuf Abah* and *Imah,* one drop comes out from the *Mo'hin* (brains) of *Abah* called *'Hokhma,* and one drop from the *Mo'hin* of *Imah* called *Binah.* After the *Shvirat HaKelim (breaking of the vessels),* the aspects of the right side were repaired, corresponding to: *'Hesed, Netsa'h,* half of *Tiferet,* of *Yesod* and of *Malkhut* by the *Tipah* of *Abah.* Later, the *aspects* of the left side were repaired, corresponding to: *Gevurah, Hod,* half of *Tiferet,* of *Yesod* and *Malkhut* by the *Tipah* of *Imah.*
טל *Tal*	H	**Thirty nine** *Miluy* (spelling) of the name ו – ה - י - ָ. יוד הא ואו = 39
טלא דבדולחא *Tela Debadul'ha*	A	**Second of the seven Tikunim of the head of Arikh Anpin** From the head of *Partsuf* (configuration) *Arikh Anpin,* seven emanations come out to act and influence on

Hebrew / Aramaic *Phonetic*	L	Dictionary

the guidance, called the *Tikunim* of *Arikh Anpin*.

The second *Tikun* (action) of *Partsuf Arikh Anpin* is achieved by the passing of the seven lower *Sephirot* of *Partsuf 'Atik* into its head before they are clothed in him. These seven *Tikunim* (actions) of the head of *Arikh Anpin* are revealed from the seven lower *Sephirot* of *'Atik*

The second *Tikun* - טלא דבדולחא (*Tela Debadul'ha*) is realized by *Gevurah* of *'Atik* in *'Hokhma Stimaah*. It includes kindness and rigor; kindness because it is on the right column, rigor; because of *Gevurah* of *'Atik*, which is the root of all the *Gevurot*.

טלית *Talit*	H	**Talit - Praying shawl** The *Talit* represents the *Or Makif* (encircling light). When *Partsuf Z"A* is in the growth stage, the *NHY* (Netsa'h, Hod, Yesod) of *Imah* come down on his back, this makes his hair come out from his head, and go downward until his chest. At the level of his thorax, it corresponds to the *Talit*, at the level of *Ra'hel*, it corresponds to the *Tsitsit*.
טמא *Tameh*	H	**Impure** State of distance from the *Kedushah* and closeness to the *Sitra A'hra* (negative force).
טמאים *Tmeim*	H	**Impure (plur)** See Tameh
טנת"א *TaNTA*	H	**Ta'amim, Nekudot, Tagin, and Autiot.** Initials

Hebrew / Aramaic Phonetic	L	Dictionary
טעמים *Ta'amim*	H	**Cantillation notes** From the lights that were invested inside of *Adam Kadmon* emerged numerous worlds in the way of his senses; which are called his branches. These "branches" are the lights that spread forth from *Adam Kadmon,* by way of its apertures in the head. They spread out from his eyes, ears, nose, and mouth. From the aspect of the name *"A"V* of *SaG,* came out three branches in the aspects of the *Ta'amim (cantillation).* They came out through the ears, nose, and mouth: the higher from the ears, the middle from the nose, and the lower from the mouth. In the categories of lights that came out of *Adam Kadmon* as the *Ta'amim, Nekudot (vowels), Tagin (crowns), and Autiot (letters),* the *Ta'amim* are of the highest level. *See Orot HaOzen. Orot Ha'Hotem, Orot HaPeh*
טעמים, נקודות, תגין, אותיות *Ta'amim Nekudot, Tagin, Autiot.*	H	**Cantillation signs, vowels, crowns and letters.** From the lights that were invested inside *Adam Kadmon,* emerged numerous worlds in the way of his senses; which are called his branches. These "branches" are the lights that spread forth from *Adam Kadmon,* by way of its apertures in the head. They spread out from his eyes, ears, nose, mouth and forehead. The *Ta'amim* (cantillation marks) are of the highest level and are subdivided in three: higher, middle and lower. The *Nekudot* (vowels) are second, also in three levels: higher, middle and lower. The *Tagin* (crowns)

Hebrew / Aramaic *Phonetic*	L	Dictionary

are third, and appear on top of some letters only. The *Autiot* (letters) are fourth.

The *Sephirot* that came out from the forehead of *Adam Kadmon* for the *Tikun* are of the aspect of the *Tagin* and of the name of *MaH* *(45)*. From the ears, nose and mouth they are of the aspect of the *Ta'amim,* of the name of *SaG* *(63)*. From the eyes, they are of the aspect of the *Autiot*, of the name of *BaN* *(52)*.

The reading of the Torah is incomplete without the *Ta'amim, Nekudot, Tagin,* and *Autiot*. The *Autiot* are the expression of the *Ma'hshava* (thought). In combination with the *Ta'amim, Nekudot, Tagin,* or with other letters, they transform the higher lights into action.

טפל *Taffel*	H	**Subordinate - Accessory**

Subordinate - Accessory

The *Taffel* is always subordinate to the *'Ikar*, which is the main or the essential. Some emanations are subordinate to other more important lights.

Hebrew / Aramaic *Phonetic*	L	Dictionary
י-ה YaH	H	**YH** One of the names of G-od, represented by the Sephira 'Hokhma.
י-ה-ו-ה Adona-y	H	**Y-H-V-H** Tetragamon (י-ה-ו-ה) Main name of G-od, reveals kindness and mercy, represented by the Sephira Tiferet.

Y-H-V-H Tetragamon (י-ה-ו-ה)

Main name of G-od, reveals kindness and mercy, represented by the *Sephira Tiferet*.

The creative forces or energies are the different powers in the letters of the name of G-od י-ה-ו-ה, and the various letters added to make their different spellings. Depending on which letters are used, the numerical value of the name changes, and each one of these possibilities becomes different in its nature and actions.

The letters that are added for the different spellings of the letters are: י ה ו א ד

The different spellings of the letters are:

The letter י *(Yud)* can only be spelled one way: יוד

The letter ה *(He)* can be spelled with a י *(Yud)* or an א *(Aleph)* or a ה *(He)*: הא הה הי

The Letter ו *(Vav)* can be spelled with a יו *(Yud and Vav)* or with או *(Aleph and Vav)* or with ו *(Vav)*: ואו ויו וו

The four *Miluyim* (spelling) are:

עב ,סג ,מה בן *'A"V (72), SaG (63), MaH (45), BaN (52)*

יוד הי ויו הי – עב   - *'A"V* = 72

יוד הי ואו הי – סג   - *SaG* = 63

יוד הא ואו הא - מה   - *MaH* = 45

יוד הה וו הה – בן   - *BaN* = 52

Hebrew / Aramaic Phonetic	L	Dictionary
		Each name can also be divided and subdivided as: *'A"V of 'A"V, SaG of 'A"V, MaH of 'A"V …* *BaN of BaN of SaG, SaG of MaH of 'A"V etc.* The lights or forces that are clothed in these letters or their combinations emanate masculine or feminine configurations that make the guidance of the worlds.
י-ה-ו-ה **צבאות** *Adona-y Tsebaot*	H	**Y-H-V-H Tsebaot** One of the names of G-od, represented by the *Sephira Netsa'h.*
יודין *Yudin*	H	**Of the letter י (yud)** *Miluy* (spelling) when the letter י *(yud) is used.* See 'A"V
יום *Yom*	H	**Day** Each new day, is of a new emanation that governs it. For each day, there are new *Zivugim* (unions) of different aspects of *Z"uN (Zeir Anpin and Nukvah).* Each day, according to the actions of man, the *Tefilot* during the week, *Shabbat* or Holidays, and depending on time, various configurations allow different *Zivugim*, and therefore outflows of abundance of variable intensities. Each day can also be described in term of permutation of the names of G-od, and by the various *Sephirot and Partsufim* that govern on this day.
יוסף *Yosef*	H	**Joseph** Corresponds to the *Sephira Yesod.*

Hebrew / Aramaic Phonetic	L	Dictionary
יוצר Yotser	H	**Creator** G-od the one and only Creator.
יושר Yosher	H	**Straightness** *See straight Sephirot*
יחוד Yi'hud	H	**Unification – Union** The union of the *Sephirot* or *Partsufim* for the *Zivug* and for the descent of the abundance.

The union of the *Sephirot* or *Partsufim* for the *Zivug* and for the descent of the abundance.

A *Yi'hud* is also the unification of names or letters, as to provoke a specific action or reaction. In his book "*Sha'ar Rua'h HaKodesh*" the Ari Z'al explains the significance of the *Yi'hudim*, their different actions, and also warns of the danger of using these names without a proper preparation. By concentrating on various permutation of letters or names of angels, one could make these superior forces act according to his will.

There is also the revelation of the *Yi'hud* (unicity) of G-od. At the end of times, after all the *Tikunim*, it will be time for the *Moshia'h* to reveal himself, and all the world will see this complete unification to G-od's perfection caused by the revelation of His truth; which is the ultimate goal of the creation.

The lights or illumination of the *Dikna* (beard) will have this supreme function at the end of times: To reveal this *Yi'hud* – of the divine sovereignty.

See Giluy Yi'hudo

Hebrew / Aramaic Phonetic	L	Dictionary

יחודו

Yi'hudo

H **His unicity**

The light of G-od is unique, of equal force, quality and beyond all description. It is perfect, and cannot be measured by any definition or limiting terms. If we think about definitions, we introduce a notion of limit or absence of its opposite. However, the concept of limitlessness is beyond our human comprehension, and we therefore have to use terms accessible to our understanding. Being ourselves distinct separate beings, we cannot grasp the concept of the "non-distinct", everything we know is finite, by having a measure or an opposite. When we use terms as 'quality', it is to differentiate the various transformations of His unicity when it is at our level, and to help us understand its effects upon the guidance of the worlds.

At the end of times, after all the *Tikunim* (rectifications), it will be time for the *Moshia'h* to reveal himself. All the world will see the complete unification to G-od's perfection by the revelation of His truth; which is the ultimate goal of the creation.

The aim is to allow man to merit by his own efforts, to get closer to his Creator, and live the *Dvekut* – the adhesion with G-od. In this way, man will attain perfection and be directly involved in the ultimate goal of this existence, which is the revelation of G-od's Unicity and Sovereignty – *Giluy Ye'hudo.*

Hebrew / Aramaic Phonetic	L	Dictionary

יחודים H **Unifications – Unions**
Yi'hudim   See Yi'hud

יחיד H **Unique – Singular**
Ya'hid   See E'had, Yi'hudo

יחיד H **One and Unique**
ומיוחד   Can only apply to G-od.
Ya'hid   See E'had, Yi'hudo
Umeyu'had

יחידה H **Fifth level of the soul**
Ye'hidah   The soul has five names: *Nefesh, Rua'h, Neshama, 'Hayah* and *Ye'hidah*, which correspond to its five levels. The soul is the spiritual entity inside the body, the latter being only his outer garment.

Since it is men that provoke the union of the four worlds, it is necessary for their souls to have their origin from them, and from the five *Partsufim*:

Soul / Level	Partsuf	World
Nefesh	Nukvah	'Asiah
Rua'h	Zeir Anpin	Yetsirah
Neshama	Imah	Beriah
'Hayah	Abah	Atsilut
Ye'hidah	Arikh Anpin	Atsilut

Each level of the soul is subdivided in five levels. As for the level of *Nefesh;* there are *Nefesh* of *Nefesh, Rua'h* of *Nefesh, Neshama* of *Nefesh, 'Hayah* of *Nefesh* and *Ye'hidah* of *Nefesh.*

153

Hebrew / Aramaic Phonetic	L	Dictionary

Each one of these levels of the soul subdivides for each level of *Partsuf* and for each world. Therefore, there are five levels of the souls for *Partsuf Nukvah* and there are five levels of *Partsufim* for the world of *'Asiah* etc. Also, as there are in each world ten *Sephirot*, each soul has its origin corresponding to one of them.

Therefore, a soul could be from the level of *Nefesh* of *Malkhut* of *Nukvah* of *'Asiah,* or *Rua'h* of *'Hesed* of *Abah* of *'Yetsirah*, or *Neshama* of *Abah* of *Z"A* of *Yetsirah* etc.

Ye'hidah is the fifth level and can only be acquired after the preceding levels.

The higher levels of the soul cannot be acquired at once. Most men only have the level of *Nefesh,* and if they merit, they will acquire the next levels - but one by one.

To reach the next higher level of his soul, man must do the *Tikun* of the preceding level. If he needs to acquire the level of *Imah* of *'Asiah*, he must first do the *Tikun* of *Malkhut* of *'Asiah* and *Z"A* of *'Asiah,* and so on. To acquire his level of *Neshama*, he must do the *Tikun* of all the levels of the *Sephirot* and *Partsufim* of his *Nefesh* and *Rua'h* etc.

| ימים | H | **Days** |
| Yamim | | See Yom |

| יניקה | H | **Suckling** |
| Yenikah | | All the *Tikunim (rectifications)* of the masculine and |

Hebrew / Aramaic Phonetic	L	Dictionary

feminine *Partsufim (configurations)* are achieved by way of *Zivug* (union), gestation and birth. Afterwards, is the suckling and finally the growth for the *Partsuf* to be fully independent.

During the *Zivug*, the lights of *MaH (45)* needed for the *Tikun* are drawn to the lights of *BaN (52)*, and are kept in the upper *Partsuf Nukvah* that will give birth to the *Partsuf.*

During the gestation inside of *Nukvah*, they are arranged and completed until there is nothing more to add. After the gestation, when it is totally repaired, the *Partsuf* is revealed. The details of the lights and *Kelim* are now distinct, they come out to their positions; this is the birth (*Leida*).

During the gestation, the *Mo'hin* (brains) are of the lowest level and are called *NHY (Netsa'h, Hod, Yesod)* of the *Mo'hin;* they are of the aspect of *Nefesh*.

During the suckling, the lights grow and the *Mo'hin* are of a higher level and are called *HGT ('Hesed, Gevurah, Tiferet)* of the *Mo'hin;* they are of the aspect of *Rua'h*.

The *Sephirot* repaired in the suckling are: *Hod, Yesod* and *Malkhut*, they are repaired after all the other *Sephirot*, as a newborn that cannot walk when first born; he needs the sustenance (suckling) to strengthen his legs to stand on them.

During the time of the gestation, *Z"A* is not really acting as it is being built, at the time of suckling it starts to act, and at the growth it is ready to act completely. *See Gadlut*

155

Hebrew / Aramaic Phonetic	L	Dictionary

יסוד
Yesod

H **Sephira (Foundation)**

Ninth of the *Sephirot*.

Quality: Guidance that makes the equilibrium between *Sephira Netsa'h and Hod*.

Link or connection between all the superior *Sephirot* and *Malkhut*.

Column: Center – *Ra'hamim* (mercy)

Position: Middle – Bottom

Other *Sephirot* on the same column: *Keter, Tiferet, Malkhut*

Partsufim made from this *Sephira:*

One of the *Sephirot* that make the *Partsuf Z"A.*

Corresponding name: *Shada- y - י-שד-*

Corresponding *Miluy* of name: *MaH -מה (45)*

Corresponding vowel: *Shirik*

Physical correspondence: Masculine organ

Level of the soul: *Rua'h.* See Sephira, Partsuf

יסודות
Yesodot

H ***Plural of Yesod***

See Yesod

יעקב
Ya'acov

H ***Partsuf Ya'acov***

Partsuf Ya'acov is a masculine *Partsuf* to the left of *Partsuf Z"A.*

From an emanation of the longer *Sephira Yesod* of *Partsuf Israel Saba,* inside *Partsuf Z"A, Ya'acov* came out. His *Keter* is at the level of *Tiferet* of *Partsuf Z"A,* and he extends until *Sephira Malkhut* of *Partsuf Z"A.* The face of *Partsuf Z"A* is to the back of *Ya'acov,* sometimes *Ya'acov* comes to his side, his face in

Hebrew / Aramaic L Phonetic	Dictionary

front of *Ra'hel.*

Ya'acov corresponds to the *Tefilin* of *Rabenu Tam,* *Ra'hel* to the *Tefilin* of *Rashi.*

There are different *Zivugim* (union) *between Partsuf Ya'acov* and the feminine *(Ra'hel, Leah)* during *Sha'hrit* - *Ya'acov* and *Ra'hel*

Arvit – *Ya'acov* and *Leah* (from the chest up)

Tikun Hatsot – *Ya'acov* and *Leah* (from the chest down). See *Partsuf, Zivug*

יצירה H **World of formation – of the angels**

Yetsirah

From the first configuration of *Adam Kadmon,* four worlds unfolded.

On these four worlds, the four letters of the Name (ה-י-ה-ו) *B'H*, govern.

י in *Atsilut;* by it, all the repaired levels are put in order.

ה descends from it (*Atsilut*) to *Beriah,* and guides it.

ו to *Yetsirah,* and

ה to *'Asiah.*

The third world to unfold is called *Yetsirah;* the world of formation, the world of the angels. It is under *Atsilut* and *Beriah* and on top of *'Asiah.*

It consists of five main *Partsufim: Arikh Anpin, Abah, Imah, Zeir Anpin* and *Nukvah.* One more *Partsuf, 'Atik Yomin,* is on top of them.

In the emanation of the lights from the eyes of *Adam Kadmon,* first the individual *Keli* (recipient) for each *Sephira* came out, and then the lights. The *Kelim*

157

Hebrew / Aramaic Phonetic	L	Dictionary

could not contain their lights and broke. The seven lower broken *Sephirot*, which did not contain their lights, descended to the world of *Beriah*, the lights also fell, but stayed in *Atsilut*. The breaking of the *Kelim* caused a descent of all the worlds, *SaG (63)*, *MaH (45)* and *BaN (52)* descended to the lower worlds, *MaH* descended in *Yetsirah*, *Beriah* fell in the higher part of *Yetsirah,* which became the *Beriah* of today, *Yetsirah* in the higher parts of *'Asiah,* which became the *Yetsirah* of today,

There is a screen (divider) that separates one world from another. From this screen, the ten *Sephirot* of the lower world come out from the ten *Sephirot* of the higher world. The three superior worlds of *Atsilut*, *Beriah* and *Yetsirah,* are interior to the fourth world of *'Asiah*.

In parallel to the four worlds (*ABYA*), there are four types of existence in our world; mineral corresponding to *'Asiah (action)*, vegetal corresponding to *Yetsirah (formation)*, animal corresponding to *Beriah (creation),* and man corresponding to *Atsilut (emanation)*.

The world of *Yetsirah* is of the aspect of *MaH* (45). Thus, *Yetsirah* is of the aspect of *Partsuf Z"A*.

יצר
Yetser

H ***Instinct – Impulse***

The *Yetser Hatov* corresponds to the good or positive impulse in man, the *Yetser Hara'* is his bad or negative impulse.

Hebrew / Aramaic *Phonetic*	L	Dictionary

The good deeds of man have an effect on the four higher worlds, his bad deeds; on the four lower worlds. It is only when man sins, that the negative side can grow in strength. The negative aspect grows inside him; this is his *Yetser Hara'*, it cuts him off from the higher worlds, and uproots him from the *Kedushah*.

The *Yetser Hara'* almost constantly tries to seduce him, and make him stumble, while the *Yetser Hatov*, on the other side, tries to attract him to *Torah* and *Mitsvot* and to help him do the *Tikun* (rectification) of his *Neshama*.

The two aspects of *Yetser Tov* and *Yetser Hara'* are necessary for the guidance of justice, and to give man the possibility of free choice.

ירושלים   H   *Jerusalem*

Yerushalaim   The closest place to G-od's emanations.

ירחי עיבור   H   *Months of pregnancy*

Yar'hei   All the *Tikunim (rectifications)* of the masculine and
'Ibur   feminine *Partsufim (configurations)* are achieved by way of *Zivug* (union), gestation and birth.

During the *Zivug*, the lights of *MaH (45)* needed for the *Tikun* are drawn to the lights of *BaN (52)*, and are kept in the upper *Partsuf Nukvah* that will give birth to the *Partsuf*.

During the gestation inside of *Nukvah*, they are arranged and completed until there is nothing more to

Hebrew / Aramaic *Phonetic*	L	Dictionary

add. After the gestation, when it is totally repaired, the *Partsuf* is revealed. The details of the lights and *Kelim* are now distinct, they come out to their positions; this is the birth (*Leida*).

A *Partsuf* includes three components: *Kelim* (recipients), sparks, and lights. At the beginning, in the *'Olam Hanikudim*, only six *Sephirot* of *Partsuf Z"A* came out; the parts needed for his *HBD* ('Hokhma, Binah, Da'at) stayed inside *Imah*.

At the time of the *Shvirat HaKelim (breaking of the vessels)*, the lights went back up, the *Kelim* and the sparks descended lower to the world of *Beriah*.

The *Tikun* was to reunite these three aspects again, by three gestations of seven, nine, and twelve months. *See Partsuf, Zivug*

ירידה H **Descent**

Yeridah

Because of the breaking of the vessels, there was a descent of the *Kelim* (recipients) from the world of *Atsilut* to the lower world of *Beriah*, the lights that were not contained in the *Kelim* fell, but stayed in *Atsilut*.

SaG (63) , *MaH* (45) and *BaN* (52) also descended to the lower worlds, *SaG* in *Beriah*, *MaH* in *Yetsirah,* and *BaN* in *'Asiah*.

However, *KHB* (Keter, 'Hokhma, Binah) remained in what is called the "first *Atsilut*". The seven lower *Sephirot* fell in the higher parts of *Beriah*, which became the *Atsilut* of today, *Beriah* fell in the higher part of *Yetsirah*,

160

Hebrew / Aramaic Phonetic	L	Dictionary
		which became the *Beriah* of today, *Yetsirah* in the higher parts of *'Asiah,* which became the *Yetsirah* of today, *'Asiah* fell even lower and became the *'Asiah* of today. There are other types of descents, as the one of the *'Hasadim* and *Gevurot* from *Sephira Da'at* to *Yesod,* and the one of *Mayin Dukhrin* (masculine waters) to the *Mayin Nukvin* (feminine waters) for the *Zivug* and *Tikun* of the *Partsufim.* *See Zivug, Tikun, Shvirat HaKelim*
יש *Yesh*	H	**There is** *See Yesh Meein*
יש מאין *Yesh Meein*	H	**Creation from nothing** There is a special force called *"Tsu'r T'K"*, which has the power to create separate entities from nothing. This force is not related to the *Sephirot*. It was first explained in the *"Sepher HaYetsrira"*, which is the oldest Kabbalistic writing. It is only after being created that the guidance is taken over by the *Sephirot*.
ישסו"ת *ISOT*	A	**Partsufim Israel Saba and Tevunah** Initials
ישסו"ת ב *ISOT 2*	A	**Second Partsufim of Israel Saba and Tevunah** Initials
ישר *Yashar*	H	**Direct – Straight – Linear** *See Or Yashar*

161

Hebrew / Aramaic Phonetic	L	Dictionary
ישראל Israel	A	**Partsuf Israel** All of Partsuf Zeir Anpin is called Israel, or sometimes only its top part. See Partsuf Zeir Anpin
ישראל Israel	H	**Israel** The land of Israel corresponds to Partsuf Nukvah – Ra'hel, and is the closest to G-od's emanations.
ישראל סבא א Israel Saba 1	A	**Partsuf Israel Saba** Malkhut of Partsuf Abah is sometimes an independent Partsuf. See Partsufim Israel Saba and Tevunah
ישראל סבא ב Israel Saba 2	A	**Partsuf Israel Saba 2** Malkhut of Israel Saba is sometimes an independent Partsuf.- See Partsufim Israel Saba and Tevunah, ISOT
ישראל סבא ותבונה Israel Saba Ve Tevunah	A	**Partsufim Israel Saba and Tevunah** The Sephirot Malkhuts of Partsuf Abah and Imah become distinct Partsufim (configurations): Israel Saba and Tevunah. Their role is to be the Mo'hin (brains) of Partsuf Z"A. They are at the level of the navel of the chest of Partsuf Arikh Anpin, and are also called by their initials ISOT or ISOT 2. The first ISOT are Israel Saba and Tevunah, the second ISOT are Israel Saba 2 and Tevunah 2. - From Sephira Malkhut of Abah - Israel Saba - From Malkhut of Israel Saba - Israel Saba 2 - From Sephira Malkhut of Binah -Tevunah

Hebrew / Aramaic Phonetic	L	Dictionary

- From *Malkhut* of *Tevunah* - *Tevunah* 2

ISOT start from the chests of *Abah* and *Imah* and extend downward. Half of *Tiferet*, and *NHY* (Netsa'h, Hod, Yesod) of *Abah* and *Imah* dress inside *ISOT* as their *Mo'hin*. *ISOT* dress inside the *NHY* of *ISOT* 2.

The *Mo'hin* (brains) of *Z"A* are given to him by the *Zivug* (union) of *Abah* and *Imah*. Depending on the state of growth of *Z"A*, they are from *ISOT*, or directly from *Abah* and *Imah*. When *NHY* of *ISOT* 2 are clothed in *Z"A* as his *Mo'hin*; it is the first growth, but when *NHY* of *ISOT* 1 are clothed in him, it is considered as if *Abah* and *Imah* were clothed in him directly as *Mo'hin*, and this is the second growth.

The *Zivug* of *Abah* and *Imah* is constant; the one of *ISOT* is occasional.

Hebrew / Aramaic *Phonetic*	L	Dictionary
כבד *Kaved*	H	***Heavy*** When the *Sephirot* came out the first time from the mouth of *Adam Kadmon,* the most tenuous part of the lights returned to their origin in the mouth but not completely, each one leaving its trace. This trace, which did not return became heavier and thickened.
כוונה *Kavanah*	H	***Intention – Concentration*** There are different levels of *Kavanah*. The basic *Kavanah* is to understand the words, and concentrate on the intention of the blessing or the *Tefilah*. The higher level is to meditate on the different systems of permutation of names and *Partsufim* (configurations), to get a particular action or result. The order of the *Tefilot* is based on the systems of ascension of the worlds as explained in the Kabbalah. At this level, we understand that our *Tefilot* have a direct influence on the superior worlds and on their guidance. Starting from the first act in the morning of *Netilat Yadayim* (washing of the hands three times in alternation), until the end of the *Tefilah*, there is a constant elevation and adhesion of the worlds of *'Asiah, Yetsirah* and *Beriah* to *Atsilut.* When saying a blessing with the Kabbalistic meditation on the appropriate words or names, we act and participate directly on the *Tikun* of the action or thing being blessed. The *Hekhalot* (portals) are the different levels of

Hebrew / Aramaic Phonetic	L	Dictionary

ascension of the *Tefilot* before reaching the seventh highest *Hekhal (portal), Kodesh Hakodashim*. Their principal function is to allow the adhesion and attachment, in various and particular ways during the *Tefilot*, until the *'Olam Atsilut* (during the *'Amidah*).

During the *Tefilot*, he who knows the system of ascension of the *Hekhalot* (portals), concentrates on the words where are hinted the precise action of the *Hekhal (portal)*. He aims to help in the realization of the particular *Zivug* (union) of the *Tefilah*.

When one understands the systems and actions of the *Tefilot*, he realizes the importance of our rituals, because only man, by praying and the accomplishment of the *Mitsvot,* can influence these incredible forces. *See Tefilah*

‎כוונות   H   ***Intentions – Concentration***
Kavanot   *See Kavanah*

‎כולל   H   ***Kolel***
Kolel   One of the seven main types of *Gematriot*.
The *Ragil* value of the word + the numbers of letters.
Ex : ‎הארץ   = 1106 + 4 = 1110. *See Gematria*

‎כורסיא   A   ***Throne***
Kursaya   *See Kisey*

‎כח   H   ***Force – Strength***
Koa'h   The different emanations of a particular light is dependent on the manifestations of the various levels of its force.

Hebrew / Aramaic Phonetic	L	Dictionary
כחב Ka'HaB	H	**Keter, 'Hokhma, Binah** Initials
כיסא Kisey	H	**Throne** There are three main types of thrones: *Kisey HaDin* - throne of justice *Kisey Hakavod* - throne of glory *Kisey Ra'hamim* - throne of mercy See Kisey HaDin, Kisey Hakavod, Kisey Ra'hamim
כיסא הדין Kisey HaDin	H	**Throne of justice – rigor** From the throne of justice, the guidance is from the left pillar – the pillar of rigor.
כיסא הכבוד Kisey HaKavod	H	**Throne of glory** "In the presence of G-od"
כיסא הרחמים Kisey Ra'hamim	H	**Throne of mercy** From the throne of mercy, the guidance is from the middle pillar – the pillar of mercy.
כלה Kalah	H	**Bride** *Sephira Malkhut. Partsuf Leah or Ra'hel.*
כלי Keli	H	**Recipient – Vessel** The light of G-od is unique and of equal force and quality. A *Sephira* is in a way a "filter" which transforms this light in a particular force or attribute, by which the Creator guides the worlds.

Hebrew / Aramaic Phonetic	L	Dictionary

Each *Sephira* is composed of a vessel called *Keli,* which holds its part of light called *Or.* There is no difference in the *Or* itself, the difference comes from the particularity, or position of the *Sephira.*

A *Partsuf,* as a *Sephira,* includes three components: *Keli,* sparks, and light. The *Keli* is the recipient of the light inside the *Sephira.*

The *Keli* has three levels: Interior, intermediate and exterior. *NHY* (Netsa'h, Hod, Yesod) are the exterior *Keli, HGT* ('Hesed, Gevurah, Tiferet) the intermediate *Keli,* and *HBD* ('Hokhma, Binah, Da'at) the interior *Keli.* The *Kelim* of *HGT* dress inside the *Kelim* of *NHY* and make their interior, but they are exterior to the *Kelim* of *HBD,* which are clothed inside them. In the same way, their lights are clothed in each other.

For each level, there are three aspects as:

NHY of *NHY* - exterior *Keli* of *NHY*

HGT of *NHY* - middle *Keli* of *NHY*

HBD of *NHY* - interior *Keli* of *NHY*

NHY of *HGT* - exterior *Keli* of *HGT,* etc.

Each one of these levels has particular actions and functions.

See Shvirat HaKelim, Keli 'Hitson, Keli Pnimi, Keli Tikhon.

כלי חיצון Keli 'Hitson	H	***Exterior recipient - vessel*** The exterior *Keli* are the *NHY* (Netsa'h, Hod, Yesod) of the *Keli.* They dress the more interior *Kelim* of *HGT* ('Hesed, Gevurah, Tiferet) which dress the *Kelim* of *HBD* ('Hokhma, Binah, Da'at).

167

Hebrew / Aramaic Phonetic	L	Dictionary
		NHY is the aspect of *Nefesh*. NHY of NHY is the aspect of *Nefesh* of the exterior *Keli*. Each one of these levels has particular actions and functions. This aspect of the *Keli* is revealed during the gestation
כלי פנימי *Keli* *Pnimi*	H	**Interior Keli** The interior *Keli* are the *HBD* ('Hokhma, Binah, Da'at) of the *Keli*. They dress in the *NHY* (Netsa'h, Hod, Yesod) of the *Keli* and in the more interior *Kelim* of *HGT* ('Hesed, Gevurah, Tiferet) *HBD* is the aspect of *Neshama*. *HBD* of *HBD* is the aspect of *Neshama* of the *interior Keli*. This aspect of the *Keli* is revealed during the growth.
כלי תיכון *Keli* *Tikhon*	H	**Intermediate Keli** The intermediate *Keli* are the *HGT* ('Hesed, Gevurah, Tiferet) of the *Keli*. They dress in the *NHY* (Netsa'h, Hod, Yesod) of the *Keli* and on the more interior *Kelim* of *HBD* ('Hokhma, Binah, Da'at). *HGT* is the aspect of *Rua'h*, *NHY* of *HGT* is the aspect of *Rua'h* of the *intermediate Keli*. This aspect of the *Keli* is revealed during the suckling
כלים *Kelim*	H	**Recipients – Vessels** See *Keli*
כניסה *Kenisah*	H	**Entrance** The arriving of the lights is also called their entrance.

Hebrew / Aramaic *Phonetic*	L	Dictionary
כנסת ישראל *Kneset Israel*	H	**Assembly of Israel** People of Israel.
כתבי האר"י *Kitve HaAri*	H	**Writings of the Ari** *See Ari Z'al*
כתפין *Ktafin*	A	**Shoulders** When *Partsuf Nukvah* descends from *Sephira Da'at* of *Z"A* to be constructed, she is built by the rears of the *NHY (Netsa'h, Hod, Yesod)* of *Z"A*. The *Sephira Yesod* of *Z"A* takes position in *Da'at* of *Nukvah,* between her shoulders.
כתר *Keter*	H	**Sephira – Crown** First and most important of the *Sephirot*. Quality: Complete kindness to all, even to the not deserving. Column: Center – *Ra'hamim* (mercy) Position: Top – center Other *Sephirot* on the same column: *Tiferet, Yesod, Malkhut*. *Partsufim* made from this *Sephira:* - *'Atik Yomin* and his *Nukvah* - *Arikh Anpin* and his *Nukvah* Corresponding name: *AHY-H* - אהי-ה Corresponding *Miluy* of name: *'A"V* - עב (72)

169

Hebrew / Aramaic Phonetic	L	Dictionary
		Corresponding vowel: *Kamatz* Physical correspondence: Head Level of the soul: *Ye'hidah. See Sephira, Partsuf*
כתר, חכמה, בינה *Keter, 'Hokhma Binah*	H	**Keter, 'Hokhma, Binah** The three first *Sephirot*, often referred as the *Ga'R*; *Shalosh Rishonot* (the three first ones). The roots of all the created are in the seven lower *Sephirot* (*Za"T*), the three first *Sephirot* are like a crown on the *Za"T* to repair and direct them. In the three first *Sephirot* there is not really a notion of damage, they are above men's deeds, and are not affected by their sins. In the *Shvirat HaKelim* (breaking of the vessels), the inferior part of *'Hokhma* and *Binah* did not contain their lights, they fell but did not break. These lower parts correspond to what is needed for the guidance of the seven lower *Sephirot*, if it had contained their lights, these *Sephirot* would not have broken, and the notions of *Kilkul* (damage) and *Tikun* (repair) not existed. *See Mo'hin.*
כתרים *Ketarim*	H	**Sephirot - Crowns** After the *Shvirat HaKelim* (breaking of the vessels) the *Sephirot Keter* of different *Sephirot* got together to make the *Partsuf 'Atik Yomin*. This *Partsuf* was realized by the *Ketarim* of the *Sephirot* of the aspect of *MaH* and *BaN*.

Hebrew / Aramaic Phonetic	L	Dictionary

ל"ב
נתיבות
חכמה
LaV
Netivot
'Hokhma

H **32 Paths of wisdom**

Thirty two paths of lights from the *Sephira 'Hokhma*. They are the twenty two letters plus the ten *Sephirot*. In the *Parasha Bereshit* the name of *Elokim* in mentioned 32 times.

לאה
Leah

H **Leah - Partsuf Nukvah**

The *Partsuf Nukvah*, which represents the feminine – the principle of receiving, comprises of two distinct *Partsufim* (configurations): *Ra'hel* and *Leah*. *Partsuf Ra'hel* is of the aspect of kindness, *Partsuf Leah* of the aspect of rigor.

Partsuf Leah is on top of *Partsuf Ra'hel,* at the level of *Da'at* of *Partsuf Z"A* and extends down to half of his *Tiferet*. It is from an emanation of the *Yesod* of *Partsuf Tevunah*, inside of *Z"A,* that *Leah* came out.

All the abundance that comes down to the world, proceeds from the various *Zivugim* (unions) of *Z"uN* (*Z"A* and *Nukvah*).

There are five different *Zivugim*: Two with *Ra'hel* and three with *Leah*. The *Zivugim* with *Ra'hel* are of a higher level; being of the aspect of kindness, the ones with *Leah* are more of the aspect of rigor.

In the *Tefilah* of *Min'ha*, there is the *Zivug* of *Israel* and *Leah*.

In the *Tefilah* of *'Arvit*, there is the *Zivug* of *Ya'acov* and *Leah* (from the chest up).

In *Tikun 'Hatsot*, there is the *Zivug* of *Ya'acov* and

171

Hebrew / Aramaic Phonetic	L	Dictionary
		Leah (from the chest down). *See Malkhut, Nukvah, Zivug, Kavanah*
לב Lev	H	**Heart** Usually identifies a center position or a main part.
לבוש Levush	H	**Garment** The *Levush* (garment) is an emanation given to a *Partsuf* to protect it from the negative forces. The difference between the *Levush* and the encircling light is that the encircling light sustains the *Keli*, while the *Levush* is like a curtain that protects him. There is also a *Levush* or envelope, which is necessary for the soul to attach to the body of man during his reincarnation (*Gilgul*). When another soul attaches to him ('*Ibur*), it could use the same *Levush* (garment) to remain in him. *See Gilgul*
לבושים Levushim	H	**Garments** *See Levush*
לבנת הספיר Livnat Hasapir	H	**Livnat Hasapir** Name of a *Hekhal* (portal). First of seven *Hekhalot*, corresponding to *Sephira Yesod* and *Malkhut*. Each world (*ABYA*) is built from four aspects: *Partsuf*, *Levush* (garment), *Or Makif* (encircling lights), and *Hekhalot*. In each *Partsuf*, there are interiority and exteriority, the exteriority is always of the aspect of *Malkhut*, and the *Hekhalot* are the ramifications of the *Malkhuts* of the *Partsufim*.

Hebrew / Aramaic Phonetic	L	Dictionary

The *Hekhalot* are also the different levels of ascension of the *Tefilot* before reaching the seventh *Hekhal (portal), Kodesh Hakodashim.*

Their principal function is to allow the adhesion and attachment, in various and particular ways during the *Tefilot*, until the *'Olam Atsilut* (during the *Amidah*)

The *Neshamot* and the angels have their root in the *Hekhalot*, each one depending on its respective level.

See Hekhal, Tefilah

להאיר

Lehair

H ***Illuminate***

A *Sephira* can "illuminate" or transmit its light to another *Sephira* or *Partsuf*.

להחיות

LeHa'hayot

H ***To Live – Sustain***

After the *Shvirat HaKelim (breaking of the vessels)*, the *Kelim* fell to the lower worlds. To sustain them after they broke, 288 sparks of the lights came down as well. A connection with their own original lights was needed to keep them alive. For their livelihood, the negative forces get strength by attaching to the exteriority of the *Sephirot*; they nourish from their lights and gain more power to act negatively.

All and everything is sustained by one and only one source; the light of G-od, which is bestowed through the *Partsufim* and *Sephirot*.

להחמיר

LeHa'hmir

H ***To be more stringent***

A strict observance of all the details when accomplishing a *Mitsva* or *Tefilah. See Kavanah*

Hebrew / Aramaic Phonetic	L	Dictionary
להנהיג LeHanhig	H	**To guide** See Hanhagah
להתיר LeHatir	H	**To allow** Permissible to do, or to observe.
לוצאטו Luzzatto	H	***Rabbi Moshe 'Haim Luzzatto – Ram'hal*** Born in Padua, Italy in 1707, died in Israel in 1746. From an early age, Rabbi Moshe 'Haim Luzzatto showed an exceptional talent for the study of Kabbalah, it is said that when he was only fourteen, he already knew all the Kabbalah of the Ari Z'al by heart, and nobody knew about it, not even his parents. He was a very prolific writer and wrote on the all aspects of the Torah and the Kabbalah. Some of his main works are *"Kala'h Pit'he'Hokhma" "Klalut Hallan" "Adir Bamaron"*.
ליאדי Liadi	H	***Rabbi Shneur Zalman of Liadi – The Alter Rebbe*** Born in Russia, 1745, died in Russia in 1813. The *"Baal HaTanya"*, founder of the 'Habad - Lubavitch movement. He was a descendant of the *Maharal of Prague*. He studied under the *Maggid of Mezritch* the writings of the Ari and composed the *"Tanya"*.
לידה Leida	H	***Birth*** All the *Tikunim* of the *Partsufim* (masculine and feminine) are achieved by way of *Zivug* (union), gestation and birth. During the *Zivug*, the lights of MaH (45) needed for the *Tikun* are drawn to the lights

Hebrew / Aramaic Phonetic	L	Dictionary

of *BaN (52)*, and are kept in the upper *Nukvah* that will give birth to the *Partsuf*. During the gestation, inside of *Nukvah*, they are arranged and completed until there is nothing more to add. After the time of the gestation, when it is totally repaired the *Partsuf* is revealed, the details of the lights and the *Kelim* are distinct, and they come out to their positions; this is the birth (*Leida*).

There is afterwards the suckling, and finally the growth, so that the *Partsuf* will be fully independent.

See Partsufim

למטה
Lemata

H **To lower**

A process of descent.

למעלה
Lema'la

H **To higher**

A process of ascent.

לפרקים
Lifrakim

H **Intermittently**

Some actions or illuminations are occasional. The *Zivug* (union) of *Partsuf Abah* and *Imah* is constant, but the one of *Partsuf ISOT* is occasional. The *Zivug* of *Abah* and *Imah* for the liveliness of the worlds is constant, but the one for the *Mo'hin* (brains) is occasional.

לקבל
Lekabel

H **To receive**

The word Kabbalah comes from the verb *Lekabel* (to receive), but to receive it is first necessary to want, and to become a *Keli* (recipient) able to receive and contain this knowledge. A *Kabbalist* is a person that is

Hebrew / Aramaic *Phonetic*	L	Dictionary

accepted to receive this knowledge, and is able to hold it by living in the path of *Torah* and rightness to strengthen himself constantly.

When one decides that he wants to know his Creator, in learning this science he realizes his smallness compared to these incredible forces, the perfection of the Lord and His infinite love for His creatures.

Since the intention of the Creator is to bestow goodness on His creatures, all the levels of creation were put in place so His kindness could emanate to them, yet in such a way that they would be able to receive it.

The *Ein Sof* (infinite), *B'H* influences when there is instigation from the receiver, the latter corresponding to the aspect of *BaN* (52). This influence is transmitted by different illuminations (*Sephirot*), and then by *Nukvah* after her *Zivug* (union) with *Z"A,* to the receiver (man).

See Kabbalah

Hebrew / Aramaic *Phonetic*	L	Dictionary
מ"ב MaV	H	**MaV (42)** Name of 42 letters made by the four letters of the name י-ה-ו-ה, the *Miluy* (spelling) of each one of the four letters for a total of ten letters, and the *Miluy* of each one of these ten letters for a total of twenty eight. This name is hinted in the recital of the *Kadish* during the *Tefilah*. It makes possible the ascent of each world to the next higher world.
מ"ד M"D	A	**Mayin Dukhrin (masculine waters)** Initials
מ"ה MaH	H	**MaH (45)** ***Miluy (spelling) of the name י-ה-ו-ה with a total of 45*** The creative forces or energies are the different powers in the four letters of the name of G-od י-ה-ו-ה, and the various letters added to make their different spellings. Depending on which letters are used, the numerical value of the name changes, and each one of these possibilities becomes different in its nature and actions. The letters that are added for the different spellings of the letters are: י ה ו א ד The different spellings of the letters are: The letter י *(Yud)* can only be spelled one way: יוד The letter ה *(He)* can be spelled with a י *(Yud)* or an א *(Aleph)* or a ה *(He)*: הא הה הי The Letter ו *(Vav)* can be spelled with a יו *(Yud and*

177

Hebrew / Aramaic *Phonetic*	L	Dictionary
		Vav) or with או *(Aleph and Vav)* or with a ו *(Vav):* ואו ויו וו The four *Miluyim* (spellings) are: עב ,סג , מה, בן - - *'A"V (72), SaG (63), MaH (45), BaN (52)* יוד הי ויו הי – עב - *'A"V* = 72 יוד הי ואו הי – סג - *SaG* = 63 יוד הא ואו הא - מה - *MaH* = 45 יוד הה הה וו הה – בן - *BaN* = 52 Each name can also be divided and subdivided as: *'A"V of 'A"V, SaG of 'A"V, MaH of 'A"V …* *BaN of BaN of SaG, SaG of MaH of 'A"V etc.* The name of *MaH (45)* is the *Miluyim* (spelling) of א, which is a (ו) (Vav) line in the middle (mercy) that unites two י (Yud) (kindness and rigor). It is of a masculine aspect and represents mercy. יוד הא ואו הא - מה - *MaH* = 45 After the breaking of the *Kelim* (recipients) and the separation from their lights, it was necessary for the guidance of the world that reparation be done. From the forehead of *Adam Kadmon* came out ten *Sephirot* of the aspect of the name of *MaH (45);* corresponding to the masculine - reparation. In contrast, the *Sephirot* of *BaN (52)* correspond to the feminine aspect - rigor, and are the root of deterioration. The *Tikun* *(reparation)* was the union of *MaH* and *BaN* in complex arrangements, as to allow the feminine *BaN*

Hebrew / Aramaic *Phonetic*	L	Dictionary

to be repaired by the masculine *MaH* and for the *Sephirot* to stand in the three-column arrangement of kindness, rigor and mercy

There is no existence that is not composed of the aspects of *MaH (45)* or *BaN (52);* the influencer and the receiver, the masculine and the feminine etc. The *Ein Sof, B'H* influences when there is instigation from the receiver. This influence is transmitted by different illuminations of the aspect of *MaH*, and then by *Nukvah* after her *Zivug* with *Z"A.* From *Z"A,* is the renewal of the aspect of *MaH*, and from *Nukvah;* the renewal of the aspect of *BaN.* These two aspects of *MaH* and *BaN* are necessary for the guidance of justice, and to give man the possibility of free choice.

The *Mayin Nukvin* are of the aspect of *BaN (52)*, the *Mayin Dukhrin,* of the aspect of *MaH (45).* After the damage of the broken *Kelim* (recipients) *SaG, MaH* and *BaN* descended to the lower worlds, *MaH)* descended to *Yetsirah,* thus *Yetsirah* is of the aspect of *MaH.*

All the emanations and *Sephirot* that came out of *Adam Kadmon (Primordial man)* by way of his apertures were of the various aspects of these four names. They have different actions and *Tikunim,* and all the *Partsufim (configurations)* will be constructed by their union.

See Orot HaMetsa'h, Sephirot Shel MaH

179

Hebrew / Aramaic Phonetic	L	Dictionary

מ"ן   A   *Mayin Nukvin (feminine waters)*
M"N   Initials

מאציל   H   *Emanator*
Maatsil   His light, force or energy is without end, and of such holiness and intensity, that it is not possible for any being to exist in its proximity.
His first act in this creation was then to set limits to His light, so that it would not emanate with its full force.

Since the intention of the Creator is to bestow goodness on His creatures, all the levels of creation were put in place so His kindness could emanate to them, yet in such a way that they would be able to receive it.
The *Sephirot* are the links between the Emanator and the guidance of the world. By them, are manifested the actions of the *Ein Sof*, - the Emanator to the receivers.
His emanations are transmitted by different illuminations of the aspect of *MaH (45)*, and then by *Nukvah* after her *Zivug* with *Partsuf Z"A*.

מגיד   H   *Celestial mentor*
Maggid   A *Maggid* reveals himself to teach celestial secrets.
The Ram'hal had the revelation of a *Maggid*, under his dictation he wrote thousands of pages and revealed magnificent secrets.

Hebrew / Aramaic Phonetic	L	Dictionary

מדבר **H** *Speaking*
Medaber

In parallel to the four worlds of *Atsilut, Beriah, Yetsirah* and *'Asiah,* there are four types of existence in our world: mineral (דומם), vegetal (צומח), animal (חי), and the speaking (מדבר)..

Mineral corresponding to *'Asiah,* vegetal corresponding to *Yetsirah,* animal corresponding to *Beriah,* and the speaking corresponding to *Atsilut.*

מדה **H** *Attribute - Quality – Measure*
Midah

The light of G-od is unique, of equal force, quality and beyond all description. Since the concept of limitlessness is above our human comprehension, we therefore have to use terms accessible to our understanding. In Kabbalah the term 'quality' is used, to differentiate the various transformations of this "simple light", and to help us understand its effects upon the guidance of the worlds. The *Sephirot* or *Partsufim* are called the attributes or qualities of G-od. A *Sephira* is in a way a "filter" which transforms this light in a particular force or quality, by which the Creator guides the worlds. *See Sephirot, Partsufim*

מדרגה **H** *Level*
Madregah

A level of importance.

The actions or manifestations of the lights and emanations depend on their level of importance.

מדרגות **H** *Levels*
Madregot

See Madregah

181

Hebrew / Aramaic *Phonetic*	L	Dictionary

מדת הדין H **The attribute (quality) of judgment**

Midat HaDin

The light of G-od is unique, of equal force, quality and beyond all description. In Kabbalah the term 'quality' is used, to differentiate the various transformations of this "unique light", and to help us understand its effects upon the guidance of the worlds.

The *Sephirot* or *Partsufim* (configurations) are called the attributes or qualities of G-od. A *Sephira* is in a way a "filter" which transforms this light in a particular force or quality, by which the Creator guides the worlds. One of these manifestations of this light once filtered by the *Sephira Gevurah* emanates rigor.

The *Sephirot* are arranged in three columns: right, left and middle, representing the guidance of the world in the manner of *'Hesed*, *Din* and *Ra'hamim* - Kindness, rigor and mercy. In the attribute of rigor, the guidance is from the left pillar – the pillar of rigor, it contains the *Sephirot*: *Binah*, *Gevurah*, *Hod*. The corresponding name to this attribute is: *Elohi-m* - אלהי-ם

Some *Partsufim* are masculine and bestow kindness, others are feminine and bestow rigor. By their union, different equilibriums of these two forces (Kindness and rigor), make the guidance. Complete rigor will be the destruction of anything not perfect, while complete kindness will permit everything without restriction. Thus we see that everything that is, and happens, is always composed of a variable measure and balance of these two forces.

Hebrew / Aramaic Phonetic	L	Dictionary

Rigor is mostly manifested by all the feminine aspects as: the name of *BaN (52)*, the *Sephira Gevurah* and by all the concealments of the masculine aspects which represent bounty.

There are particular moments, or days of rigor during the year. This is dependent on the different position of the *Partsufim.* In the absence of *Zivug* (union) when the masculine and feminine *Partsuf* are back to back, it corresponds to dissimulation and rigor.

מדת H ***The attribute of (quality) bounty***
החסד
Midat   The light of G-od is unique, of equal force, quality and
Ha'Hesed   beyond all description. In Kabbalah the term 'quality' is used, to differentiate the various transformations of this "unique light", and to help us understand its effects upon the guidance of the worlds.

The *Sephirot* or *Partsufim* are called the attributes or qualities of G-od. A *Sephira* is in a way a "filter" which transforms this light in a particular force or quality, by which the Creator guides the worlds.

The linear *Sephirot* are arranged in three columns: right, left and middle, representing the guidance of the world in the manner of *'Hesed, Din* and *Ra'hamim* - Kindness, rigor and mercy. Some *Partsufim* are masculine and bestow kindness, others are feminine and bestow rigor. By their union, different equilibriums of the two forces of Kindness and rigor make the guidance. When the masculine and feminine *Partsuf* are face to face it is the ideal level and corresponds to

183

Hebrew / Aramaic Phonetic	L	Dictionary

the bestowing of abundance.

In the attribute of bounty, the guidance is from the right pillar – the pillar of kindness.

The corresponding name to this attribute is:

YHV-K – יה-ו-ה-י

See Sephirot, Partsufim

מדת הרחמים

Midat Hara'hamim

H   ***The attribute of (quality) Mercy***

The light of G-od is unique, of equal force, quality and beyond all description. In Kabbalah the term 'quality' is used, to differentiate the various transformations of this "unique light", and to help us understand its effects upon the guidance of the worlds.

The *Sephirot* or *Partsufim* are called the attributes or qualities of G-od. A *Sephira* is in a way a "filter" which transforms this light in a particular force or quality, by which the Creator guides the worlds.

The linear *Sephirot* are arranged in three columns: right, left and middle, representing the guidance of the world in the manner of *'Hesed, Din* and *Ra'hamim* - Kindness, rigor and mercy. Some *Partsufim* are masculine and bestow kindness, others are feminine and bestow rigor. By their union, different equilibriums of the two forces of Kindness and rigor make the guidance.

In the attribute of mercy the guidance is from the middle pillar – the pillar of *Ra'hamim*. This Guidance makes the balance between the guidance of rigor and bounty. *See Sephirot, Partsufim*

Hebrew / Aramaic Phonetic	L	Dictionary
מהות *Mahut*	H	**Essence** Nature or inner quality.
מוח *Moa'h*	A	**Brain** See Mo'hin
מוחא סתימאה *Mo'ha Stimaah*	A	**Third of the three heads of Arikh Anpin** The three heads of *Arikh Anpin* are the roots of the direction of kindness, rigor and mercy. They emanate from *Arikh Anpin* to *Abah* and *Imah,* and from there, to the *Mo'hin* (brains) of *Z"A*. These three heads are the first *Tikun* (action) of *Partsuf Arikh Anpin* they are: 1- *Gulgolta* - *Keter* of *Arikh Anpin* 2- *Avirah* - In the space between *Keter* and *'Hokhma* of *Arikh Anpin,* there is *Da'at* of *'Atik* 3- *Mo'ha* - *'Hokhma* of *Arikh* For each head there are three levels of lights: Interior, encircling (*Makif*), and encircling of the encircling (*Makif* le *Makif*). The name י-ה-ו-ה represents the interiority. The name א-ה-י-ה the encircling. Depending on their vowels they correspond to one of the three heads. They differentiate by their *Nekudot* (vowels). When the first letters have the vowels as pronounced; *Segol* instead of *Tsere* and *Pata'h* instead of *Kamatz,* The *Miluy* has vowels as pronounced, The *Miluy* has *Pata'h* as a vowel. This is the third head - *Mo'ha Stimaah*.

Hebrew / Aramaic Phonetic	L	Dictionary

מוחין

Mo'hin

H **Brains**

The *Mo'hin* are the directive force given to the *Partsuf*. There are interior and encircling *Mo'hin*. The interior *Mo'hin* are the *Sephirot NHY* (Netsa'h, Hod, Yesod) of the superior *Partsuf* that enter inside the lower *Partsuf* to be his brains or intelligence. The encircling *Mo'hin* stand on the outside.

There are two distinct *Mo'hin* that come to Z"A: *Mo'hin* of *Imah* arrive first, and then the *Mo'hin* of *Abah*. The *Mo'hin* that are given from *Abah* and *Imah* to Z"A, are called his (צלם) *Tselem* and do not enter completely in him; only the *NHY* (Netsa'h, Hod, Yesod) do, the rest stays on top of him, encircling his head.

The *NHY* of the superior *Partsuf* which are composed of nine parts, corresponding to the צ, spread in the nine *Sephirot* of Z"A. The encircling are ל מ, they do not need to spread in him, and stand on his exterior in the three-column arrangement of kindness, rigor and mercy.

During the gestation, the *Mo'hin* are of the lowest level and are called *NHY* of the *Mo'hin*; they are of the aspect of *Nefesh*.

During the suckling, the lights grow and the *Mo'hin* are of a higher level; they are called *HGT* ('Hesed, Gevurah, Tiferet) of the *Mo'hin* and are of the aspect of *Rua'h*.

During the growth, the *Mo'hin* are now fully developed to guide Z"uN with the full force of *HBD* ('Hokhma, Binah, Da'at); they are of the aspect of *Neshama*.

Hebrew / Aramaic *Phonetic*	L	Dictionary

There are two gestations and two growths for *Partsuf Z"A*. The *Mo'hin* of the first growth are from *Tevunah*, the *Mo'hin* of the second growth are from *Imah*. It is only after the second growth, that *Z"A* has reached its full potential. This is *Gadlut* 2. See *Partsuf, Gadlut*

מוחין דגדלות *Mo'hin of Gadlut* — H **Brains of growth**

There are *Mo'hin* (brains) of *Gadlut* 1 and *Mo'hin* of *Gadlut* 2.

When *Partsuf Z"A* receives all his *Mo'hin*; interior and encircling (*Tselem*) from *Tevunah*, they are *Mo'hin* of *Gadlut* 1. When he receives all his *Mo'hin* directly from *Imah*, they are *Mo'hin* of *Gadlut* 2 and he has now attained his full growth. See *Partsuf, Gadlut*

מוחין דקתנות *Mo'hin of Katnut* — H **Brains of infancy**

There are *Mo'hin* (brains) of *Katnut* 1 and *Mo'hin* of *Katnut* 2.

When *Partsuf Z"A* only receives the *NHY* (Netsa'h, Hod, Yesod) of his *Mo'hin* - the interior, but not the encircling (*Tselem*), from *Tevunah*; they are the *Mo'hin* of *Katnut* 1.

When he receives the *NHY* (Netsa'h, Hod, Yesod) of his *Mo'hin* directly from *Imah*, they are the *Mo'hin* of *Katnut* 2. See *Partsuf, Gadlut*

מוחין מקיפין *Mo'hin Makifin* — H **Encircling Brains**

The encircling *Mo'hin* are of a higher aspect than the interior *Mo'hin*. They do not enter inside the lower *Partsuf*, and encircle him on the outside. It is the

Hebrew / Aramaic Phonetic	L	Dictionary
		encircling - למ of the of the complete Mo'hin - צלמ־ The HGT ('Hesed, Gevurah, Tiferet) that surround him, correspond to the ל The KHBD (Keter, 'Hokhma, Binah, Da'at) that encircle him, correspond to the מ *See Mo'hin*
מוחין פנימין Mo'hin Penimim	H	**Interior Brains** The interior Mo'hin enter inside the lower Partsuf. It is the NHY (Netsa'h, Hod, Yesod) of the superior Partsuf which are composed of nine parts, and correspond to the צ. They spread in the nine Sephirot of Z"A. *See Mo'hin*
מושך Moshekh	H	**Attracts – Draws** A light or emanation attracts or draws another for the purpose of Tikun or Zivug.
מזון Mazon	H	**Food – Subsistence** For their sustenance the negative forces get strength by attaching to the exteriority of the Sephirot.
מזונות Mezonot	H	**Sustenance** *See Mazon*
מזוקק Mezukak	H	**Refined** *See Zakh*
מזל Mazal	H	**Luck - Destiny – Constellation** Each day and moment is of a different emanation. These emanations vary in their positivity or negativity.

Hebrew / Aramaic *Phonetic*	L	Dictionary

The seven main planets correspond to seven *Sephirot*.

Planet		Sephira
Moon	לבנה	*'Hesed*
Mars	מאדים	*Gevurah*
Sun	חמה	*Tiferet*
Venus	נוגה	*Netsa'h*
Mercury	כוכב	*Hod*
Saturn	שבתאי	*Yesod*
Jupiter	צדק	*Malkhut*

מזל נוצר   A   ***Mazal Notser***

Mazal
Notser

There are hairs (lights) that come out from the face of *Sephira 'Hokhma Stimaah* of *Partsuf Arikh Anpin* and spread downward. They divide in thirteen, and are called the thirteen *Tikunim* (rectifications) of the *Dikna* (beard) of *Arikh Anpin*.

Mazal Notser is the eighth Tikun of the Dikna of Arikh Anpin, corresponding to (the beard on) The upper chin.

The length of the two *Mazalot (Notser and Nake)* is until the navel, where there is the head of *Partsuf Z"A*. The *Dikna* reveals the guidance of kindness, rigor and mercy, which was concealed in *'Hokhma Stimaah*, by bringing it down to *Z"A* through the two *Mazalot; Notser* and *Nake*, which are the eighth and thirteenth *Tikun*.

See Sheta'h 'Elyon

Hebrew / Aramaic *Phonetic*	L	Dictionary

מזל נקה
Mazal Nakeh

A **Mazal Nakeh**

There are hairs (lights) that come out from the face *Sephira 'Hokhma Stimaah* of *Partsuf Arikh Anpin,* and spread downward. They divide in thirteen, and are called the thirteen *Tikunim* of the *Dikna* (beard) of *Arikh Anpin. Mazal Nake is the thirteen Tikun* of the *Dikna* of *Arikh Anpin, corresponding to* (the beard under) The lower chin. The length of the two *Mazalot (Notser and Nake)* is until the navel, where there is the head of *Partsuf Z"A.*The *Dikna* reveals the guidance of kindness, rigor and mercy, which was concealed in *'Hokhma Stimaah*, by bringing it down to *Z"A* through the two *Mazalot; Notser* and *Nake,* which are the eighth and thirteenth *Tikun.* See Sheta'h Ta'hton

מחשבה
Ma'hashavah

H **Thought**

Intention, will.

"There are many thoughts in a man's heart, but it is the counsel of G-od that will stand"(Mishle–Prov. 19, 21)

מחשבות
Ma'hashavot

H **Thoughts**

See Thought

מטה
Matah

H **Lower**

In general, lower refers to inferior or less important.

מטה האלהים
Mateh Elokim

H **Scepter of Elokim**

Diagonal light or *Partsuf* on the left side of *Leah.*

This light, or *Partsuf*, is not considered as a complete *Partsuf*; its actions are temporary and at particular times only.

Hebrew / Aramaic Phonetic	L	Dictionary
מטה משה *Mateh* *Moshe*	H	**Scepter of Moshe** Diagonal light or *Partsuf* on the right side of *Leah*. This light, or *Partsuf*, is not considered as a complete *Partsuf*; its actions are temporary and at particular times only
מטטרו"ן *Matatro"n*		**Matatro"n** Name of one of the three great princes of the Angels.
מידות *Midot*	H	**Attributes – Qualities** *See Midah*
מיוחד *Meyu'had*	H	**Unique** *See Y'hudo*
מיין *Mayin*	A	**Water** Emanations allegorically called masculine or feminine waters. *See Mayin Dukhrin, Mayin Nukvin*
מיין דוכרין *Mayin* *Dukhrin*	A	**Masculine waters** One of two emanations allegorically called masculine or feminine waters. The *Tikun* (rectification) is done by the *Zivug* (union) of the masculine and the feminine. There are two conditions needed for the *Zivug* to be possible: the *Partsufim* (configurations) have to be constructed, and the feminine has to stimulate a reaction from the masculine. This stimulation happens when the *Partsuf Nukvah* brings up her *Mayin Nukvin* (feminine waters) of the feminine aspect of *BaN (52)*, which then provoke

191

Hebrew / Aramaic Phonetic	L	Dictionary

the descent of the *Mayin Dukhrin* from the masculine aspect of *MaH* (45).

The masculine reacts, stimulated by the feminine, which is in turn motivated by the actions of man. In addition, because of the *Tikunim* (rectifications) realized by men with the *Tefilot* and the *Mitsvot*, *Nukvah* brings up her *Mayin Nukvin*, and in response; *Mayin Dukhrin* come down for the completion of the *Zivug*.

Mayin Dukhrin and *Mayin Nukvin* are the essential of the *Zivug*. *Mayin Nukvin* proceeds from the feminine and *Mayin Dukhrin* from the masculine. There is no *Mayin Dukhrin* without *Mayin Nukvin*, and there is no *Mayin Nukvin* without desire.

מיין נוקבין

Mayin Nukvin

A **Feminine waters**

One of two emanations allegorically called masculine or feminine waters.

The *Tikun* (rectification) is done by the *Zivug* (union) of the masculine and the feminine. There are two conditions needed for the *Zivug* to be possible: the *Partsufim* (configurations) have to be constructed, and the feminine has to stimulate a reaction from the masculine. This stimulation happens when the *Partsuf Nukvah* brings up her *Mayin Nukvin* (feminine waters) of the feminine aspect of *BaN* (52), which then provoke the descent of the *Mayin Dukhrin* from the masculine aspect of *MaH* (45).

Hebrew / **Aramaic** *Phonetic*	**L**	**Dictionary**

The masculine reacts, stimulated by the feminine, which is in turn motivated by the actions of man. In addition, because of the *Tikunim* (rectifications) realized by men with the *Tefilot* and the *Mitsvot*, *Nukvah* brings up her *Mayin Nukvin*, and in response; *Mayin Dukhrin* come down for the completion of the *Zivug*.

Mayin Dukhrin and *Mayin Nukvin* are the essential of the *Zivug*. *Mayin Nukvin* proceeds from the feminine and *Mayin Dukhrin* from the masculine. There is no *Mayin Dukhrin* without *Mayin Nukvin*, and there is no *Mayin Nukvin* without desire.

For the construction of *Partsuf Nukvah,* twenty two letters are given to her by *Z"A*, once they build her, they end in her *Yesod* and make a *Keli*. She also receives the five ending letters: מנצפך, which are her five *Gevurot* (rigors) and contain the *Mayin Nukvin*.

After the *Nesirah*, when *Abah* and *Imah* have built her, they also give her twenty two letters, מנצפך and *Mayin Nukvin*. She is now complete and ready to act independently. *See Zivug, Malkhut, Nukvah*

מילוי   H ***Spelling***

Miluy

The creative forces or energies are the different powers in the four letters of the name of G-od י-ה-ו-ה, and the various letters added to make their different spellings. Depending on which letters are used, the numerical value of the name changes, and each one of these possibilities becomes different in its nature

Hebrew / Aramaic *Phonetic*	L	Dictionary

and actions.

The letters that are added for the different spellings of the letters are: י ה ו א ד

The different spellings of the letters are:

The letter י (*Yud*) can only be spelled one way: יוד

The letter ה (*He*) can be spelled with a י (*Yud*) or an א (*Aleph*) or a ה (*He*): הא הה הי

The Letter ו (*Vav*) can be spelled with a וי (*Yud and Vav*) or with וא (*Aleph and Vav*) or

With a ו (*Vav*): ואו ויו וו

The four *Miluyim* (spellings) are:

- בן ,מה , סג, עב - '*A"V, SaG, MaH, BaN*

עב – הי ויו הי יוד   - '*A"V* = 72

סג – הי ואו הי יוד   - *SaG* = 63

מה - הא ואו הא יוד   - *MaH* = 45

בן – הה וו הה יוד   - *BaN* = 52

Each name can also be divided and subdivided as:

'*A"V of 'A"V, SaG of 'A"V, MaH of 'A"V* ...

BaN of BaN of SaG, SaG of MaH of 'A"V etc.

The name of '*A"V* is of the highest level of the four names. Its *Miluy* is with the letter י (*Yud*) for a total of 72.

The name of *SaG* is the second level of the four names. Its *Miluy* is with the letter י (*Yud*) and א (*Aleph*) for a total of 63.

The name of *MaH* (45) is the third level of the four names. Its *Miluy* is with the letter א (*Aleph*) for a total of 45.

Hebrew / Aramaic Phonetic	L	Dictionary

The name of *BaN* *(52)* is the fourth level of the four names. Its *Miluy* is with the letter ו (*Vav*) for a total of 52.

All the emanations and *Sephirot* that came out of *Adam Kadmon (Primordial man)* by way of his apertures were of the various aspects of these four names. They have different actions and *Tikunim,* and all the *Partsufim (configurations)* will be constructed by their union. *See 'Av, SaG, MaH, BaN*

מילוי

גמטריות

Miluy of Gematriot

H **Miluy of Gematriot**

One of the seven main types of *Gematriot.*
The sum of the spelling of each letter.

Letter	Miluy	Value
ה	הא	6
א	אלף	111
ר	ריש	510
צ	צדי	104

Ex : הארץ = 731

See Gematria

מילוי של

מ"ה

Miluy shel MaH (45)

H **Spelling - Filling of the name of MaH** *(45)*

Letters that are added to each first letter of the name of י-ה-ו-ה (26) for the spelling of the name of *MaH* *(45)*. The *Miluy* of *MaH* is nineteen; *MaH* = 45 − 26 = 19

One of the three *Miluyim* of sparks of the names of *'A"V, SaG,* and *MaH* that enter the *Kelim of Z"A* after the *Shvirat HaKelim* (breaking of the vessels) to sustain them.

Hebrew / Aramaic *Phonetic*	L	Dictionary
מילוי של ס"ג *Miluy shel SaG*	H	**Spelling - Filling of the name of SaG** Letters that are added to each first letter of the name of ה-ו-ה-י (26) for the spelling of the name of *SaG* (63). The *Miluy* of *SaG* is thirty seven; *SaG* = 63 − 26 = 37 One of the three *Miluyim* of sparks of the names of *'A"V, SaG,* and *MaH* that enter the *Kelim of Z"A* after the *Shvirat HaKelim* (breaking of the vessels) to sustain them.
מילוי של ע"ב *Miluy shel 'A"V*	H	**Spelling - Filling of the name of 'A"V** Letters that are added to each first letter of the name of י-ה-ו-ה (26) for the spelling of the name of *'A"V* (72). The *Miluy* of *'A"V* is forty six; *'A"V* = 72 − 26 = 46 One of the three *Miluyim* of sparks of the names of *'A"V, SaG,* and *MaH* that enter the *Kelim of Z"A* after the *Shvirat HaKelim* (breaking of the vessels) to sustain them.
מילוים *Miluyim*	H	**Spellings** See Miluy
מים *Mayim*	H	**Water** See Mayin
מיעוט *Mi'ut*	H	**Decrease – Diminution** There is a decrease or diminution of an emanation depending on its stage of evolution.
מיתה *Mitah*	H	**Death** See Malkin Kadmain, Nitsutsot

Hebrew / Aramaic Phonetic	L	Dictionary
מיתוק *Mituk*	H	***Sweetening – Mitigation*** A mitigation or sweetening of the *Gevurot* (rigors) occurs when they are in direct contact with the *'Hasadim* (kindnesses). When the five *Gevurot* come down from *Sephira Da'at* of *Z"A*, they are sweetened (appeased) in *Sephira Yesod* of *Z"A*; two and a half in the descent, and two and a half by the *'Hasadim* returning upwards. See 'Hasadim, Gevurot
מכוסים *Mekhusim*	H	***Covered – Concealed*** Some lights or emanations are hidden or covered by others. Of the five *'Hasadim of Sephira Yesod* of *Partsuf 'Atik,* half (two and a half) are covered and the other half is revealed. At first, the *Gevurot* (rigors) were pushed out from the *Sephira Yesod* of *Partsuf 'Atik* by the *'Hasadim*. Two and a half of the *Gevurot* descended from the chest and lower, and the two and a half *'Hasadim* also descended to appease them. Therefore, there are two and a half *'Hasadim* revealed and two and a half covered that stayed in *Yesod of Atik*. The superior third of *Sephira Tiferet* is also hidden or covered by *Sephira Yesod* of *Partsuf Tevunah*. See Nukvah, Zivug
מלאך *Malakh*	H	***Angel*** See Malakhim

Hebrew / Aramaic Phonetic	L	Dictionary

מלאכים   H   *Angels*

Malakhim

The world of the angels is the third world; *'Olam Yetsirah* - the world of formation.

The angels of peace make ten groups and serve the ten *Sephirot* of the right, while the angels of destruction make ten levels and serve the ten *Sephirot* from the lower opposite side.

There are two types of angels: the angels of the nature who were created at the beginning of the world, they are in charge of the nature itself. The second type are the angels of "reward and punishment". They accomplish the will of the divine light inside the *Sephirot,* and are renewed constantly depending on the deeds of men.

The ten groups of positive angels are divided as follows: three groups in the world of *Beriah* (creation*)*, six groups in the world of *Yetsirah* (formation)*,* and one group in the world of *'Asiah* (action).

The princes of these three groups are: *Shemu'i-El, Matatro-n, Vihu-El.* They are also divided in four camps: Michael, Gabriel, Ouriel, and Rephael.

The name of the angels and the princes of the ten groups are:

Hebrew / Aramaic *Phonetic*	L	Dictionary

Group	*Angels*	Prince
1	שרפי-ם Seraphi-m	יהו-אל Yehu-El
2	אופני-ם Ofani-m	רפ-אל Repha-El
3	כרובי-ם Keruvi-m	כרו-ב Keru-v
4	שנאני-ם Shanani-m	צדקי-אל Tsadiki-El
5	תרשישי-ם Tarshishi-m	תרשי-ש Tarshi-sh
6	חשמלי-ם 'Hashmali-m	חשמ-ל 'Hashm-al
7	מלאכי-ם Malakhi-m	עוזי-אל 'Uzi-El
8	בני אלהי-ם Bene Eloh-im	חפני-אל 'Hafni-El
9	אישי-ם Ishi-m	צפני-ה Tsefani-ah
10	אראלי-ם Areli-m	מיכ-אל Mikha-El

The other entity, which is called the *Sitra A'hra* – (the other side, or the negative force) has its own four worlds of *Atsilut*, *Beriah*, *Yetsirah* and *'Asiah*, it also has *Partsufim*, *Sephirot*, *Hekhalot* and angels, as in the positive world, but of a lower force. Its destructive angels subdivide in the same order as well, depending on their importance they are from its own worlds of *Beriah*, *Yetsirah* or *'Asiah*.

199

Hebrew / Aramaic Phonetic	L	Dictionary
מלבוש *Malbush*	H	***Clothe*** *See Levush*
מלבושים *Malbushim*	H	***Clothes*** *See Levush*
מלך *Melekh*	H	***King*** *See Malkin*
מלכות *Malkhut*	H	***Sephira (Royalty)*** Tenth of the *Sephirot*. Quality: Guidance that translates all the superior emanations into one that is reflected to the creation. Link or connection between all the superior *Sephirot* and man. Column: Center – *Ra'hamim* (mercy) Position: Middle – Bottom Other *Sephirot* on the same column: *Keter, Tiferet, Yesod* *Partsufim* made from this *Sephira*: *Nukvah*, divided in two *Partsufim*: *Ra'hel* and *Leah* Corresponding name: *Adona-y* – אדנ-י Corresponding *Miluy* of name: *BaN (52)* - בן Corresponding vowel: none Physical correspondence: Crown on the masculine organ Level of the soul: *Nefesh* *See Sephira, Partsuf, Nukvah*
מלכים *Melakhim*	H	***Kings*** *See Malkin Kadmain*

Hebrew / Aramaic Phonetic	L	Dictionary
מלכין קדמאין **Malkin Kadmain**	A	**Kings of Edom – corresponding to Z'aT** The seven kings of Edom that died (Bereshit, 36, 31), correspond to the seven lower *Sephirot* (*Z'aT*) that broke. See Shvirat HaKelim
מן **Manna**	A	**Manna** Diagonal light or *Partsuf* (configuration) on the left side of *Partsuf Z"A*. This light, or *Partsuf*, is not considered as a complete *Partsuf*; its actions are temporary and at particular times only
מנצפ"ך **MNTSP"KH**	H	**Five Gevurot** The five ending letters correspond to the five *Gevurot* (rigors). See Gevurot, Mayin Nukvin
מסבב **Mesavev**	H	**Encircling** See Or Makif
מסך **Masakh**	H	**Screen** See Pargod
מעקה **Ma'akeh**	H	**Parapet (railing)** When the *Kelim* (recipients) broke, *SaG (63)*, *MaH (45)* and *BaN (52)* descended to the lower worlds, *SaG* in *Beriah*, *MaH* in *Yetsirah,* and *BaN* in *'Asiah*. They came back up to be under the curtain of *Atsilut,* and *BaN* made the מעקה (parapet) on top of them, so that the *Klipot* will not attach to the higher lights.

Hebrew / Aramaic Phonetic	L	Dictionary
מעשה בראשית Ma'ase Bereshit	H	**Works or acts of the creation** Name given for all the details of the beginning of the creation, from the *Tsimtsum*, the first worlds, the *Sephirot* etc.
מעשה המרקבה Ma'ase Hamerkava	H	**Works or acts of the Heavenly Chariot** Name given for all the details of the *Sephirot, Partsufim, Tikunim* and *Zivugim* that make the guidance.
מצוה Mitsva	H	**Commandment** The Torah contains four levels of comprehension, of which the highest is the *Sod (secret)*. At this level, we understand that our *Tefilot* and the accomplishment of each one of the *Mitsvot,* has a direct influence on the superior worlds and on their guidance. The Kabbalah teaches us that the world is guided by an extremely complex system of forces or lights, which through their interactions, provoke chain reactions that impact directly on man and the worlds. Each one of these reactions has numerous ramifications, with many details and results. Only man, by praying and the accomplishment of the *Mitsvot,* can influence these incredible forces. As there are 613 *Mitsvot,* there are 613 veins and bones to man, 613 parts to the soul, and each *Sephira* and *Partsuf* also has 613 parts. This number is not arbitrary as there are important interrelations and interactions between them.

Hebrew / Aramaic Phonetic	L	Dictionary

After the *Shvirat HaKelim (breaking of the vessels),* the goal of all the works, deeds and prayers of men in this existence, is to help and participate in the ascent of the fallen 288 sparks to their origin. This can be done by accomplishing the *Mitsvot* and the *Tefilot.* At the completion of this *Tikun* of unification between the fallen sparks and their *Kelim,* it will be the time of the resurrection of the dead and the arrival of *Moshia'h.*

The *Klipot* (husks) are the manifestation of the negative force, they obstruct the lights of the *Sephirot,* conceal man from his root, and from the light. Because of the bad deeds of the lower beings, the *Klipot* get their strength and do evil in the world by attaching to the higher lights. The *Tikunim* (rectifications) of the lower beings is to detach these *Klipot* from the *Kedushah* by accomplishing the *Mitsvot* and the *Tefilot.*

The *Tikun* of the soul is realized by the *Gilgul* (reincarnation), and by the *'Ibur* (attachment). By accomplishing what he did not accomplish of the 613 *Mitsvot,* man makes the necessary *Tikun* of his soul, which can now elevate to the higher realms, and rejoin its source. *See Tefilot, Kavanah*

מצוות H ***Commandments***
Mitsvot   *See Mitsva*

מצח H ***Forehead***
Metsa'h   *See Orot HaMetsa'h*

Hebrew / Aramaic Phonetic	L	Dictionary

מצח
הרצון
Metsa'h
HaRatson

H **Forehead of mercy**

The fourth *Tikun* (action) of the head of *Arikh Anpin* - רעוא דמצחא (*Ra'ava Demits'ha*) is realized by the *Sephira Yesod* of *Partsuf 'Atik*; his *'Hasadim* shine from the forehead of *Arikh Anpin*. When it is fully revealed, all the rigors are annulled.

מצחא
Mits'ha

A **Forehead**

See Orot HaMetsa'h

מקבל
Mekabel

H **Receiver**

Since the intention of the Creator is to bestow goodness on His creatures, all the levels of creation were put in place so His kindness could emanate to them, yet in such a way that they would be able to receive it.

The *Ein Sof, B'H* influences when there is instigation from the receiver, the latter corresponding to the aspect of *BaN (52)*. This influence is transmitted by different illuminations (*Sephirot*), and then by *Partsuf* (configuration) *Nukvah* after her *Zivug* (union) with *Partsuf Z"A*, to the receiver (man).

For the *Sephirot* there are also interactions of influencer and receiver. The lower *Partsuf* is guided and receives his *Mo'hin* (brains) from the higher *Partsuf*.

מקובל
Mekubal

H **Kabbalist - Accepted**

The word Kabbalah comes from the verb *Lekabel* (to receive), but to receive it is first necessary to be

Hebrew / Aramaic Phonetic	L	Dictionary

prepared, and to be a *Keli (recipient)* able to receive and contain this knowledge.

A *Mekubal* is a person who is accepted to receive this knowledge, and is able to hold it by living in the path of Torah and rightness to strengthen himself constantly.

מקום
Makom — H **Place – space**

Until the world was created, He and His Name were One. He willed to create, and contracted His light to create all beings by giving them a space.

When His light retracted, forming the round space, a trace of it, called the *Reshimu,* remained inside. This lower intensity light, allowed a space (*Makom*) of existence, for all the created worlds and beings. By "space" (*Makom*), one should not understand a physical space, but rather a possibility of existence since there is no existence that does not have its own space. Also one of the names of G-od.

מקור
Makor — H **Source – Origin**

Each emanation has its source in the higher realms

מקיף
Makif — H **Encircling**

See Or Makif

מקיפין
Makifin — H **Encircling**

See Or Makif

מרקבה
Merkavah — H **Heavenly chariot**

The *Partsufim* (configurations), *Sephirot* and the

Hebrew / Aramaic Phonetic	L	Dictionary
		Sephirot tree, with all their inter-relations, actions and illuminations.
משובח *Meshuba'h*	H	**First rate – Important** The emanations that come from the higher lights are of a finer and stronger force.
משל *Mashal*	H	**Allegory** Sometimes used to explain or illustrate difficult concepts.
משפיע *Mashpia'h*	H	**Influencer** Since the intention of the Creator is to bestow goodness on His creatures, all the levels of creation were put in place so His kindness could emanate to them, yet in such a way that they would be able to receive it. The *Sephirot* are the links between the Emanator and the guidance of the world. By them, are manifested the influence of the *Ein Sof*, - the Influencer to the receivers. His Influence is transmitted by different illuminations of the aspect of *MaH* (45), and then by *Partsuf* (configuration) *Nukvah* after her *Zivug* (union) with *Partsuf Z"A.*
מתלבש *Mitlabesh*	H	**Dress** *Partsufim* dress on, or in, each other. The more important *Partsuf* will dress inside the less important to direct him. *See Partsufim, Mo'hin*

Hebrew / Aramaic Phonetic	L	Dictionary

מתערין   A **Awakening**
Mit'arin   *See Eta'aruta de La'ila, Eta'aruta de Tata*

מתקלא   A **Matkala**
Matkala   Since the intention of the Creator is to bestow goodness on His creatures, all the levels of creation were put in place so His kindness could emanate to them, yet in such a way that they would be able to receive it.

With the emanation of the lights of *MaH (45)* and *BaN (52)*, He could have done the *Tikun* (rectification) of all the worlds after the *Shvirat HaKelim (breaking of the vessels)*, but then there would not have been a reason for the participation of man in this *Tikun*. To give a possibility to man to act and repair the creation, G-od restrained in a way, his outflow of kindness to this world, and this is the role of the *Matkala*.

The *Matkala* is the root of all the *Tikunim* and has its origin in *Sephira 'Hesed* and *Gevurah* of the *Radl'a* (the unknown head).

See Radl'a

Hebrew / Aramaic Phonetic	L	Dictionary
נאצל Neetsal	H	***Emanated being*** Men, angels etc.
נאצלים Neetsalim	H	***Emanated beings*** *See Neetsal*
נביא Navi	H	***Prophet*** The prophecy originates from the *Sephira Netsa'h* or the *Sephira Hod*. These *Sephirot* have three parts each. The difference between the levels of the prophets depends from which one of the three parts of these *Sephirot*, they receive the prophecy.
נביאים Neviim	H	***Prophets*** *See Navi*
נגה Nogah	H	***Nogah - Glow*** One of the four main levels of *Klipot* corresponding to the four lower worlds. *See Klipot*
נהי NeHY	H	***Netsa'h, Hod and Yesod*** Initials of the third triplet of the *Sephirot*: *Netsa'h, Hod and Yesod*. They mostly act together as the interior *Mo'hin* (brains) for a lower *Partsuf*.
נהר Nahar	H	***River – Stream*** The outflows of some emanations are sometimes described as one or more streams or rivers.
נוגה Nogah	A	***Nogah*** *See Klipah Nogah*

Hebrew / Aramaic Phonetic	L	Dictionary
נוגה Nogah	A	**Nogah** Name of a *Hekhal (portal)*. Third of seven *Hekhalot*, corresponding to *Netsa'h*. Each world (*ABYA*) is built from four aspects: *Partsuf*, *Levush* (garment), *Or Makif* (encircling lights), and *Hekhalot*. In each *Partsuf*, there are interiority and exteriority, the exteriority is always of the aspect of *Malkhut*, and the *Hekhalot* are the ramifications of the *Malkhuts* of the *Partsufim*. The *Hekhalot* are also the different levels of ascension of the *Tefilot* before reaching the seventh *Hekhal (portal), Kodesh Hakodashim*. Their principal function is to allow the adhesion and attachment, in various and particular ways during the *Tefilot*, until the *'Olam Atsilut* (during the *Amidah*) The *Neshamot* and the angels have their root in the *Hekhalot*, each one depending on its respective level.
נוטריקון Notrikun	H	**Notrikun** (acronym) *Notrikun* is a method of interpretation in which initials of different words make a new word. אל מלך נאמן = אמן
נופל Nofel	H	***Falling*** *See Shvirat HaKelim, Nitsutsot*
נופלים Noflim	H	***Fallen – Falling*** *See Shvirat HaKelim, Nitsutsot*

Hebrew / Aramaic Phonetic	L	Dictionary

נוקבא A **Feminine - Sephira Malkhut – Partsuf Ra'hel, Leah**

Nukvah

The *Partsuf* (configuration) *Nukvah* represents the feminine – the principle of receiving. It comprises of two distinct *Partsufim*: *Ra'hel* and *Leah*.

The masculine *Partsuf Zeir Anpin* and the feminine *Nukvah,* are the root of all the created. It is by them, that the guidance is manifested. Even if they are two distinct *Partsufim* and have their own *Tikunim* (actions), all the time that *Z"A* is being built, *Nukvah* is attached to him. Once the *Partsuf Zeir Anpin* has been constructed, the construction of *Nukvah* starts with the lights given to her by *Partsuf Abah, Imah* and *Zeir Anpin*. When she is complete, she separates herself from *Z"A*, and can now act as an independent *Partsuf*.

There is perfection for the masculine only when it completes itself with its feminine, and there can be abundance only when the masculine and the feminine are in harmony. This abundance comes down to the world, by the various *Zivugim* (unions) of *Zeir Anpin* with *Nukvah*. The one of *Partsuf Israel* and *Partsuf Ra'hel* is of the highest level. *Israel* represents the essential of *Z"A*, and *Ra'hel* of *Nukvah*. The abundance that is bestowed by this *Zivug* is the most complete. The other *Zivugim* of *Zeir Anpin* and *Nukvah* are of different levels, in various times, and of lesser plenitude

There are two conditions needed for the *Zivug* (union) to be possible: the *Partsufim* have to be constructed,

Hebrew / Aramaic Phonetic	L	Dictionary

and the feminine has to stimulate a reaction from the masculine. This stimulation happens because of the *Tikunim* (rectifications) realized by men with the *Tefilot* (prayers) and *Mitsvot*. *Nukvah* brings up emanations called *Mayin Nukvin* (feminine waters of the aspect of *BaN (52)*), which then provokes the descent of emanations called *Mayin Dukhrin* (masculine waters of the aspect of *MaH (45)*) from the masculine, for the completion of the *Zivug*.

This is the goal of the service of the creatures; to help prepare the *Partsufim Z"A* and *Nukvah* for the *Zivug*, and this, by the elevation and adhesion of the worlds of *Beriah, Yetsirah* and *'Asiah* to the *Hekhalot* (portals) of *Nukvah* of the world of *Atsilut,* during the *Tefilot.*

The *Nukvah (Ra'hel)* also has an aspect of *Tefilin,* and attaches on the left arm (*Gevurah*) of *Z"A*. She has four *Parashiot* in her *Tefilin,* and receives her *Mo'hin* (brains) through the *Sephira Netsa'h* and *Hod* of *Partsuf Z"A*.

See Partsuf, Zivug, Tikun, Partsuf Z"A

נחתם H ***Sealed – Imprinted***
Ne'htam See 'Hotam

נימין A ***Extremities of the hairs on the head***
Nimin From the *Partsuf (configuration) Arikh Anpin*, there are emanations that come out from its head to act and influence on the guidance called; the *Tikunim* (actions) of *Arikh Anpin*.

Hebrew / Aramaic Phonetic	L	Dictionary

One of these *Tikunim* of *Arikh Anpin* is from *Avirah* (*Sephira Da'at* of *'Atik*; between *Sephira Keter* and *'Hokhma*) It is called נימין (*Nimin*); the extremities of the hairs on the head.

From *Avirah* the thirteen נימין (*Nimin*) are divided to spread out the lights of *Sephira 'Hokhma Stimaah;* they are his hair, four on the right side, four on the left, four on the back of the neck, and one in the middle of the head containing all. These hairs are white, although hair represents rigor, here there is no rigor. This is the difference with the hair of *Z"A*, which is black and intermingled; while here, they are white and separated. The *Nimin* are called hair, because they spread out in individual conduits.

The second *Tikun* of *Z"A* is expressed by the lights that come out of him, as the hair on his head, and on his face. There are also *Nimin* and these *Tikunim* are similar to the ones of *Arikh Anpin,* but with some differences. From *Arikh Anpin* all the hair come out from *'Hokhma Stimaah*, from *Z"A*; they come out from his *HBD* (*'Hokhma, Binah, Da'at*). The hairs of *Z"A* are black and intermingled; being more of the aspect of *Gevurah*, the hairs of *Arikh Anpin* are white, and express bounty.

There are also *Nimin* of *Nukvah*; they are fifteen and their color is purple.

נִיצוֹץ	H	**Spark**
Nitsuts		One of the 288 sparks (*Nitsutsot*).

Hebrew / Aramaic L *Phonetic*	Dictionary

ניצוצות H *Sparks*

Nitsutsot

In the emanation of the lights from the eyes of *Adam Kadmon*, first the individual *Keli* (recipient) for each *Sephira* came out and then their lights. Each one of these *Sephirot* had its own *Keli*, but the seven lower *Sephirot* were aligned one under the other in a straight line, and not ready for the guidance of kindness, rigor and mercy. Therefore, they could not contain their lights and broke.

The three first *Sephirot*: *Keter*, *'Hokhma* and *Binah*, were structured in the three-column order: B ^{K} H, their lower parts did not contain their lights, fell but did not break. These lower parts correspond to what is needed for the guidance of the seven lower *Sephirot*, if they had contained their lights, the seven *Sephirot* would not have broken, and the notions of *Kilkul* (damage) and *Tikun* (repair) not existed.

This caused an important damage called *Shvirat HaKelim* – *the breaking of the vessels*. The *Kelim* (recipients) of the seven *Sephirot* which did not contain their lights, fell to the world of *Beriah* (creation), the lights also descended, but stayed in the world of *Atsilut*. The breaking of the *Kelim* caused a descent of all the worlds. However, KHB remained in what is called the "first *Atsilut*". The seven lower *Kelim* fell in the higher parts of the world of *Beriah*.

The roots of all the created are in the seven lower *Sephirot* (*Za"T*), the three first *Sephirot* are like a crown on the *Za"T* to repair and direct them. In the

Hebrew / Aramaic Phonetic	L	Dictionary

three first *Sephirot* there is not really a notion of damage, they are above men's deeds, and are not affected by their sins.

To sustain the *Kelim* after they broke, 288 sparks of their lights came down as well, because a connection to their original lights was needed to keep them alive. These sparks correspond to the four aspects of *'A"V* of the names *'A"V* (72), *SaG* (63), *MaH* (45), *BaN* (52) , 4 x 72 = 288.

It is important to understand that all that happens in our world, is similar to what occurred in this fall.

The goal of all the works, deeds and prayers of men in this existence, is to help and participate in the ascent of the fallen 288 sparks to their origin. This can be done by accomplishing the *Mitsvot* and the *Tefilot*. At the completion of this *Tikun* of unification between all the fallen sparks and their *Kelim*, it will be the time of the resurrection of the dead and the arrival of *Moshia'h*.

See Shvirat HaKelim, Tikun, Tefilah

ניצוצין A **Sparks**
Nitsutsin   See Nitsutsot

נמשך H **Drawn**
Nimshakh   See Hamshakhah

נמשל H **Moral**
Nimshal   Sometimes used to explain or illustrate difficult concepts.

Hebrew / Aramaic Phonetic	L	Dictionary

נסירה
Nesirah

H **Cutting – Separation**

When *Partsuf (configuration) Zeir Anpin* is being built, *Partsuf Nukvah* is attached to his back. Once the *Partsuf Zeir Anpin* constructed, the construction of *Nukvah* starts with the lights given to her by *Partsuf Abah, Imah* and *Zeir Anpin*. She needs to separate completely from him and come to a face to face position, for a possibility of *Zivug* (union).

At first, the *Nukvah* separates from him to get her own *Mo'hin* (brains), and there is *Nesirah* (cutting off). The *Mo'hin* inside of *Z"A* are the *Sephirot NHY (Netsa'h, Hod, Yesod)* of *Partsuf Imah*, during the construction of *Nukvah*, they leave from inside *Z"A* and dress inside *Nukvah*, who is now completely detached.

Nukvah needs to get her own aspects of *Gevurot* (rigors), they are now given to her directly by *Imah* and she is more appeased than when she was receiving them from *Z"A*. *Nukvah* has now *Gevurot* from *Imah* and *Z"A*. After the *Nesirah*, when *Abah* and *Imah* have built her, they also give her the twenty two letters and the five ending letters: מנצפך, which will make her *Keli* (recipient).

She is now complete, separated from *Z"A*, and can act as an independent *Partsuf*. Her rears being complete in the aspects of *Gevurot*, and the rears of *Z"A* in the aspects of *'Hasadim*, they are now face to face and ready for their various *Zivugim* (unions).

Hebrew / Aramaic Phonetic	L	Dictionary

נערה
Na'arah — H **Girl**

The *Malkhut* is sometimes referred as the young girl.

See Partsuf Nukvah

נפילה
Nefilah — H **Fall**

See Shvirat HaKelim, Nitsutsot

נפש
Nefesh — H **Soul - First level of the soul**

The soul has five names: *Nefesh, Rua'h, Neshama, 'Hayah* and *Ye'hidah*, which correspond to its five levels. The soul is the spiritual entity inside the body, the latter being only his outer garment.

Since it is men that provoke the union of the four worlds, it is necessary for their souls to have their origin from them, and from the five *Partsufim*:

Soul / Level	Partsuf	World
Nefesh	Nukvah	'Asiah
Rua'h	Zeir Anpin	Yetsirah
Neshama	Imah	Beriah
'Hayah	Abah	Atsilut
Ye'hidah	Arikh Anpin	Atsilut

Each level of the soul is subdivided in five levels. As for the level of *Nefesh;* there are *Nefesh* of *Nefesh, Rua'h* of *Nefesh, Neshama* of *Nefesh, 'Hayah* of *Nefesh* and *Ye'hidah* of *Nefesh.*

Each one of these levels of the soul subdivides for each level of *Partsuf* and for each world. Therefore, there are five levels of the souls for *Partsuf Nukvah*

Hebrew / Aramaic *Phonetic*	L	Dictionary

and there are five levels of *Partsufim* for the world of *'Asiah* etc. Also, as there are in each world ten *Sephirot*, each soul has its origin corresponding to one of them.

Therefore, a soul could be from the level of *Nefesh* of *Malkhut* of *Nukvah* of *'Asiah,* or *Rua'h* of *'Hesed* of *Abah* of *'Yetsirah,* or *Neshama* of *Abah* of *Z"A* of *Yetsirah* etc.

Nefesh is the first level and is acquired before the next levels.

The higher levels of the soul cannot be acquired at once. Most men only have the level of *Nefesh,* and if they merit, they will acquire the next levels - but one by one.

To reach the next higher level of his soul, man must do the *Tikun* of the preceding level. If he needs to acquire the level of *Imah* of *'Asiah,* he must first do the *Tikun* of *Malkhut* of *'Asiah* and *Z"A* of *'Asiah,* and so on. To acquire his level of *Neshama,* he must do the *Tikun* of all the levels of the *Sephirot* and *Partsufim* of his *Nefesh* and *Rua'h* etc.

נפש, רוח, נשמה *Nefesh,* *Rua'h,* *Neshama*	H	**Nefesh, Rua'h, Neshama** Three first levels of the soul.

217

Hebrew / Aramaic Phonetic	L	Dictionary
נפש, רוח, נשמה, חיה, יחידה Nefesh, Rua'h, Neshama 'Hayah, Ye'hidah	H	**Nefesh, Rua'h, Neshama, 'Hayah and Ye'hidah** The soul has five names: *Nefesh, Rua'h, Neshama, 'Hayah* and *Ye'hidah*, which correspond to its five levels. The soul is the spiritual entity inside the body, the latter being only his outer garment. Since it is men that provoke the union of the four worlds, it is necessary for their souls to have their origin from them, and from the five *Partsufim*:

Soul / Level	Partsuf	World
Nefesh	Nukvah	'Asiah
Rua'h	Zeir Anpin	Yetsirah
Neshama	Imah	Beriah
'Hayah	Abah	Atsilut
Ye'hidah	Arikh Anpin	Atsilut

Each level of the soul is subdivided in five levels. As for the level of *Nefesh;* there are *Nefesh* of *Nefesh, Rua'h* of *Nefesh, Neshama* of *Nefesh, 'Hayah* of *Nefesh* and *Ye'hidah* of *Nefesh.*

Each one of these levels of the soul subdivides for each level of *Partsuf* and for each world. Therefore, there are five levels of the souls for *Partsuf Nukvah* and there are five levels of *Partsufim* for the world of *'Asiah* etc. Also, as there are in each world ten *Sephirot,* each soul has its origin corresponding to one of them.

Therefore, a soul could be from the level of *Nefesh* of *Malkhut* of *Nukvah* of *'Asiah,* or *Rua'h* of *'Hesed* of

Hebrew / Aramaic *Phonetic*	L	Dictionary

Abah of *'Yetsirah,* or *Neshama* of *Abah* of *Z"A* of *Yetsirah* etc.

The higher levels of the soul cannot be acquired at once. Most men only have the level of *Nefesh,* and if they merit, they will acquire the next levels - but one by one.

To reach the next higher level of his soul, man must do the *Tikun* of the preceding level. If he needs to acquire the level of *Imah* of *'Asiah,* he must first do the *Tikun* of *Malkhut* of *'Asiah* and *Z"A* of *'Asiah,* and so on. To acquire his level of *Neshama,* he must do the *Tikun* of all the levels of the *Sephirot* and *Partsufim* of his *Nefesh* and *Rua'h* etc.

See *Nefesh, Rua'h, Neshama, Hayah* and *Ye'hidah*

נפשות
Nefashot   H   **Souls (first level)**

Aspect of *Nefashot* means lowest level.

נצח
Netsa'h   H   **Sephira (splendor)**

Seventh of the *Sephirot.*

Quality: Diminished kindness to who is deserving.

Column: Right – *'Hesed* (kindness)

Position: Right – bottom

Other *Sephirot* on the same column: *'Hokhma, 'Hesed.*

Partsufim made from this *Sephira:*

One of the *Sephirot* that make the *Partsuf Z"A.*

Corresponding name: YKVK *Tsebaot*

יהו-ה -צבאות

Corresponding *Miluy* of name: MaH (45) (מה)

219

Hebrew / Aramaic Phonetic	L	Dictionary
		Corresponding vowel: *'Hirik* Physical correspondence: Right leg Level of the soul: *Rua'h* See Sephira, Partsuf
נצח, הוד, יסוד *Netsa'h* *Hod* *Yesod*	H	**Netsa'h, Hod and Yesod** Third triplet of the *Sephirot,* they mostly act together as the interior *Mo'hin* (brains) for a lower *Partsuf* (configuration) to direct him, and are called by their initials; *NHY*

The *Mo'hin (brains)* are the directive force given to the *Partsuf.* There are interior and encircling *Mo'hin.* The interior *Mo'hin* are the *Sephirot NHY (Netsa'h, Hod, Yesod)* of the superior *Partsuf,* and are composed of nine parts. They enter inside the lower *Partsuf* to be his brains or intelligence and spread in its nine *Sephirot* from *'Hokhma to Yesod.* The encircling *Mo'hin* which are the other *Sephirot; HGT ('Hesed, Gevurah, Tiferet)* and *HBD ('Hokhma, Binah, Da'at)* encircle him on the outside.

The *Mo'hin* usually come in the lower *Partsuf* in three stages. First, the *NHY* enter followed by the *HGT,* and finally the *HBD.* When the *NHY* of the higher *Partsuf* are clothed inside the lower *Partsuf,* it is given to the higher *Partsuf* new *NHY* to be complete again.

Netsa'h and *Hod* have three parts each, *Yesod* only two. These individual parts can sometimes act independently. The masculine *Yesod* is longer than the feminine. The *NHY* of *Partsuf Abah* dress inside the *NHY* of *Partsuf Imah,* *Yesod* of *Abah* is inside

Hebrew / Aramaic Phonetic	L	Dictionary

Yesod of *Imah,* and is preponderant between her *Netsa'h* and *Hod.* They make the *Mo'hin* of *Z"A* and depending on his growth, they are from the *Partsufim ISOT* or directly from them. The *Mo'hin* of the level of *NHY* are called *Nefesh* of the *Mo'hin.*

The *Kelim* of the *Sephirot* have three levels: Interior, intermediate and exterior. *NHY* is the exterior *Keli,* *HGT* the intermediate *Keli,* and *HBD* the interior *Keli.*

For each level, there are three aspects as:

NHY of *NHY* - exterior *Keli* of *NHY*

HGT of *NHY* - middle *Keli* of *NHY*

HBD of *NHY* - interior *Keli* of *NHY*

NHY of *HGT* - exterior *Keli* of *HGT* etc.

NHY is the aspect of *Nefesh, HGT* of *Rua'h,* and *HBD* of *Neshama. NHY* of *NHY* is the aspect of *Nefesh* of *NHY, HBD* of *HBD* is the aspect of *Neshama* of *HBD* , and so on.

NHY are also the *A'horaim* (rears) of a *Partsuf.*

See Mo'hin, Zeir Anpin, Zivug, Gadlut

נקבה *Nekevah*	H	**Female – Feminine**

Rigor is manifested by all the feminine aspects and by the concealment of the masculine aspects, which represent bounty. Some *Partsufim* are masculine and bestow kindness, others are feminine and bestow rigor.

The *Zivug* is the union of the masculine with its feminine. All the outcomes of the higher emanations are a result of the different unions of these masculine

Hebrew / Aramaic Phonetic	L	Dictionary

and feminine lights.

The masculine corresponds to 'Hesed and MaH (45), the feminine to Gevurah and BaN (52). The Tikun (rectification) is only possible by the Zivug (union) of the masculine and the feminine.

The guidance of the world is dependent on the different positioning and interaction of the masculine and feminine Partsufim, since they have a direct effect on the measure and balance of the factors of kindness, rigor and mercy.

See Nukvah, Malkhut

נקוד
Nekud

H **Point**

See 'Olam HaNekudim

נקוד
Nikud

H **Punctuation - Point**

See Nikudot

נקודה
Nekudah

H **Point – Dot**

When Partsuf (configuration) Zeir Anpin is being built, Partsuf Nukvah is attached to his back, and her state corresponds to one dot. When Z"A ascends, she ascends with him, during the gestation, the suckling and the growth.

During the gestation, she is attached to his Sephira Yesod, (she is still as one dot), during the suckling, she is on his Tiferet, and during the growth, she is on his Da'at. It is only once his construction complete, that Z"A starts to build Nukvah by his NHY (Netsa'h, Hod, Yesod) for her to be an independent Partsuf.

Hebrew / Aramaic Phonetic	L	Dictionary

During the night *Nukvah* of the world of *Atsilut* (emanation) descends in the world of *Beriah* (creation) and corresponds to a dot. During the morning *Tefilah* of *Sha'hrit* we contribute to her reconstruction and her ascension back to *Atsilut*.

נקודות

Nekudot

H **Punctuation – Vowels – Points**

Each vowel corresponds to a *Sephira*. It in a way translates, with the combination of the letters, the inner identity of the word.

Vowel	Sephira
Kamatz	Keter
Pata'h	'Hokhma
Tsere	Binah
Segol	'Hesed
Shevah	Gevurah
'Holam	Tiferet
'Hirik	Netsa'h
Kubutz	Hod
Shuruk	Yesod
No vowel	Malkhut

See Autiot

נקודות אמצעיות

Nekudot Atsma'iot

H **Middle Nekudot**

The vowels in the middle of the letters. They correspond to the emanations of the eyes of *Adam Kadmon*.

223

Hebrew / Aramaic Phonetic	L	Dictionary
נקודות דס"ג *Nekudot de SAG*	H	**_Vowels of SAG_** From the lights that were invested inside of *Adam Kadmon* emerged numerous worlds in the way of his senses; which are called his branches. These "branches" are the lights that spread forth from *Adam Kadmon,* by way of its apertures in the head. They spread out from his eyes, ears, nose, and mouth. Inside of *Adam Kadmon*, the light of the aspect of *SaG* (63) gathered its own aspects of *MaH* (45) and *BaN* (52) together with the general aspects of *MaH* and *BaN* of *Adam Kadmon*. It brought them up above the navel and put a veil as a separation. These emanations are the *Nekudot* (vowels) and are more exactly of the aspect of *BaN* (52) of *SaG*. They correspond to the feminine aspect - rigor, and are the root of deterioration. These *Sephirot* came out as ten encircling *Sephirot* from the right eye, ten interior from the left eye, and descended lower than the navel. When they came out, the first three *Sephirot* – KHB (Keter, 'Hokhma, Binah) were able to stand in three columns, the seven lower *Sephirot* could not stand in this order and broke. See Orot HaOzen, 'Olam HaNekudim, Shvirat HaKelim
נקודות עליונות *Nekudot 'Elyonot*	H	**_Upper Nekudot_** The vowels on top of the letters. They correspond to an aspect of the emanations of the eyes of *Adam Kadmon.*

Hebrew / Aramaic Phonetic	L	Dictionary

נקודות **H** ***Lower Nekudot***
תחתונות
Nekudot The vowels below the letters. They correspond to an aspect of the emanations of the eyes of *Adam*
Ta'htonot *Kadmon.*

נקודים **H** ***Points***
Nekudim See 'Olam HaNekudim

נר"ן **H** ***Nefesh, Rua'h, Neshama***
NaRaN Initials of the first three levels of the souls.

נרנח"י **H** ***Nefesh, Rua'h, Neshama, Hayah and Ye'hidah***
NRNHY Initials of the five levels of the souls.

נשיקין **A** ***Kiss***
Neshikin See Zivug De Neshikin

נשמה **H** ***Soul - Third level of the soul***
Neshama The soul has five names: *Nefesh, Rua'h, Neshama, 'Hayah* and *Ye'hidah*, which correspond to its five levels. The soul is the spiritual entity inside the body, the latter being only his outer garment.

Since it is men that provoke the union of the four worlds, it is necessary for their souls to have their origin from them, and from the five *Partsufim*

Soul / Level	Partsuf	World
Nefesh	Nukvah	'Asiah
Rua'h	Zeir Anpin	Yetsirah
Neshama	Imah	Beriah
'Hayah	Abah	Atsilut
Ye'hidah	Arikh Anpin	Atsilut

Hebrew / Aramaic *Phonetic*	L	Dictionary

Each level of the soul is subdivided in five levels. As for the level of *Nefesh;* there are *Nefesh* of *Nefesh, Rua'h* of *Nefesh, Neshama* of *Nefesh, 'Hayah* of *Nefesh* and *Ye'hidah* of *Nefesh.*

Each one of these levels of the soul subdivides for each level of *Partsuf* and for each world. Therefore, there are five levels of the souls for *Partsuf Nukvah* and there are five levels of *Partsufim* for the world of *'Asiah* etc. Also, as there are in each world ten *Sephirot,* each soul has its origin corresponding to one of them. Therefore, a soul could be from the level of *Nefesh* of *Malkhut* of *Nukvah* of *'Asiah,* or *Rua'h* of *'Hesed* of *Abah* of *'Yetsirah,* or *Neshama* of *Abah* of *Z"A* of *Yetsirah* etc.

Neshama is the third level and can be acquired only after acquiring the level of *Nefesh* and *Rua'h.*

The higher levels of the soul cannot be acquired at once. Most men only have the level of *Nefesh,* and if they merit, they will acquire the next levels - but one by one. To reach the next higher level of his soul, man must do the *Tikun* of the preceding level. If he needs to acquire the level of *Imah* of *'Asiah,* he must first do the *Tikun* of *Malkhut* of *'Asiah* and *Z"A* of *'Asiah,* and so on. To acquire his level of *Neshama,* he must do the *Tikun* of all the levels of the *Sephirot* and *Partsufim* of his *Nefesh* and *Rua'h etc*

נשמות *Neshamot*	H	**Souls** *See Neshama*

Hebrew / Aramaic Phonetic	L	Dictionary
ס"ג SaG	H	**SaG (63)**

SaG (63)

Miluy (spelling) of the name י-ה-ו-ה **with a total of 63**

The creative forces or energies are the different powers in the four letters of the name of G-od י-ה-ו-ה, and the various letters added to make their different spellings. Depending on which letters are used, the numerical value of the name changes, and each one of these possibilities becomes different in its nature and actions.

The letters that are added for the different spellings of the letters are: י ה ו א ד

The different spellings of the letters are:

The letter י (Yud) can only be spelled one way: יוד

The letter ה (He) can be spelled with a י (Yud) or an א (Aleph) or a ה (He): הא הה הי

The Letter ו (Vav) can be spelled with a יו (Yud and Vav) or with או (Aleph and Vav) or

With a ו (Vav): ואו ויו וו

The four Miluyim (spellings) are:

עב ,סג , מה, בן - 'A"V, SaG, MaH, BaN

יוד הי ויו הי – עב   - 'A"V = 72

יוד הי ואו הי – סג   - SaG = 63

יוד הא ואו הא - מה   - MaH = 45

יוד הה וו הה – בן   - BaN = 52

Each name can also be divided and subdivided as:

'A"V of 'A"V, SaG of 'A"V, MaH of 'A"V ...

BaN of BaN of SaG, SaG of MaH of 'A"V etc.

Hebrew / Aramaic *Phonetic*	L	Dictionary

The name of *SaG* is the second level of the four names of *'A"V, SaG, MaH* and *BaN*. Its *Miluy* (spelling) is with the letter ' א *(Yud and Aleph)* for a total of 63.

סג – יוד הי ואו הי   - *SaG* = 63

In the categories of lights that came out of *Adam Kadmon* as the *Ta'amim, Nekudot, Tagin, and Autiot,* the *Ta'amim* are of the highest level. They are subdivided in three: higher, middle and lower. They came out through the ears, nose, and mouth: the higher from the ears, the middle from the nose, and the lower from the mouth. These emanations correspond to the name of *SaG*.

ס"מ *S"M*		**Initials of the main destructive Angel** There are four levels of *Klipot* (husks); they are the worlds of *S'M*, they obstruct the lights of the *Sephirot,* conceal man from his root and from the light. In parallel (opposite) to the four worlds, there are four negative worlds and ten groups of negative angels divided as follows: three groups in their world of *Beriah*, six groups in *Yetsirah,* and one group in *'Asiah*. They nourish from the extremities of the higher lights, when the latter are weakened by the bad deeds of the lower beings. These destructive angels get more powers and come to do evil in the world. *See angels*
סגול *Segol*	H	**Segol – Vowel E** The vowel that represents the *Sephira 'Hesed*

Hebrew / Aramaic Phonetic	L	Dictionary

סגולה H **Remedy – Protection**
Segulah

Names, or combinations of names of angels with special signs or incantations, written on parchment to protect, or to invoke particular powers.

By writing various permutation of letters or names of angels, one could make these superior forces act according to his will. There is a danger of using these names without a proper preparation and a good knowledge of their forces and limits. *See Kemi'a*

סדר H **Order**
Seder

Every light or emanation has its own order of spreading.

סהר H **Moon**
Sahar

It is of the aspect of *Nukvah.*

סובב H **Surround**
Sovev

See Or Makif

סוד H **Secret**
Sod

The Torah contains four levels of comprehension, of which the highest is the *Sod.* At this level, we understand that our *Tefilot* and the accomplishment of each one of the *Mitsvot,* has a direct influence on the superior worlds and on their guidance.

Through the knowledge of Kabbalah, we can get to a level of true understanding of the will of the Creator, and in a way "decode" the profound secrets of our holy Torah.

Hebrew / Aramaic Phonetic	L	Dictionary
סודות Sodot	H	***Secrets*** See Sod
סולם Sulam	H	***Ladder*** See *Rabbi Yehudah Ashlag*
סוף Sof	H	***End – Extremity*** See Siyum
סיבה Sibah	H	***Reason – Cause*** Since the intention of the Creator is to bestow goodness on His creatures, all the levels of creation were put in place so His kindness could emanate to them, yet in such a way that they would be able to receive it. With the emanation of the lights of MaH *(45)* and BaN *(52),* He could have done the *Tikun* (rectification) of all the worlds after the *Shvirat HaKelim (breaking of the vessels),* but then, there would not have been a reason for the participation of man in this *Tikun.* It is to give a possibility to man to act and repair the creation, that G-od restrained in a way his outflow of kindness to this world. The reason why the Creator created these worlds, is to bestow kindness to all his creatures, and to change all evil to goodness.
סיבות Sibot	H	***Reasons – Causes*** See Sibah
סיהרא Sihara	A	***Moon*** See Sahar

Hebrew / Aramaic Phonetic	L	Dictionary

סיום
Siyum

H **End – Extremity**

From the extremity of *Sephira Malkhut* of the world of *'Asiah*, the *Sitra A'hra* (negative force) came out.

See Malkhur, Sephirot

סיטרא אחרא
Sitra A'hra

A **Negative force**

When the *Sephirot* of *BaN (52)* came out from the eyes of *Adam Kadmon*, the first three *Sephirot – KHB (Keter, 'Hokhma, Binah)*, took strength from the lights that came out of the ears, nose and mouth of *Adam Kadmon*, and were able to stand in three columns. The seven lower *Sephirot* did not stand in this order, they were not able to retain their lights and broke. It is only when the column of mercy stands between the columns of kindness and rigor that they can attach and bind together.

This imperfect arrangement is the first origin of the *Sitra A'hra* or "evil". This type of existence could not come to be from a perfect source; it had to originate from a defective state.

The breaking of the seven lower *Sephirot* caused a descent of the worlds. However, *KHB* remained in what is called the "first *Atsilut*". The seven lower *Sephirot* fell in the higher parts of *Beriah*, which became the *Atsilut* of today, *Beriah* fell in the higher part of *Yetsirah*, which became the *Beriah* of today, *Yetsirah* in the higher parts of *'Asiah*, which became the *Yetsirah* of today, *'Asiah* fell even lower and

Hebrew / Aramaic *Phonetic*	L	Dictionary

became the *'Asiah* of today. From the end of *'Asiah*, the *Sitra A'hra* came out.

The *Sephirot* have their root in the *Kedushah* of the *Ein Sof, B'H*. The root of the *Sitra A'hra* is in the lack, or absence of the *Kedushah*. These *Klipot* (husks) obstruct the lights of the *Sephirot*, conceal man from his root and from the light.

In parallel (opposite) to the four worlds, this negative entity - *Sitra A'hra,* has its four worlds, where ten groups of negative angels divide as follows: three groups in their world of *Beriah*, six groups in *Yetsirah,* and one group in *'Asiah*. They nourish from the extremities of the higher lights when the latter are weakened by the bad deeds of the lower beings. These destructive angels get more powers and come to do evil in the world.

The existence of the *Sitra A'hra* was willed by the Creator to give man free will. With falsehood, it almost constantly tries to seduce him, and make him stumble.

The good deeds of man have an effect on the four higher worlds, his bad deeds; on the four lower worlds. It is only when man sins, that the negative side can grow in strength. In man, this negative aspect grows inside him; this is his *Yetser Hara',* it cuts him off from the higher worlds, and uproots him from the *Kedushah*.

Hebrew / Aramaic Phonetic	L	Dictionary
ספירה *Sephira*	H	**Sephira**

Sephira

The light of G-od is unique and of equal force and quality. A *Sephira* is in a way a "filter" which transforms this light in a particular force or attribute, by which the Creator guides the worlds.

Each *Sephira* is composed of a vessel called *Keli*, which holds its part of light called *Or*. There is no difference in the *Or* itself, the difference comes from the particularity, or position of the *Sephira*. There are ten *Sephirot*, their names are:

Keter
Crown

Binah   **'Hokhma**
Understanding   Wisdom

Da'at
Knowledge

Gevurah   **'Hesed**
Rigor   Bounty

Tiferet
Beauty

Hod   **Netsa'h**
Splendor   Glory

Yesod
Foundation

Malkhut
Kingship

On the right, the *'Hesed* (kindness*) column: 'Hokhma, 'Hesed, Netsa'h.*
In the middle, the *Ra'hamim* (mercy) *column: Keter, Tiferet, Yesod, Malkhut*
On the left, the *Din* (rigor) column: *Binah, Gevurah, Hod.*

Hebrew / Aramaic L Phonetic	Dictionary

There is one more *Sephira* called *Da'at*, which is counted when *Keter* is not, also in the *Ra'hamim* column.

The first and most important of the *Sephirot* is *Keter*. It is complete kindness to all, even to the not deserving.

The second *Sephira* '*Hokhma* is also kindness to all, even to the not deserving, but less than *Keter,* and not always.

The third *Sephira Binah* is kindness to all, even to the less deserving, but from her the rigors start.

The fourth *Sephira* '*Hesed* is complete kindness but to who is deserving.

The fifth *Sephira Gevurah* is full rigor to who is deserving.

The sixth *Sephira Tiferet* is kindness that makes the equilibrium between complete kindness and rigor.

The seventh *Sephira Netsa'h* is diminished kindness to who is deserving.

The eighth *Sephira Hod* is diminished rigor to who is deserving.

The ninth *Sephira* Yesod makes the equilibrium between *Sephira Netsa'h* and *Hod* for the guidance, and is the link or connection between all the superior *Sephirot* and the *Sephira Malkhut.*

The tenth *Sephira* is *Malkhut* translates all the superior emanations into one that is reflected to the creation. It is the link or connection between all the superior *Sephirot* and man.

Hebrew / Aramaic *Phonetic*	L	Dictionary

There are also configurations of one or more *Sephirot* acting in coordination, which are called *Partsufim*.

See Partsuf, Keter, 'Hokhma, Binah, 'Hesed, Gevurah, Tiferet, Netsa'h, Hod, Yesod, Malkhut

---

ספירות H **Plural of Sephira**
Sephirot   See Sephira

ספירות H **Straight Sephirot**
הישר   After entering the *'Hallal* (vacant space) and making
Sephirot the ten circular *Sephirot*, the *Kav* (ray) maintained his
HaYashar straight shape and made ten other *Sephirot*, but this time in a linear arrangement. They were arranged in three columns: right, left and middle, representing the guidance of the world in the manner of *'Hesed, Din* and *Ra'hamim* (Kindness, rigor and mercy).

This first configuration, or the first world where the emanated lights were formed into ten *Sephirot* is called *Adam Kadmon* (*Primordial Man*). It is the union between the *Reshimu* (imprint) and the *Kav* (ray). From this first configuration, all the other worlds came forth into existence.

From this emanation, the other four worlds of *Atsilut* (emanation), *Beriah* (creation), *Yetsirah* (formation) and *'Asiah* (action) will unfold.

See Sephira, Partsuf, Hanhagah, Adam Kadmon

235

Hebrew / Aramaic *Phonetic*	L	Dictionary
ספירות העיגולים *Sephirot Ha'Igulim*	H	**Encircling Sephirot** After entering the *Hallal* (vacant space), the *Kav* (ray) made ten circular *Sephirot*, encircling one another, but still maintaining a straight shape. These ten *Sephirot* are in charge of the general guidance of the worlds, and are not influenced by the actions of men.
ספירות של ב"ן *Sephirot Shel BaN*	H	**Sephirot of BaN** The lights of *BaN* (52) are of the aspect of the *'Olam HaNekudim*. From the eyes of *Adam Kadmon* came out ten *Sephirot* of the aspect of the name of *BaN* (52); ten encircling *Sephirot* from the right eye, and ten interior from the left eye, they descended lower than the navel. They correspond to the feminine aspect - rigor, and are the root of deterioration. When they came out, the first three *Sephirot* - KHB (Keter, 'Hokhma, Binah), took strength from the lights of the ears, nose and mouth of *Adam Kadmon* and were able to stand in three columns. The seven lower *Sephirot* who only took from the lights of the mouth, could not stand in this order and broke. This is called *Shvirat HaKelim* (breaking of the vessels), this imperfect arrangement is the first origin of the *Sitra A'hra* or "evil". The *Tikun* (rectification) was done by the union of the *Sephirot* of *BaN* (52) (rigor) with the *Sephirot* of *MaH* (45) (mercy) that came out from the forehead of *Adam*

236

Hebrew / Aramaic Phonetic	L	Dictionary

Kadmon. By this union, the feminine *BaN* (52) was repaired by the masculine *MaH* (45) and made the *Partsufim* (configurations). With this new arrangement the *Sephirot* were able to stand in the three-column of kindness, rigor and mercy.

See Orot Ha'Enayim, Orot HaMetsa'h

ספירות H **Sephirot of MaH** (45)
של מ"ה
Sephirot   The *Sephirot* of *MaH* (45) are of the aspect of the
Shel   'Olam HaTiKun.
MaH

After the breaking of the *Kelim* and the separation from their lights, it was necessary for the guidance of the world, that reparation be done. From the forehead of *Adam Kadmon* came out ten *Sephirot* of the aspect of the name of *MaH* (45); corresponding to the masculine - reparation. In contrast to the *Sephirot* of *BaN* (52) which correspond to the feminine aspect - rigor, and are the root of deterioration.

The *Tikun* was done by the union of the *Sephirot* of *MaH* (45) (mercy) and *BaN* (52) (rigor) in complex arrangements, as to allow the feminine *BaN* (52) to be repaired by the masculine *MaH* (45), and for the *Sephirot* to stand in the three-column arrangement of kindness, rigor and mercy. ith the proper order of the *Sephirot* in place, various configurations that are called *Partsufim* completed the creation.

See Orot Ha'Enayim, Orot HaMetsa'h, Partsuf

Hebrew / Aramaic Phonetic	L	Dictionary
ע"ב 'A"V	H	**'A"V Name of seventy two triplets of letters** Name hinted in the book of *Shemot* chapt 14. From the three *Pesukim* (verses) 18, 19, 20 (72 letters each) we take the first letter of *Pesuk* 18, the last of *Pesuk* 19, the first of *Pesuk* 20 and so on to get 72 triplets. Each one of these triplets of letters as explained in the *Zohar,* has particular powers.
ע"ב 'A"V	H	**'A"V** **Miluy (spelling) of the name י-ה-ו-ה with a total of 72** The creative forces or energies are the different powers in the four letters of the name of G-od י-ה-ו-ה, and the various letters added to make their different spellings. Depending on which letters are used, the numerical value of the name changes, and each one of these possibilities becomes different in its nature and actions. The letters that are added for the different spellings of the letters are: י ה ו א ד The different spellings of the letters are: The letter י *(Yud)* can only be spelled one way: יוד The letter ה *(He)* can be spelled with a י *(Yud)* or an א *(Aleph)* or a ה *(He):* הא הה הי The Letter ו *(Vav)* can be spelled with a וי *(Yud and Vav)* or with או *(Aleph and Vav)* or With a ו *(Vav):* ואו ויו וו

Hebrew / Aramaic *Phonetic*	L	Dictionary

The four *Miluyim* (spellings) are:

עב ,סג , מה, בן - *'A"V* , *SaG*, *MaH*, *BaN* -

עב – הי ויו הי יוד   - *'A"V* = 72

סג – הי ואו הי יוד   - *SaG* = 63

מה - הא ואו הא יוד   - *MaH* = 45

בן – הה וו הה יוד   - *BaN* = 52

Each name can also be divided and subdivided as:
'A"V of 'A"V, SaG of 'A"V, MaH of 'A"V ...
BaN of BaN of SaG, SaG of MaH of 'A"V etc.
The name of *'A"V* is of the highest level of the four
names of *'A"V*, *SaG*, *MaH* (45) and *BaN* (52). Its *Miluy*
(spelling) is with the letter י *(Yud)* for a total of 72.

עב – הי ויו הי יוד   - *'A"V* = 72

From *Adam Kadmon* emerged numerous worlds,
four of which are called: sight, hearing, smell and
speech that spread out from his eyes, ears, nose,
and mouth. The first emanation to come out is the
branch of *'A"V*, which spread out from the hair on its
head. This light is too lofty for our understanding.

To sustain the *Kelim* after they broke, 288 sparks of
the lights came down as well, because a connection
to their original lights was needed to keep them
alive. These sparks correspond to the four *'A"V* of
the names *'A"V* , *SaG*, *MaH*, *BaN,* 4 x 72 = 288.

239

Hebrew / Aramaic Phonetic	L	Dictionary
		The highest world of *Atsilut* is of the aspect of the name of *'A"V*. All the emanations and *Sephirot* that came out of *Adam Kadmon (Primordial man)* by way of his apertures were of the various aspects of these four names. They have different actions and *Tikunim,* and all the *Partsufim (configurations)* will be constructed by their union.
עב *'Av*	H	**Thick – Coarse** In the world of *Ha'Akudim* (the attached), when the *Sephirot* came out the first time from the mouth of *Adam Kadmon*, each one had its own place, but in one unique *Keli*. The most tenuous part of the lights returned to their origin in the mouth but not completely, each one leaving its trace. The parts of the lights that remained thickened.
עב, סג מה, בן *'A"V,* *SaG,* *MaH,* *BaN*	H	**Spellings of the Name י-ה-ו-ה** *'A"V (72), SaG (63), MaH (45), BaN (52)* The creative forces or energies are the different powers in the four letters of the name of G-od י-ה-ו-ה, and the various letters added to make their different spellings. Depending on which letters are used, the numerical value of the name changes, and each one of these possibilities becomes different in its nature and actions.

Hebrew / Aramaic *Phonetic*	L	Dictionary

The letter ' *(Yud)* can only be spelled one way: יוד

The letter ה *(He)* can be spelled with a ' *(Yud)* or an

א *(Aleph)* or a ה *(He)*: הא הה הי

The Letter ו *(Vav)* can be spelled with a יו *(Yud and Vav)* or with או *(Aleph and Vav)* or

With a ו *(Vav)*: ואו ויו וו

The four *Miluyim* (spellings) are:

עב ,סג , מה, בן - - *'A"V, SaG, MaH, BaN* -

יוד הי ויו הי – עב - *'A"V* = 72

יוד הי ואו הי – סג - *SaG* = 63

יוד הא ואו הא - מה - *MaH* = 45

יוד הה וו הה – בן - *BaN* = 52

Each name can also be divided and subdivided as:

'A"V of 'A"V, SaG of 'A"V, MaH of 'A"V …

BaN of BaN of SaG, SaG of MaH of 'A"V etc.

All the worlds that came out of *Adam Kadmon* by way of his apertures were of the different aspects of the four names. They have different actions and *Tikunim,* and the *Partsufim* are constructed by the union of *BaN (52)* and *MaH (45).*

See *BaN, MaH, SaG, 'A"V*

עבה *'Avey*	H	***Thick*** See *'Aviyut*

עבודה *'Avodah*	H	***Service – Duty*** From the first configuration of *Adam Kadmon* came out different emanations for the construction of the

Hebrew / Aramaic Phonetic	L	Dictionary

worlds. From his eyes came out ten *Sephirot* of the feminine aspect of *BaN* (52), the three first *Sephirot* contained their lights but the seven lower *Sephirot* did not and broke.

This caused an important damage called *Shvirat HaKelim* – *the breaking of the vessels.* The *Kelim* (recipients) of the seven *Sephirot* which did not contain their lights, fell to the lower worlds.

To sustain these *Kelim* after they broke, 288 sparks of their lights came down as well, because a connection to their original lights was needed to keep them alive. These sparks correspond to the four aspects of *'A"V* of the names *'A"V* (72), *SaG* (63), *MaH* (45), *BaN* (52) , 4 x 72 = 288.

It is important to understand that all that happens in our world, is similar to what occurred in this fall.

The goal of all the works, deeds and prayers of men in this existence, is to help and participate in the ascent of the fallen 288 sparks to their origin. This can be done by accomplishing the *Mitsvot* and the *Tefilot*. At the completion of this *Tikun* of unification between all the fallen sparks and their *Kelim*, it will be the time of the resurrection of the dead and the arrival of *Moshia'h*.

See Shvirat HaKelim, Tikun, Tefilah

עביות   H   ***Thickness – Coarseness***
'Aviyut

After the *Sephirot* came out the first time from the mouth of *Adam Kadmon,* the most tenuous part of

Hebrew / Aramaic Phonetic	L	Dictionary

the lights returned to their origin in the mouth but not completely, each one leaving its trace. This trace, which did not return, thickened, and together with the sparks that fell from the collision of the returning higher lights, made the *Kelim (recipients)*.

עבר   H   ***Past***
'Avar

There is a higher dimension where there is not a notion called time. Past, present and future are one. Man being a limited entity physically and temporally, it is not possible for him to comprehend this reality.

Everything, past, present and future has a purpose, and in the end, all will be clear and comprehensible.

עגל   H   ***Make round***
'Agol

The shape of the *'Hallal* (vacant space) after the *Tsimtsum* (retraction).

עובי   H   ***Thickness***
'Ovi

See *'Aviyut*

עובר   H   ***Embryo - Fetus***
'Ubar

The *Tikunim* (rectifications) of the masculine and feminine *Partsufim* (configurations) are achieved by way of *Zivug* (union), gestation and birth.

'Ubar is the first stage in the *Tikun* of a *Partsuf*.

During the *Zivug*, the lights of *MaH* (45) needed for the *Tikun* are drawn to the lights of *BaN* (52) and are kept in the upper *Partsuf Nukvah*.

During the gestation, inside of *Nukvah*, they are arranged and completed until there is nothing more

243

Hebrew / Aramaic Phonetic	L	Dictionary
		to add. When it is totally repaired, the *Partsuf* is revealed, and this is the birth. During the gestation, which is the first selection in the three pillar arrangement, the *Mo'hin* (brains) are of the lowest level and are called *NHY* (Netsa'h, Hod, Yesod) of the *Mo'hin;* they are of the aspect of *Nefesh.* During the time of the gestation, as a *'Ubar,* the *Partsuf* is not really acting as it is being built, at the time of suckling it starts to act, and at the growth it is ready to act completely. *See Tikun, Zivug*
עובר *'Over*	H	**Passing** There is passing when lights "travel" from one position to another. The second *Tikun* (action) of *Partsuf Arikh Anpin* is revealed by the passing of the seven lower *Sephirot* of *Partsuf 'Atik* into its head, before they are clothed in him. The lights of a higher world have to pass through a curtain to make the *Partsufim* of a lower world.
עולם *'Olam*	H	**World** A *'Olam* is a possibility and a type of existence, in a particular dimension. From the first configuration; *Adam Kadmon* (Primordial man), emanations made the four lower worlds. There is a screen (divider) that separates one world from another, and from this screen the ten *Sephirot* of the lower world came out from the ten *Sephirot* of the higher world.

Hebrew / Aramaic Phonetic	L	Dictionary

The first world to unfold from *Adam Kadmon (Primordial man)* is called *Atsilut;* the world of emanation, where there is no existence of the separated, and no *Sitra A'hra (negative force)* even at its lowest levels. The second world is *Beriah (creation)*; the world of the *Neshamot*; of the souls. The third world is *Yetsirah (formation)*; the world of formation, the world of the angels. The fourth world is *'Asiah (action)*; the world of action, the world of physical existence

Each world is built from four aspects: *Partsuf* (configuration), *Levush* (garment), *Or Makif* (encircling lights), and *Hekhalot* (portals). The five main *Partsufim* (configurations) are: *Arikh Anpin, Abah, Imah, Zeir Anpin* and *Nukvah*. One more *Partsuf, 'Atik Yomin,* is on top of them, his three first *Sephirot* are in the superior world, his seven lower *Sephirot* are inside the ten *Sephirot* of *Arikh Anpin* and make the link between a world and the one under it.

Atsilut is of the aspect of *Partsuf Abah, Beriah* of *Imah, Yetsirah* of *Z"A,* and *'Asiah* of *Nukvah.*

See Atsilut, Beriah, Yetsirah, Asiah

עולם הברודים 'Olam Haberudim	H	**World of reparation**

Also called *'Olam HaTikun*. From the eyes of *Adam Kadmon* came out ten *Sephirot* of the feminine aspect of *BaN* (52), the three first *Sephirot* contained their lights but the seven lower *Sephirot* did not and broke.

Hebrew / Aramaic *Phonetic*	L	Dictionary

This caused an important damage called *Shvirat HaKelim* – *the breaking of the vessels.* The *Kelim* (recipients) of the seven *Sephirot* which did not contain their lights, fell to the lower worlds.

After the lights of the aspect of *BaN* *(52)* and the breaking of the *Kelim* (recipients), lights of the aspect of *MaH* *(45)* came out through the forehead of *Adam Kadmon.* The union between the lights of *MaH*, which represent mercy, with the ones of *BaN*, which represent rigor, made the *Tikun* (rectification) of the broken *Sephirot.*

This *Tikun* is also the arrangement of the *Sephirot* in three columns, which will allow the beginning of the construction of the first *Partsufim.*

See Shvirat HaKelim, Tikun

עולם **H** ***The world of points***
הנקודים

'Olam   The *Sephirot* that came out through the eyes of
Hanikudim *Adam Kadmon* were of the aspects of the *Nekudim* (punctuation), and of the name of *BaN* *(52)*. This world is called the world of points because these *Sephirot* had their own *Kelim* (recipients), but were separated.

When the lights of *BaN* *(52)* came out, the *Kelim* were not in the three pillar arrangement needed for the direction of Kindness, rigor and mercy. Therefore, they could not hold the influx of these lights and broke.

See Shvirat HaKelim

Hebrew / Aramaic Phonetic	L	Dictionary
עולם העקודים 'Olam Ha'Akudim	H	**The world of the attached** In the *'Olam Ha'Akudim* (the attached), when the *Sephirot* came out the first time from the mouth of *Adam Kadmon*, each one had its own place, but in one unique *Keli* (recipient). The seven lower *Sephirot* were aligned one under the other in a straight line, not in the three pillar arrangement and not ready for the guidance of kindness, rigor and mercy. They could not hold in this configuration, and the most tenuous part of the lights returned to their origin in the mouth but not completely, each one leaving its trace. The parts of the lights that remained thickened, but were still illuminated by their own parts that ascended. The lights strike each other and produced sparks which formed the *Kelim* (recipients) for the more tenuous lights that returned a second time. This is considered as an annulment, but not as important as the one in *'Olam HaNikudim*.
עולמות 'Olamot	H	**Worlds** See *'Olam*
עונש 'Onesh	H	**Punishment** From the world of *Atsilut* unfolded all the lower worlds. The last world to unfold is *'Asiah*; the physical world with the possibility of reward, punishment and evil.

247

Hebrew / Aramaic Phonetic	L	Dictionary

There are two main kinds of guidance: The general guidance and the variable guidance.

The general guidance is for the subsistence of the worlds and is not influenced by the actions of men. This guidance is by the encircling *Sephirot.* The variable guidance is on the basis of justice, reward and punishment and is dependant on the actions of man. This guidance is by the linear *Sephirot.*

If there was only good in this world, the guidance based on the duality of reward and punishment would not be necessary, but then, men will not have free choice, and no merit for the accomplishment of the will of G-od.

עור
'Or

H **Skin**

Some emanations are described allegorically as physical parts.

When *NHY* (Netsa'h, Hod, Yesod) of *Partsuf Imah* entered in *Partsuf Zeir Anpin,* her (emanations called) skin, flesh, bones and veins included with his. A *Levush* (garment) was made for *Partsuf Zeir Anpin* and *Nukvah,* from the exteriors of *NHY* (*Partsuf Tevunah*) of *Imah.* In *NHY* there are three aspects of *Kelim* (recipients): flesh, bones and veins, and one more aspect of *Keli* from *Malkhut,* which is the skin in surplus of *Imah.*

עורף
'Oref

H **Back of the neck**

Highest part on the back until where the *Klipot* (husks) can attach. *See Klipa*

Hebrew / Aramaic Phonetic	L	Dictionary
עיבוי 'Ibuy	H	**Thickening** See 'Aviyut
עיבור 'Ibur	H	**Attachment – Gestation**

There is 'Ibur as gestation for the Partsufim (configurations), and 'Ibur as attachment for the soul.

Gestation - All the Tikunim (rectification) of the Partsufim (masculine and feminine) are achieved by way of Zivug (union), 'Ibur (gestation) and Leida (birth).

During the Zivug, the lights of MaH (45) needed for the Tikun are drawn to the lights of BaN (52), and are kept in the upper Partsuf Nukvah that will give birth to the Partsuf. When the Mayin Nukvin (feminine waters) and Mayin Dukhrin (masculine waters) stand in Nukvah, and are repaired in her interior, it corresponds to the 'Ibur (gestation).

During the gestation, inside of Nukvah, they are arranged and completed until there is nothing more to add. When it is totally repaired, the Partsuf is revealed, and this is the birth. There is afterwards the suckling, and finally the growth, so that the Partsuf will be fully independent.

Attachment - The Tikun of the soul is realized by the Gilgul (reincarnation), and by the 'Ibur (attachment). By accomplishing what he did not accomplish of the 613 Mitsvot, man makes the necessary Tikun of his soul which can now elevate to the higher realms and rejoin its source.

Hebrew / Aramaic Phonetic	L	Dictionary
		The *Gilgul* is the reincarnation of a soul from the time of birth until death, the *'Ibur* is an attachment of another soul to his, that could come and leave anytime.

For the *Mitsvot* that it was obligated to accomplish, it accomplishes them by the *Gilgul*, for the ones it did not have to accomplish, it accomplishes them by the *'Ibur,* which departs afterwards.

To help him accomplish the missing *Mitsvot*, another soul could attach to his soul (*'Ibur*), until he accomplishes it, and then departs. The missing *Mitsva* could be one he chose not to do, or one he could not do in his previous life.

There is a *Levush* (garment) or envelope, which is necessary for the soul to attach to the body of man (*Gilgul*), and when another soul attaches to him (*'Ibur*), it could use the same *Levush* to remain in him.

עיגול *'Igul*	H	***Circle - Circular*** See *'Hallal, Sephirot Ha'Igulim*
עיגולים *'Igulim*	H	***Circles - Circular*** See *Sephirot Ha'Igulim*
עיינין *'Eynin*	A	***Eyes*** See *'Enayim*
עינוג *'Inug*	A	***Pleasure – Delight*** See *Ta'anug*

Hebrew / Aramaic Phonetic	L	Dictionary
עיניים 'Enayim	H	**Eyes** The lights of the aspect of *BaN (52)* came out through the eyes of *Adam Kadmon*. See Orot Ha'Enayim, Orot Shel BaN
עיקר 'Ikar	A	**Essential** The *Taffel* (accessory) is always subordinate to the *'Ikar*, which is the main or the essential. Likewise, some emanations are subordinate to other more important lights.
עירוב 'Iruv	H	**Mixture** In *Sephira Yesod* the lights of the aspect of *'Hasadim* (kindnesses) mix with the *Gevurot (rigors)*.
על 'Al	H	**On – On top of** Sometimes, more important *Partsufim* are described as being on top of other lower *Partsufim*. In reality, this only denotes a position of superiority, since more important *Partsufim* are usually clothed inside lower *Partsufim*. See Partsuf
עלאה 'Ilaa	A	**Upper** See 'Al
עליה 'Aliyah	H	**Elevation – Ascent** There is ascent when there is reparation or amelioration. The first ascent was the one of the *Malkin* (Kings), representing the *Kelim* (recipients) of the *Sephirot* that broke from *Beriah* to *Atsilut*. This ascent was of

Hebrew / Aramaic Phonetic	L	Dictionary
		forty days:

Ten days: *Kelim of 'Hesed* and *Netsa'h,* to *Netsa'h* of *Atsilut.*

Ten days: *Kelim of Da'at* and *Tiferet,* to *Yesod* of *Atsilut*

Ten days: *Kelim of Gevurah* and *Hod,* to *Hod* of *Atsilut*

Ten days: *Kelim of Yesod* and *Malkhut,* to *Malkhut* of *Atsilut*

There is also an ascent of the worlds during the *Tefilot,* when the worlds of *Asiah, Yetsirah* and *Beriah* ascend until *Atsilut* during the *'Amidah.*

See Tefilah, Kavanah

עליון 'Elyon	H	**Higher – Superior**

Sometimes, more important *Partsufim* are described as being on top or higher than other *Partsufim.* In reality, this only denotes a position of superiority, since more important *Partsufim* are usually clothed inside lower *Partsufim.* See Partsuf

עליונים 'Elyonim	H	**Higher – Superiors** See 'Elyon

עלמא 'Alma	A	**World** See 'Olam

עמר 'Omer	H	**Counting of the 'Omer**

During the counting of the *'Omer* we rebuild during the 49 days, the seven parts of the seven *Sephirot* of *Partsuf Z"A* from *'Hesed* to *Malkhut* (7 x 7 = 49).

Hebrew / Aramaic *Phonetic*	L	Dictionary
עמר נקי *'Amer Naki*	A	**Fifth of seven Tikunim of the head of Arikh Anpin** From the *Partsuf (configuration) Arikh Anpin*, there are emanations that come out from its head to act and influence on the guidance; called the *Tikunim* of *Arikh Anpin*. The second *Tikun* (action) of *Arikh Anpin*, is achieved by the passing of the seven lower *Sephirot* of *Partsuf 'Atik* into its head before they are clothed in him. These seven *Tikunim* of the head of *Arikh Anpin* are revealed from the seven lower *Sephirot* of *'Atik*. The fifth *Tikun* - עמר נקי (*'Amer Naki*) is realized by the first parts of *Netsa'h* and *Hod*, which are positioned higher than *Yesod;* it shapes the hair that spreads out from *'Hokhma Stimaah*.
ענן דול *'Anan Gadol*	H	**'Anan Gadol - A large cloud** One of the four main levels of *Klipot* corresponding to the four lower worlds. See *Klipot*
ענני כבוד *'Anane Kavod*	H	**The Clouds of Glory** Diagonal light or *Partsuf,* on the right side of *Partsuf Z"A.* This light, or *Partsuf* is not considered as a complete *Partsuf,* its actions are temporary and at particular times only.
ענף *'Anaf*	H	**Branch** Light or *Sephira* that is an outcome of a root.

Hebrew / Aramaic *Phonetic*	L	Dictionary
ענפי א"ק *'Anafe* *A"K*	H	**Branches of Adam Kadmon** *Adam Kadmon* being at such close proximity to the *Ein Sof*, we cannot grasp anything of its nature. Our understanding only starts from the emanations that came out of him in the way of his senses, which are called his branches. These four branches are called: sight, hearing, smell and speech. They spread out from his eyes, ears, nose, and mouth. In the language of Kabbalah we use names of body parts solely to describe the inner sense, or the position they represent. It is understood, of course, that there is no physical existence at these level. These four emanations are of the aspects of the names of *'A"V (72)*, *SaG (63)*, *MaH (45)* and *BaN (52)*. The first one to come out is the branch of *'A"V*, which spread out from the hair on its head. This light is too lofty for our understanding. From the ears, came out lights of the aspect of the name *SaG (63)*; ten linear *Sephirot* from the left ear, and ten encircling *Sephirot* from the right ear. From the nose, came out lights also of the aspect of the name of *SaG (63)*; ten encircling *Sephirot* from the right nostril and ten linear from the left nostril. The lights of the encircling *Sephirot* are of a finer aspect, which is why they came out of the right side; the side of *'Hesed* (kindness), as opposed to the left; which is of the side of *Gevurah* (rigor). In the emanations (lights) of the ears and nose, there is not yet a concept of *Keli* (vessel).

Hebrew / Aramaic *Phonetic*	L	Dictionary
		From the mouth, came out lights also of the aspect of the name of *SaG* (63); ten internal *Sephirot*, and ten encircling *Sephirot*.
		From the eyes, came out lights of the aspect of the name *BaN (52)*. These feminine lights caused the *Shvirat HaKelim* (breaking of the vessels).
		From the forehead, came out lights of the aspect of the name of *MaH* (45), these masculine lights will make the *Tikun* (rectification) of the broken *Sephirot*, and together with *BaN* make all the *Partsufim* (configurations) for the guidance of the worlds.
		From all these emanations, the other four worlds of *Atsilut* (emanation), *Beriah* (creation), *Yetsirah* (formation) and *'Asiah* (action) will unfold.
ענפים *'Anafim*	H	***Branches*** Lights or *Sephirot* that are an outcome of a root.
עסמ"ב *'ASMaB*	H	***'A"V (72), SaG (63), MaH (45), BaN (52)*** *Initials*
עפר *'Afar*	H	***Soil – Dust*** The body is called soil. It obstructs the spiritual aspect, which is the *Neshama,* from seeing and understanding.
עץ הדעת טוב ורע *'Ets Hada'at Tov ve Ra*	H	***The Tree of Knowledge of Good and Bad*** The *Bne* Israel went in exile in Egypt to make the *Tikun* (rectification) of "*'Ets Hada'at*" which is of the aspect of *Yesod* of *Partsuf Z"A* .

Hebrew / Aramaic Phonetic	L	Dictionary
עץ החיים 'Ets Ha'Haim	H	**Tree of Life** It is of the aspect of *Tiferet* of *Partsuf Z"A.* During the night the "Tree of Life" ascends higher and the "Tree of death" governs,. It is only in the morning that the governance is given back to the Tree of Life and that all the souls return in men's bodies. (Zohar, Bamidbar) It is also the name of the master work of the Ari Z'al. *See Ari Z'al*
עצם השמים 'Etsem Hashamaim		**'Etsem HaShamaim** Name of a *Hekhal (portal).* Second of seven *Hekhalot,* corresponding to *Hod.* Each world (*ABYA*) is built from four aspects: *Partsuf, Levush* (garment), *Or Makif* (encircling lights), and *Hekhalot.* In each *Partsuf,* there are interiority and exteriority, the exteriority is always of the aspect of *Malkhut,* and the *Hekhalot* are the ramifications of the *Malkhuts* of the *Partsufim.* The *Hekhalot* are also the different levels of ascension of the *Tefilot* before reaching the seventh *Hekhal (portal), Kodesh Hakodashim.* Their principal function is to allow the adhesion and attachment, in various and particular ways during the *Tefilot,* until the *'Olam Atsilut* (during the *'Amidah*) The *Neshamot* and the angels have their root in the *Hekhalot,* each one depending on its respective level.

Hebrew / Aramaic Phonetic	L	Dictionary
עצמות 'Atsamot	H	**Bones** Some emanations are described allegorically as physical parts. There are 613 veins and bones to man. Similarly, there are 613 commandments in the Torah , 613 parts to the soul, and 613 lights in each *Sephira* or *Partsuf*, this number is not arbitrary, as there are important interrelations and interactions between them. When *NHY (Netsa'h, Hod, Yesod)* of *Partsuf Imah* entered in *Partsuf Zeir Anpin*, her skin, flesh, bones and veins included with his. A *Levush (garment)* was made for *Partsuf Zeir Anpin* and *Nukvah,* from the exteriors of *NHY (Partsuf Tevunah)* of *Imah*. In *NHY* there are three aspects of *Kelim (recipients)*: flesh, bones and veins, and one more aspect of *Keli* from *Malkhut*, which is the skin in surplus of *Imah*.
עצמות 'Atsmut	H	**Essence – Nature** The inner light of each *Sephira* or *Partsuf* is identical. The lights are transformed only once inside, by the nature of the *Sephira* or *Partsuf*.
עקב 'Ekev	H	**Heel** Some *Neshamot* came out from the heel of *Adam Kadmon*, corresponding to a left part of *Kayin*.
עקוד 'Akud	H	**Bound – Tied** See Olam Ha'Akudim
עקודים 'Akudim	H	**Bound - Tied** See Olam Ha'Akudim

257

Hebrew / Aramaic Phonetic	L	Dictionary
ערב רב 'Erev Rav	H	**The mixed multitude** Diagonal light or *Partsuf* on the right side of *Ya'acov*. This light, or *Partsuf*, is not considered as a complete *Partsuf*; its actions are temporary and at particular times only.
ערבים 'Arevim	H	**Guarantors - Mutual responsibility** "*Kol Israel 'Arevim ze la ze*", every Jew is a guarantor for his fellow Jew. The majority of the *Tikunim* (rectifications), as explained in the Kabbalah, are not realized by one, but more by the actions of many. The *Geulah* (liberation) will come as a result of the efforts of all Israel.
ערלה 'Orla	H	**Foreskin** When the *'Orla* covers the *Sephira Yesod*, the *'Hasadim* cannot spread from the chest and down. Similarly, the foreskin has to be removed from the masculine organ which is also called the *Yesod*.
עשו Essav	H	**Essav** Diagonal light or *Partsuf* on the left side of *Ya'acov*. This light, or *Partsuf*, is not considered as a complete *Partsuf*; its actions are temporary and at particular times only.
עשיה 'Asiah	H	**World of action – of man** From the first configuration of *Adam Kadmon,* four worlds unfolded. On these four worlds, the four letters of the Name (ה-ו-ה-י) *B'H*, govern.

Hebrew / Aramaic Phonetic	L	Dictionary

' in *Atsilut;* by it, all the repaired levels are put in order.

ה descends from it (*Atsilut*) to *Beriah,* and guides it.

ו to *Yetsirah,* and

ה to *'Asiah.*

The fourth world to unfold is called *'Asiah* - action, the world of physical existence.

It is under *Atsilut, Beriah* and *Yetsirah.*

It consists of five main *Partsufim: Arikh Anpin, Abah, Imah, Zeir Anpin* and *Nukvah.* One more *Partsuf, 'Atik Yomin,* is on top of them.

In the emanation of the lights from the eyes of *Adam Kadmon,* first the individual *Keli* (recipient) for each *Sephira* came out, and then the lights. The *Kelim* could not contain their lights and broke. The seven lower broken *Sephirot,* which did not contain their lights, descended to the world of *Beriah,* the lights also fell, but stayed in *Atsilut.* When the *Kelim* broke *SaG (63), MaH (45)* and *BaN (52)* descended to the lower worlds, *BaN* descended in *'Asiah.* It also caused a descent of the worlds, *'Asiah* fell lower and its lower levels became *'Asiah* of today. From the last level of the *Sephirot* of *'Asiah (Malkhut* of *'Asiah),* the *Sitra A'hra* (negative force) came out.

There is a screen (divider) that separates one world from another. From this screen, the ten *Sephirot* of the lower world come out from the ten *Sephirot* of the higher world. The three superior worlds of *Atsilut,*

Hebrew / Aramaic *Phonetic*	L	Dictionary
		Beriah and *Yetsirah,* are interior to the fourth world of *'Asiah.* In parallel to the four worlds (*ABYA*), there are four types of existence in our world; mineral corresponding to *'Asiah (action)*, vegetal corresponding to *Yetsirah (formation)*, animal corresponding to *Beriah (creation)*, and man corresponding to *Atsilut (emanation)*. The world of *'Asiah* is of the aspect of *BaN (52)*. Thus, *'Asiah* is of the aspect of *Partsuf Nukvah – Sephira Malkhut.*
עשר *'Eser*	H	**Ten** Number of *Sephirot* in each world, in each *Sephira, Partsuf* or configuration.
עשר מכות *'Eser* *Makot*	H	**Ten plagues** Each plague corresponds to a *Sephira.*
עת *'Et*	H	**Time – Moment** Each moment can be described in term of permutation of the names of G-od, and by the various *Sephirot and Partsufim.*
עת רצון *'Et* *Ratson*	H	**Moment of bounty** Time when the configuration of bounty is prevailing. One of them is at the time of *Min'ha* of *Shabbat.* *See Tefilah*

Hebrew / Aramaic Phonetic	L	Dictionary
עתיד 'Atid	H	**Future** There is a higher dimension where there is not a notion called time. Past, present and future are one. Man being a limited entity physically and temporally, it is not possible for him to comprehend this reality. Everything, past, present and future has a purpose, and in the end, all will be clear and comprehensible. *See Giluy Yi'hudo*
עתיק 'Atik	A	**Partsuf – Ancient** Sometimes *Partsuf 'Atik Yomin* is only called *'Atik.* *See 'Atik Yomin*
עתיק יומין 'Atik Yomin	A	**Partsuf – Ancient** The *Partsuf 'Atik* is superior to all the *Partsufim*. It was constructed by the *Zivug* (union) of *'A"V* and *SaG* of *Adam Kadmon*. It has ten *Sephirot*, his aspect of *MaH* (45) corresponds to the masculine principle, his aspect of *BaN* (52) to the feminine, he is called *'Atik* and his *Nukvah*. His *Nukvah* is never separated from him, her back attached to his back, *'Atik* is thus all face; the face of *BaN* (52) corresponding to his back, the face of *MaH* (45) to his front. His masculine aspect is not clothed inside *Atsilut*. The first three *Sephirot* of his *Nukvah* are above *Atsilut,* and make together the *Radl'a* - רישה דלא אתידע (the unknown head).

Hebrew / Aramaic Phonetic	L	Dictionary

His seven lower *Sephirot* dress inside *Partsuf Arikh Anpin* in the following manner: '*Hesed* in *Keter*, *Gevurah* in '*Hokhma*, *Tiferet* in *Binah*, the first part of *NHY* (Netsa'h, Hod, Yesod) in '*Hesed*, *Gevurah* and *Tiferet*, the second part of *NHY* in *Netsa'h, Hod* and *Yesod*, the third part of *NH* (Netsa'h, Hod), and *Malkhut* of '*Atik* in *Malkhut* of *Arikh Anpin*.

The *Partsuf* '*Atik* makes the connection between the worlds, in *Atsilut* it is the *Malkhut* of *Adam Kadmon* which becomes its *Partsuf* '*Atik*. It is the same in the three other worlds of *Beriah, Yetsirah* and '*Asiah*, the *Malkhut* of the world above becomes the *Partsuf* '*Atik* of the world below.

See Partsuf

עתיקא A ***Partsuf Arikh Anpin***
'Atika   In the two *Adarot* of Rabbi Shim'on Bar Yo'hay in the *Zohar, Arikh Anpin* is called '*Atika*.

See Partsuf Arikh Anpin

Hebrew / Aramaic Phonetic	L	Dictionary
פאה Peah	H	***Edge or side of the face*** *See Shete Peot*
פב"א Panim B A'hor	H	***Face to back*** Initials
פב"פ Panin B Panim	H	***Face to Face*** Initials
פה Peh	H	***Mouth*** *See Orot HaPeh*
פה פנוי Peh Panuy	H	***Free mouth*** *Peh Panuy* is the twelfth *Tikun* (action) of the *Dikna* (beard) of *Arikh Anpin,* it corresponds to the free mouth. There are hairs (lights) that come out from the face of *'Hokhma Stimaah* of *Arikh Anpin,* and spread downward. They divide in thirteen, and are called the thirteen *Tikunim* of the *Dikna* of *Arikh Anpin.* **אל רחום ..** **מי אל כמוך . . נושא עון...** Each one of these *Tikunim* has its particular function or action for the general guidance. The *Dikna* reveals the guidance of kindness, rigor and mercy, which was concealed in *'Hokhma Stimaah,* by bringing it down to *Z"A* through the two *Mazalot; Notser* and *Nake,* which are the eighth and thirteenth *Tikun.*

Hebrew / Aramaic Phonetic	L	Dictionary
פנוי *Panuy*	H	***Vacant*** See 'Hallal
פנים *Panim*	H	***Face or Front*** Closeness or readiness.

פנים H ***Face to back***
באחור
Panim B
A'hor

There is a notion of closeness and interaction, depending on whether the *Partsufim* (configurations) face or turn their back to each other. The three possibilities are: face to face, face to back, or back to back.

Face to back denotes a readiness to get close from one side only. It is a position of waiting or longing for the face to face, which is the ideal situation.

The guidance of the world is dependent on the different positioning and interaction of these masculine and feminine *Partsufim*, since they have a direct effect on the measure and balance of the factors of kindness, rigor and mercy.

פנים H ***Face to Face***
בפנים
Panin B
Panim

There is a notion of closeness and interaction, depending on whether the *Partsufim* (configurations) face or turn their back to each other. The three possibilities are: face to face, face to back, or back to back.

Face to face is the ideal level and corresponds to the bestowing of abundance.

Hebrew / Aramaic *Phonetic*	L	Dictionary

When the *Partsuf Nukvah* is ready for the *Zivug* (union), she comes face to face with the masculine; this is the ideal positioning for the *Zivug*.

The guidance of the world is dependent on the different positioning and interaction, of these masculine and feminine *Partsufim*, since they have a direct effect on the measure and balance of the factors of kindness, rigor and mercy.

פנימי H **Inner – Internal**

Pnimi

There are interior aspects, and exterior aspects. All the lights subdivide among themselves in interiority and exteriority aspects. Depending on the context, the exterior or the interior aspect could be superior.

For man, the *Neshama* is the interiority, and the body exteriority.

For the worlds, the interior aspect is superior to the exterior. The *Kav* is interiority and the *Reshimu* exteriority. The exterior aspects of a world are the *NHY* (*Netsa'h, Hod, Yesod*), the interior are the *HGT* ('*Hesed, Gevurah, Tiferet*) and *HBD* ('*Hokhma, Binah, Da'at*). The three superior worlds of *Atsilut, Beriah* and *Yetsirah,* are interior to the fourth world of '*Asiah*.

For the *Mo'hin* of the *Partsufim,* the exterior aspect which are the *HGT* and *HBD,* are superior. The interior aspects are the *NHY.*

See Or Pnimi, Keli Pnimi, Partsuf

Hebrew / Aramaic *Phonetic*	L	Dictionary
פנימיות *Pnimiut*	H	**Internality** What is inside or interior. Also applies to deeper meaning or spirituality. *See Pnimi, Or Pnimi, Keli Pnimi, Partsuf*
פסול *Pasul*	H	**Disqualified** State of distance from the *Kedushah* and closeness to the *Sitra A'hra* (negative force).
פסולים *Pesulim*	H	**Disqualified** *See Pasul*
פעולה *Pe'ulah*	H	**Action** The Kabbalah teaches us that the world is guided by an extremely complex system of forces or lights. By their actions or interactions, are provoked chain reactions that impact directly on man and the worlds. Each one of these actions has numerous ramifications, with many details and results.
פעולות *Pe'ulot*	H	**Actions** *See Pe'ulah*
פקיחו דעינין *Peki'hu De'inin*	A	***Sixth of the seven Tikunim of the head of Arikh Anpin*** From the *Partsuf (configuration) Arikh Anpin*, there are emanations that come out from its head to act and influence on the guidance; called the *Tikunim* of *Arikh Anpin*. The second *Tikun* (action) of *Arikh Anpin* is achieved by the passing of the seven lower *Sephirot* of *'Atik*

Hebrew / Aramaic *Phonetic*	L	Dictionary

into its head before they are clothed in him. These seven *Tikunim* of the head of *Arikh Anpin* are revealed from the seven lower *Sephirot* of *'Atik*

The sixth *Tikun* - פקיחו דעינין (*Peki'hu De'inin*) is realized by the parts of *Netsa'h* and *Hod* which are positioned lower than *Yesod*. This *Tikun* is achieved by the eyes, there, the *'Hasadim* are multiplied and always open so as to influence constantly.

פרגוד H **Curtain**

Pargod

A curtain denotes a limit, a difference of level, or a separation of lights.

When the vowels (emanations) of the aspect of the name of *SaG* (63) were ready to come out from *Partsuf Adam Kadmon*, *SaG* assembled his own *MaH* (45) and *BaN* (52), and the general *MaH* and *BaN* with them, from the navel and up. It then spread there a curtain (as a limit), starting in the front at the level of his chest, and extending down to his rear until the level of his navel.

After the spreading of the lights and the unfolding of the worlds, the lights of *Malkhut* collided at the bottom of the world of *Atsilut*. A curtain was made between *Atsilut* and *Beriah* by the striking of these lights. From there, other *Partsufim* similar to the ones in *Atsilut* were formed in the lower worlds, but of a lower force since the lights were dimmed by the divider.

Hebrew / Aramaic Phonetic	L	Dictionary
		The curtain at the bottom of *Atsilut* is made from the lights of *Imah,* the lights of *Atsilut* pass through it and make *Beriah.* Thus, *Beriah* is of the aspect of *Imah.*
		From *Beriah* to *Yetsirah* there are two curtains: a curtain from *Imah* to *Z"uN,* and a curtain from *Z"A* to *Nukvah.* Thus, *Yetsirah* is from the aspect of *Z"A.*
		From *Yetsirah* to *'Asiah;* one curtain on two curtains: one curtain from *Imah* to *Z"uN,* one curtain from *Z"A* to *Nukvah* and one curtain from *Nukvah* to the world under her. Thus, *'Asiah* is of from the aspect of *Nukvah.*
פרישות *Prishut*	H	***Separation*** After the *Zivug* there is a state of separation before the next *Zivug.* See Zivug
פרסא *Parsa*	A	***Curtain*** See Pargod
פרצוף *Partsuf*	H	***Configuration - Countenance*** The light of G-od is unique and of equal force and quality. A *Sephira* is in a way a "filter" which transforms this light in a particular force or attribute, by which the Creator guides the worlds. A *Partsuf* is a configuration of one or more *Sephirot* acting in coordination. Some *Partsufim* are masculine and bestow kindness, others are feminine and bestow rigor. The masculine corresponds to *'Hesed* and *MaH (45),* the feminine to

Hebrew / Aramaic Phonetic	L	Dictionary

Gevurah and *BaN* *(52)*. By their union, different equilibriums of these two forces (Kindness and rigor), make the guidance. Complete rigor will be the destruction of anything not perfect, while complete kindness will permit everything without restriction. However, these two aspects are necessary for the guidance of justice, and to give man the possibility of free choice

For the guidance, the *Tikunim* of the *Partsufim* are the actions, illuminations and inter-relations of the *Partsufim* and their influence on the worlds. These *Tikunim* result in various illuminations of different intensities, depending on time and the actions of man.

The construction of a *Partsuf* is achieved by way of *Zivug* (union), gestation and birth. During the *Zivug*, the lights of *MaH* *(45)* needed for the *Tikun* are drawn to the lights of *BaN* *(52)*, and are kept in the upper *Nukvah*. During the gestation, inside of *Nukvah*, they are arranged and completed until there is nothing more to add. When it is totally repaired, the *Partsuf* is revealed, and this is the birth. There is afterwards the suckling, and finally the growth so that the *Partsuf* will be fully independent

For the abundance to come down to the world, *Partsuf Zeir Anpin* needs to unite with *Nukvah*. There can be abundance only when the masculine and the feminine are in harmony. The guidance of the world is dependent on the different positioning and interaction of the masculine and feminine *Partsufim*, since they have a direct effect on the measure and balance of the factors of kindness, rigor and mercy.

The *Partsufim* of *Zeir Anpin* and *Nukvah* are the root of all the created. It is by their *Tikunim* that the guidance of justice is manifested. Each day, according to the actions of man, the *Tefilot* during the week, *Shabbat* or *Holidays*, and depending on time, various configurations allow different *Zivugim* (unions) of *Partsufim*, and therefore outflows of abundance of variable intensities.

There are five main *Partsufim:*

- *Arikh Anpin*
- *Abah*
- *Imah*
- *Zeir Anpin*
- *Nukvah*

And one on top of them: *'Atik Yomin* (clothed inside *Arikh Anpin*).

From these five *Partsufim;* emerge seven more. They all emanate from the ten *Sephirot* as follows:

From *Keter:*

- ***'Atik Yomin*** and his ***Nukvah***
- ***Arikh Anpin*** and his ***Nukvah***

Hebrew / Aramaic *Phonetic*	L	Dictionary

From *'Hokhma*:
- ***Abah***
- From *Malkhut* of *Abah* - ***Israel Saba***
- From *Malkhut* of *Israel Saba* - ***Israel Saba* 2**

From *Binah*:
- ***Imah***
- From *Malkhut* of *Binah* -***Tevunah***
- From *Malkhut* of *Tevunah* - ***Tevunah* 2**

Israel Saba and *Tevunah* are also called by their initials *ISOT* or *ISOT* 2.

From *'Hesed, Gevurah, Tiferet, Netsa'h, Hod,* and *Yesod*:
- ***Zeir Anpin*** also called ***Israel***

From *Zeir Anpin* - ***Ya'acov***

From *Malkhut*:
- ***Nukvah***, divided in two *Partsufim*: ***Ra'hel* and *Leah***

פרצופים *Partsufim*	H	***Configurations*** *See Partsuf*
פרקין *Prakin*	A	***Parts*** Some *Sephirot* have three parts, while others have two. These different parts have their own interactions and illuminations. *See Mo'hin*

Hebrew / Aramaic *Phonetic*	L	Dictionary
פשוט *Pashut*	H	**Simple**

Simple

Before the creation, G-od's light or energy is called "simple light". Simple; because absolutely perfect, with no distinctions, measures or qualities.

At first, the Creator was alone, occupying all space with His light. His light without end or variations, filled everything. If we think about differentiations, we introduce a notion of limit, or absence of its opposite. Being ourselves distinct separate beings, we cannot grasp the concept of the "non-distinct", everything we know is finite by having a measure or an opposite. However, since the concept of limitlessness is beyond our human comprehension, we therefore have to use terms accessible to our understanding.

In Kabbalah the term 'quality' is used, to differentiate the various transformations of this "simple light", and to help us understand its effects upon the guidance of the worlds. *See Partsuf, Zivug*

פתח *Pata'h* — H — Pata'h – Vowel A

The vowel that represents the *Sephira 'Hokhma.*

פתח *Peta'h* — H — Opening – Entrance

Entrance to a dimension. Possibility of permissibility, or understanding.

Hebrew / Aramaic Phonetic	L	Dictionary
צבאות Tsevaot	H	**Troops - Army** Army of angels. One of the Names of G-od in combination with other names.
צדיק Tsadik	H	**Righteous** State of outmost closeness to the *Kedushah* and distance from the *Sitra A'hra (negative force)*. Also attributed to the *Sephira Yesod*. See Tsadikim
צדיקים Tsadikim	H	**Righteous** The *Neshamot* of the ten *Tsadikim* that were killed by the Romans, have the power during the *Tefilot* (prayers) to elevate *Mayin Nukvin* (feminine waters) of the aspect of *BaN (52)*, which then provokes the descent of the *Mayin Dukhrin* (masculine waters) of the aspect of *MaH (45))*. This is essential for the preparation of the *Zivug* (union) of the *Partsufim* (configurations) during the *Tefilah*. See Tefilah, Kavanah
צו"ר ט"ק Tsu'r T'K		**Tsu'r T'K** There is a special force called *"Tsu'r T'K"*, that has the power to create separate entities from nothing. This force is not related to the *Sephirot*. It was first explained is the *"Sepher HaYetsrira"*, (Book of Formation) which is one of the first Kabbalistic writing. It is only after being created that the guidance is taken over by the *Sephirot*.
צומח Tsomea'h	H	**Vegetal** In parallel to the four worlds of *Atsilut, Beriah, Yetsirah* and *'Asiah,* there are four types of existence

Hebrew / Aramaic Phonetic	L	Dictionary
		in our world: mineral (דומם), vegetal (צומח), animal (חי), and the speaking (מדבר).. Mineral corresponding to 'Asiah, vegetal corresponding to Yetsirah, animal corresponding to Beriah, and the speaking corresponding to Atsilut.
צורה Tsurah	H	**Form** Shape or identification.
ציון Tsion	H	**Zion** The land of Israel, the closest place to G-od's emanations.
צינור Tsinor	H	**Conduit** A Sephira is in a way a "conduit" which transforms the light in a particular force or quality, by which the Creator guides the worlds.
צינורות Tsinorot	H	**Conduits** See Tsinor
ציצית Tsitsit	H	**Fringe** The Tsitsit correspond to Partsuf (configuration) Ra'hel. When Partsuf Z"A is in the growth stage, the NHY (Netsa'h, Hod, Yesod) of Imah come down on his back, this makes his hair (lights) come out from his head, and go downward until his chest. When they are at the level of his thorax; it corresponds to the Talit, when they are at the level of Ra'hel; it corresponds to the Tsitsit. See Talit

Hebrew / Aramaic Phonetic	L	Dictionary

‎ציר H **Axis**
Tsir

Two Vav and one Yud that make the Keli (recipient).

The construction of a *Partsuf* is done by the twenty two letters. For the construction of *Nukvah,* twenty two letters are given to her by *Z"A,* once they build her, they end in her *Yesod* and make a *Keli.* The five ending letters: ‎מנצפך, are her five *Gevurot* (rigors), and also contain the *Mayin Nukvin* (feminine waters). After the *Nesirah* (separation), when *Partsuf Abah* and *Imah* have built her, they also give her twenty two letters, ‎מנצפך and *Mayin Nukvin.*

The twenty two letters given by *Z"A* make an axis in a shape of two letters *Vav* (‎ו) and one *Yud* (‎י); as a letter *Dalet* (‎ד), and likewise from *Abah* and *Imah.* The two *Dalet* (‎ד) complement each other and make a final letter *Mem* (‎ם), which has a shape of a *Keli.* (*Gematria* of the three letters = 22). With this in place, *Z"uN* are now ready for the guidance of the world.

‎צירי H **Tsere – Vowel E**
Tsere

The vowel that represents the *Sephira Binah*

‎צירים H **Axis**
Tsirim

See Tsir

‎צל"ם H **Mo'hin (brains) of Z"A**
Tselem

The *Tselem* are the *Mo'hin* (brains) given to *Z"A* by the *Zivug* (union) of *Partsuf Abah* and *Imah.*

There are two distinct *Mo'hin* that come to *Z"A, Mo'hin* of *Imah* that arrive first, and then the *Mo'hin* of *Abah.*

Hebrew / Aramaic Phonetic	L	Dictionary

Depending on the state of growth of *Z"A,* they are from *Partsuf ISOT,* or directly from *Abah* and *Imah.* A first part; *NHY (Netsa'h, Hod, Yesod)* of the *Mo'hin* enter inside the *Partsuf,* while the other two parts *HGT (*'Hesed, Gevurah, Tiferet)* and *KHBD (Keter, 'Hokhma, Binah, Da'at)* encircle him on the outside.

The *NHY* of the superior *Partsuf* which are composed of nine parts, corresponding to the צ, spread in the nine *Sephirot* of *Z"A.* The encircling are מ ל, they do not need to spread in him, and stand on his exterior in the three-column arrangement of kindness, rigor and mercy.

During the gestation, the *Mo'hin* are of the lowest level and are called *NHY* of the *Mo'hin;* they are of the aspect of *Nefesh.*

During the suckling, the lights grow and the *Mo'hin* are of a higher level and are called *HGT* of the *Mo'hin;* they are of the aspect of *Rua'h.*

During the growth, the *Mo'hin* are fully developed to guide *Z"uN* with the force of *HBD ,* they are of the aspect of *Neshama.*

There are two gestations and two growths for *Partsuf Z"A.* The first *Mo'hin* of the first growth are from *Partsuf Tevunah,* and of the second growth, from *Partsuf Imah.* It is only after the second growth, that *Z"A* has reached its full potential. This is *Gadlut* 2.

See *Partsuf Z"A, Mo'hin, Gadlut*

Hebrew / Aramaic Phonetic	L	Dictionary

צלע H **Rib**
Tsela'

Representation of the *Partsuf Nukvah* in *Bereshit.*
The rib taken from *Adam HaRishon*, is a description of the *Nesirah* (separation), when the *Nukvah* separates from *Z"A* to become an independent *Partsuf.* See Nesirah

צמצום H ***Contraction - Retraction***
Tsimtsum

In the beginning, there was no existence except His presence, the Creator was alone, occupying all space with His light. His light without end, borders or limit filled everything. He was not bestowing his influence, because there was no one to receive it. When He willed to create, He started to influence. His light being of such holiness and intensity, it is not possible for any being to exist in its proximity.

The "*Tsimtsum*" is the first act of the *Ein Sof* (Infinite) in the creation. It is the retraction of His light from a certain space and encircling it, so as to reduce its intensity and allow created beings to exist. After this contraction, a ray of His light entered this empty space and formed the first *Sephirot.*

By these boundaries, He revealed the concepts of rigor and limit, needed by the created beings, and gave a space for all the created to exist. This round

Hebrew / Aramaic Phonetic	L	Dictionary
		space is called "*Hallal*", and contains all possibilities of existence for separated entities, given that they are distanced from the intensity of His light. *See Kav, Rechimu, Adam Kakmon, Sephira*
צפורני רגליים *Tsipornei Raglayim*	H	**Toe nails** From inside of *Adam Kadmon*, lights of the aspect of the name *BaN (52)* descended, cleaved out at the level of the lights of the eyes that went down, and shone outwards through the skin of *Adam Kadmon*. From the navel and the *Yesod* of *Adam Kadmon* the light divided to *Keter*, *'Hokhma* and *Binah*, the remaining seven lower *Sephirot* received from the lights of the toes of *Adam Kadmon*.

Hebrew / Aramaic Phonetic	L	Dictionary

קבועים H **Fixed – Unchanging**
Kvu'im
Emanations or lights not affected by man or time.

קבלה H **Kabbalah**
Kabbalah
The Kabbalah is the mystical and esoteric explanation of the Torah. It teaches the unfolding of the worlds, the various ways of guidance of these worlds, the role of man in the creation, the will of the Creator and so on. No other writings explain in details, the creation of this world and the ones above it, the lights or energies that influence its guidance, nor the final goal of everything. These writings are based on ancient Jewish texts and mostly on the *Zohar*.

The word Kabbalah comes from the verb Lekabel (to receive), but to receive it is first necessary to want, and to become a *Keli* (recipient) able to receive and contain this knowledge.

The Kabbalah, explains to us the true guidance of the world, so that we may understand the will of G-od. How, and why He created the world, in what way He governs it, the provenance of the souls and angels, the purpose of the existence of evil, the reasons for the dualism of reward and punishment, etc.

The Kabbalah teaches us that the world is guided by an extremely complex system of forces or lights, which through their interactions, provoke chain reactions that impact directly on man and the worlds. Each one of these reactions has numerous ramifications, with many details and results.

279

Hebrew / Aramaic Phonetic	L	Dictionary
		A true understanding of the will of the Creator is possible through the knowledge of Kabbalah, which teaches us the profound secrets of our holy *Torah*, and what we are allowed to know of G-od: His will, how He guides the world, and how we can participate and influence this guidance.
		The Kabbalah also demonstrates to us the importance of man, because only he, by getting closer to the Creator, can influence these incredible forces
קבלה מעשית Kabbalah Ma'asit	H	***Practical Kabbalah***
		The "other" type of Kabbalah, where names or combinations of names of angels are used with special signs or incantations, sometimes written on parchment, to invoke particular powers and alterate normal states of events. *See Kmi'a*
קדוש Kadosh	H	***Holly – Saintly***
		State of closeness to the *Kedushah* and distance from the *Sitra A'hra* (negative force). *See Kedushah*
קדוש ברוך הוא Kadosh Barukh Hu	H	***Saintly and Blessed He is***
		One of the names of G-od.
		The light of the *Ein Sof* (infinite) which is revealed by the *Partsuf* (configuration) *Zeir Anpin*.
קדושה Kedushah	H	***Sanctity – Holiness***
		The *Sephirot* have their root in the *Kedushah* of the *Ein Sof*, B'H.

Hebrew / Aramaic Phonetic	L	Dictionary

The root of the *Sitra A'hra* (negative force) is in the lack, or absence of the *Kedushah*. Its existence was willed by the Creator to give man free will. It creates *Klipot* (husks) that attach to the exteriority of the *Sephirot*, nourish from their lights, and gain more power to act negatively

By accomplishing the *Mitsvot* and the *Tefilot* (prayers), men do the *Tikunim* (rectifications) necessary to detach these *Klipot* from the *Kedushah*.

The ultimate goal is to create a maximum distance from the *Sitra A'hra* (negative force), and closeness to the *Kedushah*.

קדיש H *Kadish*

Kadish

During the *Tefilot*, when one knows the system of ascension of the *Hekhalot* (portals), he concentrates on the words or the names where are hinted the precise action of the *Hekhal* (portal). He aims to help in the realization of the particular *Zivug* (union) of the *Tefilah*.

The *Hekhalot* are also the different levels of ascension of the four world of *ABYA* before reaching the *'Olam Atsilut* during the *Amidah*.

To get from one world to the next a secret name called *MaV* (42) hinted during the *Kadish*, makes this ascension possible.

This secret name of 42 letters is made with the four letters of the name י-ה-ו-ה, the *Miluy* (spelling) of each one of the four letters for a total of ten letters, and the

Hebrew / Aramaic Phonetic	L	Dictionary

Miluy of each one of theses ten letters for a total of twenty eight. This name is hinted when we answer *Yehe Sheme* ..... until - *Be'alma.* The *Kadish* makes possible the ascent of each world to the next higher world, and the descent afterwards from the world of *Atsilut* to *'Asiah.* See Kavanah, Tefilah

קדש H **Holy of Holies**
קדשים
Kodesh
Kodashim

Attribute given to *Partsuf Arikh Anpin* of *Atsilut.*

קדש H ***Kodesh Kodashim***
קדשים
Kodesh
Kodashim

Name of a *Hekhal* (portal).

Seventh of seven *Hekhalot,* corresponding to *Keter, 'Hokhma* and *Binah.*

Each world *(ABYA)* is built from four aspects: *Partsuf, Levush* (garment), *Or Makif* (encircling lights), and *Hekhalot.* In each *Partsuf,* there are interiority and exteriority, the exteriority is always of the aspect of *Malkhut,* and the *Hekhalot* are the ramifications of the *Malkhuts* of the *Partsufim.*

The *Hekhalot* are also the different levels of ascension of the *Tefilot* before reaching the seventh *Hekhal* (portal), *Kodesh HaKodashim.*

Their principal function is to allow the adhesion and attachment, in various and particular ways during the *Tefilot,* until the *'Olam Atsilut* (during the *'Amidah*)

The *Neshamot* and the angels have their root in the *Hekhalot,* each one depending on its respective level.

Hebrew / Aramaic Phonetic	L	Dictionary

קו   H   *Ray – Line*

Kav   After the *Tsimtsum*, a straight ray of light called *"Kav"*, emerged from the *Ein Sof* (infinite) and entered on one side of the *"'Hallal"* (vacant space), where there were still a *Reshimu* (imprint) of the original light. The combination of the *Kav* and the *Reshimu* is what will give existence to the *Sephirot* with which He governs the worlds.

After entering the *'Hallal,* the *Kav* made ten circles encircling one another, but still maintaining a straight shape. These ten circles are called *Sephirot Ha'Igulim* (encircling *Sephirot*). They are in charge of the general guidance of the worlds, and are not influenced by the actions of men.

From the *Kav*, another ten *Sephirot* were formed, but this time in a linear arrangement, and later in three columns: right, left and middle, representing the guidance of the world in the manner of *'Hesed, Din* and *Ra'hamim* (Kindness, rigor and mercy). This guidance is dependent on time, and the actions of men.

The first configuration, by which the emanated light was formed into ten *Sephirot*, is called *Adam Kadmon* (Primordial Man). It is the union between the *Kav* and the *Reshimu*, and from this first configuration, all the worlds came forth into existence.

The *Kav* is the innermost interiority of all this creation.

Hebrew / Aramaic Phonetic	L	Dictionary
קובוץ *Kubutz*	H	**Kubutz - Vowel U** The vowel that represents the *Sephira Hod*.
קודשא בריך הוא *Kudsha Berikh Hu*	A	**Saintly and Blessed He is** *See Kadosh Barukh Hu*
קול *Kol*	H	**Voice** When saying a blessing with the Kabbalistic meditation on the appropriate words or names, we act and participate directly on the *Tikun* (rectification) of the action or thing being blessed. *See Kavanah, Kadish*
קוץ של יוד *Kots shel Yud*	H	**Extremity of the letter Yud** Superior extremity of the letter Yud of the *Tetragamon*, which represents the *Sephira Keter* or the *Partsuf Arikh Anpin*.
קורדובירו *Kordovero*		**Rabbi Moshe Kordovero** Born in 1522, died in Tsfat in 1570. He was the founder of the Kabbalah academy in Tsfat, one of his best known student was Rabbi 'Haim Vital. He foresaw the coming of the teachings of the Ari Z'al and admitted in advance their truthfulness. Some of his main works are "Tomer Deborah", "Pardes Rimonim"
קטורת *Ketoret*	H	**Incense** During the *Tefilah*, by naming the eleven types of incenses used in the Temple, the *Klipot* are put aside to allow the process of ascension of the worlds.

Hebrew / Aramaic *Phonetic*	L	Dictionary

קטן H **Katan**

Katan

One of the seven main types of *Gematriot.*

Tens and hundreds are reduced to one digit.

From	To	Value
א	ט	1 - 9
י	צ	1 - 9
ק	ת	1 - 4
ך	ץ	5 -9

Ex : הארץ = 17

See Gematria

קטנות H **Smallness – Infancy**

Katnut

Inside of *Imah, Partsuf Z"A* goes through a period of gestation, followed by a first and a second period of infancy.

See Mo'hin of Katnut, Katnut rishon shel Z"A, Katnut sheni shel Z"A

קטנות H **First infancy of Partsuf Z"A**

ראשון של

ז"א

Katnut rishon shel Z"A

At first *Partsuf Z"A* is in a state of *Dormita* (somnolence), to act, it needs to get its *Mo'hin* (brains) from *Partsuf ISOT* or *Abah* and *Imah*, and to get to a stage of growth.

Inside of *Imah, Partsuf Z"A* goes through a period of gestation, followed by a first period of infancy. Following this first infancy, *Z"A* will receive his *Mo'hin* from *NHY (Netsa'h, Hod, Yesod)* of *ISOT.*

285

Hebrew / Aramaic Phonetic	L	Dictionary
קטנות שני של ז"א Katnut sheni shel Z"A	H	**Second infancy of Partsuf Z"A** After its first growth, there is for *Partsuf Z"A* a second period of infancy and a second of growth. Following its second gestation inside Imah, it is the second infancy and the second growth, and his *Mo'hin* are directly from *NHY (Netsa'h, Hod, Yesod)* of *Partsuf Abah* and *Imah*. During the time of the second infancy, *Z"A* is only starting to act as it is being built, and at the growth it is ready to act. It is only after the second growth, that *Z"A* has reached its full potential.
קיפול רגלים של אריך אנפין Kipul Reglaim shel Arikh Anpin	H	**Folding of the legs of Arikh Anpin** After the *Shvirat HaKelim* (breaking of the vessels), when the lights were separated from their *Kelim*, the first act of reparation for this damage was to reunite again these fallen lights and *Kelim*. To repair them *Partsuf Arikh Anpin* folded his legs *(NHY (Netsa'h, Hod, Yesod))* and drew them upwards. *Partsuf Arikh* brought up his three lower *Sephirot* – *NHY* (legs) and the lower third of his Tiferet, on to clothe his *HGT ('Hesed, Gevurah, Tiferet)*, this is called the folding of the legs; three *(NHY)* on three *(HGT)*. This folding made an attraction that drew the *Kelim* of *Z"A* upward on the *Sephirot* of *HGT* and *NHY* of *Arikh Anpin* that were folded on themselves in *Atsilut*. This folding of the legs of *Partsuf Arikh Anpin* was the first force given to the broken *Kelim* of the seven

Hebrew / Aramaic Phonetic	L	Dictionary

Sephirot to ascend to *Atsilut*.

After this first reparation in *Partsuf Arikh Anpin*, they were taken by *Partsuf Abah* and *Imah* which repaired them completely.

Partsuf Arikh Anpin is the root of all the *Partsufim*, and all the other *Partsufim* are attached to him.

קליטה H **Insemination – Reception**
Klitah

After the folding of the legs of *Partsuf Arikh Anpin* to reunite the seven *Sephirot* that broke, *Partsuf Abah* and *Imah* continued to repair them for three days. They are called the three days of *Klitah* (insemination).

The first day *Abah* repaired the *Sephirot* of the right side, the second day Imah repaired the left side, and on the third day they were joined (the right and the left side).

Each day sparks of the superior lights entered *Z'uN* (*Zeir Anpin* and *Nukvah*) to sustain them. These sparks are the *Miluyim* (spellings) of the name of *MaH* (45) less the total of the *Tetragamon* (26) which makes nineteen sparks. Three days were needed for these sparks of the *Miluyim* of *MaH* (45) to enter: six of the nineteen sparks entered on the first day, six on the second, and seven on the third. On the third day, one more because of the joining of the lights (of the right and left columns).

More *Miluyim* of sparks were needed for the complete reparation of *Partsuf Z"A:* the *Miluy* of *SaG* (63) which

Hebrew / Aramaic Phonetic	L	Dictionary
		is thirty seven (63 - 26), and the *Miluy* of "A"V (72) forty six (72 – 26).
קליפה Klipah	H	**Husk (negative force)** See Klipot
קליפה נוגה Klipah Nogah	H	**Husk – Glow** One of the four main levels of *Klipot.*
קליפות Klipot	H	**Husks (negative forces)** The *Klipot* are the manifestation of the negative force. They obstruct the lights of the *Sephirot,* and conceal man from his root and from the light. Because of the bad deeds of the lower beings, the *Klipot* get their strength and do evil in the world by attaching to the higher lights. The *Tikunim* (rectification) of the lower beings are to detach these *Klipot* from the *Kedushah* by accomplishing the *Mitsvot* and the *Tefilot.* When men act negatively, they cause a deterioration that reach the lower worlds and give strength to the *Klipot* to attach and nourish from the *Sephirot* of the higher worlds. There are four main levels of *Klipot:* - נגה - *(Nogah)* - Glow - ענן דול - *('Anan Gadol)* - A large cloud - אש מתלקחת - *(Eish Mitlaka'hat)* - A dividing fire - רוח סערה - *(Rua'h She'ara)* - A wind of storm.

Hebrew / Aramaic Phonetic	L	Dictionary
		They correspond to the four lower worlds, which also comprise of *Sephirot* and *Partsufim* as in the positive worlds. *See Sitra A'hra*
קלקול **Kilkul**	H	***Deterioration – Damage*** *Kilkul* is the opposite of *Tikun* (rectification). In the *Shvirat HaKelim* (breaking of the vessels), the *Kilkul* was caused by the disposition of the seven lower *Sephirot* in a straight line (one under the other), instead of the three-column arrangement, and when the inferior part of the three first *Sephirot* did not contain their lights. If these *Sephirot* had contained their lights, the seven lower *Sephirot* would not have broken and all the future notions of *Kilkul* and *Tikun* not existed. *See Shvirat HaKelim*
קמ"ג **KaMa"G**	H	***KM"G (143)*** *Miluy* (spelling) of the name א-ה-י-ה, with the letter א. אלף הא יוד הא . *See Miluy*
קמיע **Kmi'a**	H	***Amulet*** Names, or combinations of names of angels, with special signs or incantations, written on parchment to protect or to invoke particular powers.
קמץ **Kamatz**	H	***Kamatz – Vowel A*** The vowel that represents the *Sephira Keter*.

289

Hebrew / Aramaic Phonetic	L	Dictionary
קנ"א KaN"A	H	**KN"A (151)** *Miluy* (spelling) of the name ה-י-ה-א, with the letter ה אלף הה יוד הה
קס"א KaS"A	H	**KS"A (161)** *Miluy* (spelling) of the name ה-י-ה-א, with the letter י אלף הי יוד הי
קצוות Ktsavot	H	**Edges – Extremities** Edges could be of a *Partsuf* or a world. When the *'Hasadim* come down to group in *Yesod* of *Z"A*, they return upwards on their columns (*Netsa'h* and *Hod)*, until they ascend in all the six edges of *Z"A*.
קרדינותא Kardinuta	A	**Darkness** See *'Hoshekh*
קרומא דאוירא Kroma Deavirah	A	**Third of seven Tikunim of the head of Arikh Anpin** From the head of *Partsuf* (configuration) *Arikh Anpin*, seven emanations come out to act and influence on the guidance, called the *Tikunim* of *Arikh Anpin*. The second *Tikun* (action) of *Arikh Anpin* is achieved by the passing of the seven lower *Sephirot* of *'Atik* into its head before they are clothed in him. These seven *Tikunim* of the head of *Arikh Anpin* are revealed from the seven lower *Sephirot* of *'Atik*.

Hebrew / Aramaic *Phonetic*	L	Dictionary

The third *Tikun* - קרומא דאוירא *(Kroma Deavirah)* is realized by *Tiferet* of *'Atik;* it has two actions: to cover *'Hokhma Stimaah* (of *Arikh*), so that the illumination of *Da'at* of *'Atik* will not be too strong, and for its illumination (of *'Hokhma Stimaah*) when spreading down, not to be too overwhelming for the lower beings.

קשיות H **Hardness**
Kashiut
  See Kashin

קשין A **Hard**
Kashin
Some rigors are called "דינין קשין" *(Dinin Kashim)* – Hard rigors.

קשר **Attachment - Relation – Similitude**
Kesher
All the *Sephirot* and *Partsufim* have a certain degree of attachment between them.

Hebrew / Aramaic Phonetic	L	Dictionary

ראיה H **Seeing**
Reiya

From the lights that were invested inside of *Adam Kadmon* emerged numerous worlds in the way of his senses, which are called his branches.

These "branches" are the lights that spread forth from *Adam Kadmon* by way of its apertures in the head, four of which are called: sight, hearing, smell and speech. They spread out from his eyes, ears, nose, and mouth.

In the language of Kabbalah, we use names of body parts solely to illustrate the esoteric powers of these forces. It is understood, of course, that there is no physical existence at these level. When we say ears, mouth, or any other physical expression, the goal is to describe the inner sense, or the position they represent.

These emanations and configurations are drawn from the four letters of the Name of G-od. B'H, and their different spellings, which are called *Miluyim*.

The lights that came out from the eyes are of the feminine aspect of *BaN* (52), which caused the breaking of the vessels *(Shvirat HaKelim)*.

See Orot Ha'Enaim, Shvirat HaKelim

ראש H **Head**
Rosh The three first *Sephirot; Keter,'Hokhma,* and *Binah* are called the head of a Partsuf.

Hebrew / Aramaic Phonetic	L	Dictionary

ראשית H **Beginning – First**

Reshit "The beginning of wisdom is to awe (venerate) G-od."
(*Tehilim* 111, 10)

רגיל H **Ragil (regular)**

Ragil One of the seven main types of *Gematriot*. This one is considered as simple or regular *Gematria*, and is the most frequently used.

The numbers of the letters are as follows:

From	To	Value
א	ט	1 - 9
י	צ	10 -90
ק	ת	100 - 400
ך	ץ	500 -900

Ex : הארץ = 1106

See Gematria

רגלי אריך A **Legs of Arikh Anpin**
אנפין
Ragle Arikh   *See Kipul Reglaim shel Arikh Anpin*
Anpin

רגליים H **Legs**

Reglayim   *See Kipul Reglaim shel Arikh Anpin*

רגלין A **Legs**

Raglin   *See Kipul Reglaim shel Arikh Anpin*

רדל"א A **The Unknown Head**

Radl'a Initials of *"Reisha de lo Idtyada'"*. It is mostly called by its initials.

293

Hebrew / Aramaic Phonetic	L	Dictionary

Partsuf 'Atik Yomin is superior to all the *Partsufim* (configurations), it is realized by the *Malkhut* of *Adam Kadmon.* It has ten Sephirot, his front corresponding to his masculine aspect, and his back corresponding to his feminine aspect (his *Nukvah*). His masculine aspect is not clothed inside *Atsilut.*

In *Arikh Anpin,* are clothed the seven lower *Sephirot* of the *Nukvah* of *'Atik Yomin.* The first three *Sephirot* of *Nukvah* of *'Atik Yomin: Keter, 'Hokhma* and *Binah* did not dress inside *Arikh,* and remained on top of his head, they make the *Radl'a* – the unknown head; it is called this way because we can not grasp any understanding of it.

רוח   H   ***Soul - Second level of the soul***

Rua'h

The soul has five names: *Nefesh, Rua'h, Neshama, 'Hayah* and *Ye'hidah,* which correspond to its five levels. The soul is the spiritual entity inside the body, the latter being only his outer garment.

Since it is men that provoke the union of the four worlds, it is necessary for their souls to have their origin from them, and from the five *Partsufim* (configurations):

Soul / Level	Partsuf	World
Nefesh	Nukvah	'Asiah
Rua'h	Zeir Anpin	Yetsirah
Neshama	Imah	Beriah
'Hayah	Abah	Atsilut
Ye'hidah	Arikh Anpin	Atsilut

Hebrew / Aramaic *Phonetic*	L	Dictionary

Each level of the soul is subdivided in five levels. As for the level of *Nefesh;* there are *Nefesh* of *Nefesh, Rua'h* of *Nefesh, Neshama* of *Nefesh, 'Hayah* of *Nefesh* and *Ye'hidah* of *Nefesh.*

Each one of these levels of the soul subdivides for each level of *Partsuf* and for each world. Therefore, there are five levels of the souls for *Partsuf Nukvah* and there are five levels of *Partsufim* for the world of *'Asiah* etc. Also, as there are in each world ten *Sephirot,* each soul has its origin corresponding to one of them.

Therefore, a soul could be from the level of *Nefesh* of *Malkhut* of *Nukvah* of *'Asiah,* or *Rua'h* of *'Hesed* of *Abah* of *'Yetsirah,* or *Neshama* of *Abah* of *Z"A* of *Yetsirah* etc.

Rua'h is the second level and is acquired before the next levels.

The higher levels of the soul cannot be acquired at once. Most men only have the level of *Nefesh,* and if they merit, they will acquire the next levels - but one by one.

To reach the next higher level of his soul, man must do the *Tikun* of the preceding level. If he needs to acquire the level of *Imah* of *'Asiah,* he must first do the *Tikun* of *Malkhut* of *'Asiah* and *Z"A* of *'Asiah,* and so on. To acquire his level of *Neshama,* he must do the *Tikun* of all the levels of the *Sephirot* and *Partsufim* of his *Nefesh* and *Rua'h* etc.

Hebrew / Aramaic Phonetic	L	Dictionary
רוח סערה *Rua'h* *Se'arah*	H	**Rua'h Se'arah - A wind of storm** One of the four main levels of *Klipot* corresponding to the four lower worlds. *See Klipot*
רוחני *Ru'hani*	H	**Spiritual** The Torah contains four levels of comprehension, of which the highest is the *Sod* (secret). At this level, we understand that our *Tefilot* and the accomplishment of each one of the *Mitsvot,* has a direct influence on the superior worlds and on their guidance. A spiritual person will give importance to this higher meaning of things, and live in the path of rightness to strengthen himself constantly.
רוחניות *Ru'haniut*	H	**Spirituality** *See Ru'hani*
רושם *Roshem*	H	**Imprint –seal** *See Reshimu*
רזא *Secret*	A	**Raza** *See Sod*
רחבה של זקן *Re'hava shel Zakan*	A	**Width of the beard** *Re'hava shel Zakan* is the sixth *Tikun* (action) of the *Dikna* (beard) of *Arikh Anpin,* it corresponds to: The width of the beard. There are hairs (lights) that come out from the face of *'Hokhma Stimaah* of *Arikh Anpin,* and spread downward. They divide in thirteen, and are called the thirteen *Tikunim* of the *Dikna* of *Arikh Anpin.*

Hebrew / Aramaic Phonetic	L	Dictionary

אל רחום ..

מי אל כמוך. . נושא עון...

Each one of these *Tikunim* has its particular function or action for the general guidance.

The *Dikna* reveals the guidance of kindness, rigor and mercy, which was concealed in *'Hokhma Stimaah,* by bringing it down to *Z"A* through the two *Mazalot; Notser* and *Nake,* which are the eighth and thirteenth *Tikun.*

רחוק H *Distant – Far*

Ra'hok

Denotes a back to back position, or an important difference in power or level.

רחל H *Ra'hel - Partsuf Nukvah*

Ra'hel

The *Partsuf Nukvah,* which represents the feminine – the principle of receiving, comprises of two distinct *Partsufim* (configurations): *Ra'hel* and *Leah. Partsuf Ra'hel* is of the aspect of kindness, *Partsuf Leah* of the aspect of rigor.

Partsuf Ra'hel is under *Partsuf Leah* at the level of *NHY* of *Partsuf Z"A.*

All the abundance that comes down to the world, proceeds from the various *Zivugim* (unions) of *Z"uN* (*Z"A* and *Nukvah*).

There are five different *Zivugim:* Two with *Ra'hel* and three with *Leah.* The *Zivugim* with Ra'hel are of a higher level; being of the aspect of kindness, the ones with Leah are more of the aspect of rigor.

In the *Tefilah* of *Sha'hrit,* there is the *Zivug* of *Ya'acov*

297

Hebrew / Aramaic Phonetic	L	Dictionary
		and *Ra'hel*. In the *Tefilah* of *Musaf Shabbat*, there is the *Zivug* of *Z"A* and *Ra'hel*. See *Malkhut, Nukvah, Zivug, Kavanah*
רחמים *Ra'hamim*	H	**Mercy** From the *Kav* (ray) ten Sephirot were formed in a linear arrangement, and later in three columns: right, left and middle, representing the guidance of the world in the manner of *'Hesed, Din* and *Ra'hamim* (Kindness, rigor and mercy). This guidance is dependent on time, and the actions of men. The *Ra'hamim* (mercy) column is in the middle and is composed of the *Sephirot Keter, Tiferet, Yesod, Malkhut*. Complete rigor will be the destruction of anything not perfect, while complete kindness will permit everything without restriction. *Ra'hamim* makes the balance and equilibrium between the kindness and rigor columns for a possible existence.
ריח *Reya'h*	H	**Smelling** From the lights that were invested inside of *Adam Kadmon* emerged numerous worlds in the way of his senses; which are called his branches. These "branches" are the lights that spread forth from *Adam Kadmon*, by way of its apertures in the head, four of which are called: Sight, hearing, smell and speech. They spread out from his eyes, ears, nose, and mouth. In the language of Kabbalah, we use names of body

Hebrew / Aramaic Phonetic	L	Dictionary
		parts solely to illustrate the esoteric powers of these forces. It is understood, of course, that there is no physical existence at these level. When we say ears, mouth, or any other physical expression, the goal is to describe the inner sense, or the position they represent.
		These emanations and configurations are drawn from the four letters of the Name of G-od B'H, and their different spellings, which are called *Miluyim*.
		From the nose, came out lights of the aspect of *SaG* (middle Ta'amim). *See Orot Ha'Hotem*
רישא *Reisha*	A	***Head*** *See Rosh*
רישא דלא אתידע *Reisha de lo Idtyada'*	A	***The Unknown Head*** *See Radl"a*
רמ"ק *RAMA"K*		***Ramak*** Initials of Rabbi Moshe Kordovero *See Rabbi Moshe Kordovero*
רמח"ל *Ram'hal*	H	***Ram'hal*** Initials of Rabbi Moshe 'Haim Luzzatto *See Rabbi Moshe 'Haim Luzzatto*
רע *Ra'*	H	***Evil – Bad*** *See Sitra A'hra*

299

Hebrew / Aramaic Phonetic	L	Dictionary
רעוא *Ra'ava*	A	***Desire – Will*** See Ratson
רעוא דמצחא *Ra'ava Demits'ha*	A	***Fourth of the seven Tikunim of the head of Arikh Anpin*** From the head of *Partsuf* (configuration) *Arikh Anpin*, seven emanations come out to act and influence on the guidance, called the *Tikunim* of *Arikh Anpin*. The second *Tikun* (action) of *Arikh Anpin* is achieved by the passing of the seven lower *Sephirot* of *'Atik* into its head before they are clothed in him. These seven *Tikunim* of the head of *Arikh Anpin* are revealed from the seven lower *Sephirot* of *'Atik* The fourth *Tikun* - רעוא דמצחא *(Ra'ava Demits'ha)* is realized by *Yesod* of *'Atik;* his *'Hasadim* shine from the forehead of *Arikh Anpin*. When it is fully revealed, all the rigors are annulled.
רפ"ח *Rapa'h*	H	***288 (numeric value)*** See Nitsutsot
רפ"ח נצוצות *Rapa'h Nitsutsot*	H	***288 sparks*** See Nitsutsot
רצון *Ratson*	H	***Will – Desire*** All the Kabbalists agree to say that it is not possible to understand, or to have the slightest notion of the Nature of G-od, since our comprehension cannot attain that level. However, we can learn to understand

Hebrew / Aramaic Phonetic	L	Dictionary

His will, how and why He created the world, in what way He directs it, the provenance of the souls and angels, the purpose of the existence of evil, the reasons for the dualism of reward and punishment, etc.

At first, the Creator was alone, occupying all space with His light. He was not bestowing His influence, because there was no one to receive it. When He willed to create, He started to influence. The Kabbalah is the only science that, in the least details, explains to us the true guidance of the world, so that we may understand His will.

The will of the Creator is to bestow goodness on His creatures, all the levels of creation were put in place so His kindness could emanate to them, yet in such a way that they would be able to receive it. While man by his nature, is himself a *Keli* (recipient) with a will to receive without limits. It is by understanding His will, that we realize the importance of man, because only he, by getting closer to the Creator and observing His commandments, can influence these incredible forces that impact directly on the guidance of the worlds. Desire has also to be present for the *Tikun* of the *Partsufim,* the feminine has to stimulate a reaction from the masculine. This stimulation happens when the *Nukvah* brings up her *Mayin Nukvin* (feminine waters) of the aspect of *BaN* (52), which then provoke the descent of the *Mayin Dukhrin* (masculine waters) of the aspect of *MaH* (45)).

Hebrew / Aramaic *Phonetic*	L	Dictionary
רצון *Ratson*	H	**Ratson** Name of a *Hekhal* (portal). Sixth of seven *Hekhalot*, corresponding to *Tiferet*. Each world *(ABYA)* is built from four aspects: *Partsuf*, *Levush* (garment), *Or Makif* (encircling lights), and *Hekhalot*. In each *Partsuf*, there are interiority and exteriority, the exteriority is always of the aspect of *Malkhut*, and the *Hekhalot* are the ramifications of the *Malkhuts* of the *Partsufim*. The *Hekhalot* are also the different levels of ascension of the *Tefilot* before reaching the seventh *Hekhal* (portal), *Kodesh Hakodashim*. Their principal function is to allow the adhesion and attachment, in various and particular ways during the *Tefilot*, until the *'Olam Atsilut* (during the *'Amidah*) The *Neshamot* and the angels have their root in the *Hekhalot*, each one depending on its respective level. *See Hekhalot*
רצון להשפיע *Ratson* *Lehashpia'*	H	**Will to bestow** The will of the Creator is to bestow goodness on His creatures, all the levels of creation were put in place so His kindness could emanate to them, yet in such a way that they would be able to receive it. From the *Kav* (ray) ten *Sephirot* were formed in a linear arrangement, and later in three columns: right, left and middle, representing the guidance of the world in the manner of *'Hesed*, Din and *Ra'hamim*

Hebrew / Aramaic Phonetic	L	Dictionary

(Kindness, rigor and mercy). This guidance is dependent on time, and the actions of men.

There is no existence that is not composed of the aspects of *MaH* (45) or *BaN* (52): The influencer and the receiver, the masculine and the feminine etc. The *Ein Sof*, B'H influences when there is instigation from the receiver, the latter corresponding to the aspect of *BaN* (52). This influence is transmitted by different illuminations of the aspect of *MaH* (45), and then by *Nukvah* after her *Zivug* (union) with *Partsuf Z"A*, to the worlds.

Different equilibriums of the two forces of kindness and rigor make the guidance. Complete rigor will be the destruction of anything not perfect, while complete kindness will permit everything without restriction. Thus we see that everything that is, and happens, is always composed of a variable measure and balance of these two forces.

These complex possibilities have only one purpose: To allow man to merit by his own efforts to get closer to his Creator and receive his goodness.

See Sephirot, Tefilah, Zivug

רצון לקבל H ***Desire to receive***
Ratson Lekabel
By his nature man is himself a *Keli* (recipient) with a will to receive without limits, and containing a spiritual light; his soul. A guidance based on this desire will permit anything without restriction, and not allow man

Hebrew / Aramaic Phonetic	L	Dictionary

to merit by his own efforts to get closer to his Creator. The perfect goal for man is to elevate his bodily desires by sanctifying his ways, and resemble his Creator, by becoming a giver with a will to bestow goodness to all.

רקיע
Raki'a

H **Heavens – Firmament**

It is of the aspect of *Yesod* of *Tevunah*.

רש"ש
Rashash

Rashash

Initials of Rabbi Shalom Sharabi

See Kavanot, Rabbi Shalom Sharabi

רשות
Reshut

H **Authority – Domain**

There is a "second" authority called *Sitra A'hra* or "evil". Even if it is the opposite of everything good, it is important to understand that the origin of "evil" is from an emanation of the superior lights and thus, it does not really have a complete independent authority. It nourishes itself from the lower extremities of the *Kedushah*, and needs permission to act, from above.

There is really only one unique authority, and it is the one of the Creator.

See Sitra A'hra

רשותא
Reshuta

A **Authority – Domain**

See Reshut

Hebrew / Aramaic Phonetic	L	Dictionary

רשימו A **Imprint – trace**
Reshimu

After the *Tsimtsum* (retraction), when His light retracted forming the round space, a trace of it, called *Reshimu,* remained inside. This lower intensity light, allowed a space of existence (*Makom*), for all the created worlds and beings.

The roots of all future existence and events are in the *Reshimu*. Nothing can come into existence, without having its root in this imprint.
The combination of the *Kav* and the *Reshimu* is what will give existence to the *Sephirot* with which He governs the worlds.
See Kav

רשע H **Wicked –Sinner**
Rasha'

As long as one undertakes the *Tikun* (rectification) of his soul in three reincarnations, he will come back again as needed, to complete his *Tikun*. However, if he maintains his wrong behavior, he will not come back after the third reincarnation.
See Tikun

Hebrew / Aramaic Phonetic	L	Dictionary
שבולת הזקן Shibolet HaZakan	H	**Part of the beard under the lower lip** Corresponds to a level on the face of *Adam Kadmon*. From the aspect of *BaN (52)* inside *Adam Kadmon*, *Sephirot* ascended and came out trough his eyes; ten *Sephirot* from the right eye, and ten from the left. These *Sephirot* took from the higher lights: *KHB (Keter, 'Hokhma, Binah)* received from the lights of the ears, nose and mouth that were on the beard of the chin, and the seven lower *Sephirot* received from the lights of the mouth and lower.
שבירה Shvira	H	**Breaking** See Shvirat HaKelim
שבירת הכלים Shvirat HaKelim	H	**Breaking of the vessels** From the first configuration of *Adam Kadmon* came out different emanations for the construction of the worlds. From his eyes came out ten *Sephirot* of the aspect of the name of *BaN (52);* they correspond to the feminine aspect - rigor, and are the root of deterioration. When they came out, the higher parts of the first three *Sephirot* of *Keter, 'Hokhma* and *Binah* received and contained their lights, because they were in the three-column arrangement The seven lower *Sephirot* were not in the three pillar arrangement needed for the direction of Kindness, rigor and mercy. Therefore, they could not hold the influx of their lights and broke, their lights stayed in the world of *Atsilut*, their *Kelim* (recipients) fell to the lower worlds.

This caused an important damage called *Shvirat HaKelim* – the breaking of the vessels; this imperfect arrangement is the first origin of the *Sitra A'hra* or "evil".

The lower parts of the three first *Sephirot: Keter, 'Hokhma* and *Binah* did not contain their lights, they fell but did not break. These lower parts correspond to what is needed for the guidance of the seven lower *Sephirot*, if they had contained their lights, the seven *Sephirot* would not have broken, and the notions of *Kilkul* (damage) and *Tikun* (repair) not existed.

The roots of all the created are in the seven lower *Sephirot* (*Za"T*), the three first *Sephirot* are like a crown on the *Za"T* to repair and direct them. In the three first *Sephirot* there is not really a notion of damage, they are above men's deeds, and are not affected by their sins.

It is important to understand that all that happens in our world, is similar to what occurred in this fall. If the *Kelim* had contained their lights, the *Za"T* would not have broken, and the world would have been in a perfect state from the start.

The separation between *G"aR* (three first *Sephirot*), which are considered the *Mo'hin* (brains), and *Za"T* (the seven lower *Sephirot*), - the body, is like the death of a man, when his soul departs and goes up, while his body descends into the earth. The *Or* (light) that gives life to the *Keli* (recipient) is comparable to the soul that keeps the body alive.

Hebrew / Aramaic Phonetic	L	Dictionary

After the *Shvirat HaKelim (breaking of the vessels),* the first *Tikun (rectification)* was the *Zivug* (union) of the *Sephirot* of *MaH (45)* and *BaN (52)* in complex arrangements, as to allow the feminine *BaN (52)* to be repaired by the masculine *MaH (45),* and for the *Sephirot* to stand in the three-column arrangement of kindness, rigor and mercy.

To sustain the *Kelim* after they broke, 288 sparks of the lights came down as well, because a connection to their original lights was needed to keep them alive. The goal of all the works, deeds and prayers of men in this existence, is to help and participate in the ascent of these sparks to their origin. There are 613 lights in each *Sephira* or *Partsuf* , similarly, there are 613 *Mitsvot,* 613 parts to the soul, and 613 veins and bones to man , this number is not arbitrary, as there are important interrelations and interactions between them.

With the emanation of the lights of *MaH (45)* and *BaN (52)*, He could have done the *Tikun* (rectification) of all the worlds after the *Shvirat HaKelim (breaking of the vessels),* but then, there would not have been a reason for the participation of man in this *Tikun*. It is to give a possibility to man to act and repair the creation, that G-od restrained in a way his outflow of kindness to this world. At the completion of this *Tikun* of unification between the fallen sparks and their *Kelim*, it will be the time of the resurrection of the dead and the arrival of *Moshia'h.*

Hebrew / Aramaic Phonetic	L	Dictionary

שבעת מלכין
Shev'at
Malkin

A **Seven kings of Edom – corresponding to Z'aT**

See Malkin Kadmain

שבשפה התחתונה
Shebashafa
Hata'htonah

H **On the lower lip**

Shebashafa Hata'htonah is the fourth *Tikun* (action) of the *Dikna* (beard) of *Arikh Anpin,* it corresponds to the hair on the lower lip.

There are hairs (lights) that come out from the face of *Sephira 'Hokhma Stimaah* of *Partsuf Arikh Anpin,* and spread downward. They divide in thirteen, and are called the thirteen *Tikunim* of the *Dikna* of *Arikh Anpin.*

אל רחום ..

מי אל כמוך. . נושא עון...

Each one of these *Tikunim* has its particular function or action for the general guidance.

The *Dikna* reveals the guidance of kindness, rigor and mercy, which was concealed in *'Hokhma Stimaah,* by bringing it down to *Z"A* through the two *Mazalot; Notser* and *Nake,* which are the eighth and thirteenth *Tikun.*

שבת
Shabbat

H **Shabbat**

The seventh day, *Shabbat* corresponds to the seventh *Sephira; Malkhut.*

Hebrew / Aramaic *Phonetic*	L	Dictionary
שבתי צבי *Shabbetai Tsevi*		**Shabbetai Tsevi *(1626-1676)*** False *Messiah* who was called the "Kabbalistic *Messiah*". He converted to Islam before his death. This movement caused a severe division in the Jewish community, and mistrust in the teachings of the Kabbalah.
שד-י *Shada-y*	H	**Shada-y** One of the names of G-od, represented by the *Sephira Yesod*.
שוא *Shevah*	H	**Shevah – Silent vowel** The vowel that represents the *Sephira Gevurah*
שורוק *Shuruk*	H	**Shuruk– Vowel U** The vowel that represents the *Sephira Yesod.*
שורש *Shoresh*	H	**Root** Every thing and existence has its root in the higher realms.
שטח עליון מזל נוצר *Shata'h 'Elyon Mazal Notser*	H	**Upper chin** *Shata'h 'Elyon – Mazal Notser* is the eighth *Tikun* (action) of the *Dikna* (beard) of *Arikh Anpin,* it corresponds to the beard on the upper chin. There are hairs (lights) that come out from the face of *'Hokhma Stimaah* of *Arikh Anpin,* and spread downward. They divide in thirteen, and are called the thirteen *Tikunim* of the *Dikna* of *Arikh Anpin.* אל רחום .. מי אל כמוך . . נושא עון...

Hebrew / Aramaic *Phonetic*	L	Dictionary

Each one of these *Tikunim* has its particular function or action for the general guidance.

The *Dikna* reveals the guidance of kindness, rigor and mercy, which was concealed in *'Hokhma Stimaah*, by bringing it down to *Z"A* through the two *Mazalot; Notser* and *Nake,* which are the eighth and thirteenth *Tikun.*

שטח H **Lower chin**
תחתון
מזל נקה   *Sheta'h Ta'hton* is the thirteen *Tikun* (action) of the
Sheta'h   *Dikna* (beard) of *Arikh Anpin;* it corresponds to the
Ta'hton   beard under the lower chin (*Mazal Nake*).
Mazal   There are hairs (lights) that come out from the face of
Nake   *'Hokhma Stimaah* of *Arikh Anpin,* and spread downward. They divide in thirteen, and are called the thirteen *Tikunim* of the *Dikna* of *Arikh Anpin.*

.. **אל רחום**

מי אל כמוך. . נושא עון...

Each one of these *Tikunim* has its particular function or action for the general guidance.

The *Dikna* reveals the guidance of kindness, rigor and mercy, which was concealed in *'Hokhma Stimaah*, by bringing it down to *Z"A* through the two *Mazalot; Notser* and *Nake,* which are the eighth and thirteenth *Tikun.*

שינוי H **Change – Difference**
Shinuy   The most significant change is in the transformation of the higher emanations.
The light of G-od is unique and of equal force and

Hebrew / Aramaic Phonetic	L	Dictionary

quality. A *Sephira* is in a way a "filter" which transforms this light in a particular force or attribute, by which the Creator guides the worlds.

Each *Sephira* is composed of a vessel called *Keli*, which holds its part of light called *Or*. There is no difference in the *Or* itself; the difference comes from the particularity, or position of the *Sephira*.

שיעור H
Shi'ur

Measurement

When a *Partsuf* (configuration) is in the stage of *Gadlut* (growth) and has grown to its full size, we say that it has reached its "full measure".

שכולם
שוין H
Shekulam Shavim

They are all equal

Shekulam Shavim is the eleventh *Tikun* (action) of the *Dikna* (beard) of *Arikh Anpin,* it corresponds to they are all equal.

There are hairs (lights) that come out from the face of *'Hokhma Stimaah* of *Arikh Anpin,* and spread downward. They divide in thirteen, and are called the thirteen *Tikunim* of the *Dikna* of *Arikh Anpin.*

אל רחום ..

מי אל כמוך. . נושא עון...

Each one of these *Tikunim* has its particular function or action for the general guidance.

The *Dikna* reveals the guidance of kindness, rigor and mercy, which was concealed in *'Hokhma Stimaah*, by bringing it down to *Z"A* through the two *Mazalot; Notser* and *Nake,* which are the eighth and thirteenth *Tikun.*

Hebrew / Aramaic Phonetic	L	Dictionary
שכינה *Shekhina*	H	**Divine presence** One of the names of G-od. The light of the *Ein Sof* which is revealed by the *Sephira Malkhut* is called *Shekhina*. The goal of all *Tefilot* and *Mitsvot* is to make the *Yi'hud* (union) between *Kudsha Beriah Hu (Z"A)* and the *Shekhina (Malkhut)*.
שכינתיה *Shkhinteh*	A	**Divine presence** See Shekhina
שכר *Sakhar*	H	**Reward** From the world of *Atsilut* (emanation) unfolded all the lower worlds. The last world to unfold is *'Asiah* (action); the physical world with the possibility of reward, punishment and evil. There are two main kinds of guidance: The general guidance and the variable guidance. The general guidance is for the subsistence of the worlds and is not influenced by the actions of men. This guidance is by the encircling *Sephirot*. The variable guidance is on the basis of justice, reward and punishment and is dependant on the actions of man. This guidance is by the linear *Sephirot*. If there was only good in this world, the guidance based on the duality of reward and punishment would not be necessary, but then, men will not have free choice, and no merit for the accomplishment of the will of G-od.

Hebrew / Aramaic Phonetic	L	Dictionary

שלם   H   ***Complete***

Shalem

A *Partsuf* (configuration) is considered complete when it has reached its full potential.

For *Partsuf Z"A,* there are two gestations and two growths. The first *Mo'hin* (brains) of the first growth are from *Partsuf Tevunah,* and of the second growth, from *Partsuf Imah.*

During the first growth *Partsuf Z"A* is not considered complete, It is only after the second growth that *Z"A* has reached this stage; this is *Gadlut* 2.

שלמות   H   ***Completeness***

Shelemut

See Shalem

שמועיא"ל   **Shemou'ie"l**

Shemou'ie"l

Name of one of the three great princes of the Angels.

שמות   H   ***Names***

Shemot

A name identifies and characterizes a light or a manifestation.

שמיעה   H   ***Hearing***

Shemi'ah

From the lights that were invested inside of *Adam Kadmon* emerged numerous worlds in the way of his senses; which are called his branches.

These "branches" are the lights that spread forth from *Adam Kadmon,* by way of its apertures in the head, four of which are called: Sight, hearing, smell and speech. They spread out from his eyes, ears, nose, and mouth.

In the language of Kabbalah, we use names of body

Hebrew / Aramaic Phonetic	L	Dictionary
		parts solely to illustrate the esoteric powers of these forces. It is understood, of course, that there is no physical existence at these level. When we say ears, mouth, or any other physical expression, the goal is to describe the inner sense, or the position they represent.
		These emanations and configurations are drawn from the four letters of the Name of G-od. *B'H*, and their different spellings, which are called *Miluyim*.
		From the ears came out lights of the aspect of *SaG* (63) (higher *Ta'amim*). *See Orot HaOzen*
שמש *Shemesh*	H	**Sun** It is of the aspect of *Partsuf Z"A*.
שמשא *Shamsha*	A	**Sun** *See Shemesh*
שני נחירים *Shene Ne'hirim*	H	**Two nostrils** One of seven *Tikunim* of the head of *Arikh Anpin*. *See 'Hotma*
שני תפוחים שנפנו *Shene Tapu'him Shenifenu*	H	**Two upper sided of the cheeks** *Shene Tapu'him Shenifenu* is the seventh *Tikun* (action) of the *Dikna* (beard) of *Arikh Anpin*, it corresponds to the two upper sides of the cheeks. There are hairs (lights) that come out from the face of *'Hokhma Stimaah* of *Arikh Anpin*, and spread downward. They divide in thirteen, and are called the thirteen *Tikunim* of the *Dikna* of *Arikh Anpin*.

315

Hebrew / Aramaic Phonetic	L	Dictionary
		אל רחום .. מי אל כמוך. . נושא עון... Each one of these *Tikunim* has its particular function or action for the general guidance. The *Dikna* reveals the guidance of kindness, rigor and mercy, which was concealed in *'Hokhma Stimaah*, by bringing it down to *Z"A* through the two *Mazalot; Notser* and *Nake,* which are the eighth and thirteenth *Tikun.*
שער *Se'ar*	H	*Hair* See Se'arot
שער *Sha'ar*	H	*Gate – Portal* Entrance to a dimension. Gate to enter a knowledge.
שערות *Se'arot*	H	*Hairs* There are emanations that come out from the head or face of the *Partsufim* (configurations). They are called hair and beard because they spread out in individual conduits. The first emanation to come out from *Adam Kadmon* is of the aspect of the name *"A"V* (72), which spread out from the hair on its head. This emanated light is too lofty for our understanding. There are hairs (lights) that come out from the face of *Arikh Anpin,* and spread downward. They divide in thirteen and are called the thirteen *Tikunim* (actions) of the *Dikna* (beard) of *Arikh Anpin.*

Hebrew / Aramaic Phonetic	L	Dictionary

The *Tikunim* of *Z"A* are similar to the ones of *Arikh Anpin,* but with some differences. From *Arikh Anpin* all the hair come out from *'Hokhma Stimaah,* from *Z"A,* they come out from his *HBD* ('Hokhma, Binah, Da'at). The hairs of *Z"A* are black and intermingled, being more of the aspect of *Gevurah,* the hairs of *Arikh Anpin* are white and express bounty.

| שערות הגרון Se'arot HaGaron | H | **Hair on the throat** |

Se'arot HaGaron is the tenth *Tikun* (action) of the *Dikna* (beard) of *Arikh Anpin;* it corresponds to the hair on the throat.

There are hairs (lights) that come out from the face of *'Hokhma Stimaah* of *Arikh Anpin,* and spread downward. They divide in thirteen, and are called the thirteen *Tikunim* of the *Dikna* of *Arikh Anpin.*

אל רחום ..

מי אל כמוך. . נושא עון...

Each one of these *Tikunim* has its particular function or action for the general guidance.

The *Dikna* reveals the guidance of kindness, rigor and mercy, which was concealed in *'Hokhma Stimaah,* by bringing it down to *Z"A* through the two *Mazalot; Notser* and *Nake,* which are the eighth and thirteenth *Tikun.*

See Tikun, Partsufim

317

Hebrew / Aramaic Phonetic	L	Dictionary
שערות שבין מזל למזל Se'arot sheben Mazal leMazal	H	**Hair between the upper and lower chin** *Se'arot sheben Mazal leMazal* is the ninth *Tikun* (action) of the *Dikna* (beard) of *Arikh Anpin,* it corresponds to the hair between the upper and lower chin. There are hairs (lights) that come out from the face of *'Hokhma Stimaah* of *Arikh Anpin,* and spread downward. They divide in thirteen, and are called the thirteen *Tikunim* of the *Dikna* of *Arikh Anpin.* אל רחום .. מי אל כמוך. . נושא עון... Each one of these *Tikunim* has its particular function or action for the general guidance. The *Dikna* reveals the guidance of kindness, rigor and mercy, which was concealed in *'Hokhma Stimaah,* by bringing it down to *Z"A* through the two *Mazalot; Notser* and *Nake,* which are the eighth and thirteenth *Tikun.*
שערות שבשפה עליונה Se'arot she baShafa 'Elyonah	H	**Hair on the upper lip** *Se'arot she baShafa 'Elyonah* is the second *Tikun* (action) of the *Dikna* (beard) of *Arikh Anpin,* it corresponds to: The hair on the upper lip. There are hairs (lights) that come out from the face of *'Hokhma Stimaah* of *Arikh Anpin,* and spread downward. They divide in thirteen, and are called the thirteen *Tikunim* of the *Dikna* of *Arikh Anpin.* אל רחום .. מי אל כמוך. . נושא עון...

Hebrew / Aramaic Phonetic	L	Dictionary

Each one of these *Tikunim* has its particular function or action for the general guidance.

The *Dikna* reveals the guidance of kindness, rigor and mercy, which was concealed in *'Hokhma Stimaah*, by bringing it down to *Z"A* through the two *Mazalot; Notser* and *Nake,* which are the eighth and thirteenth *Tikun.*

שפע H
Shefa'

Abundance

For the abundance to come down to the world, *Partsuf Zeir Anpin* needs to unite with *Nukvah.* There can be abundance only when the masculine and the feminine are in harmony.

Each day, according to the actions of man, the *Tefilot* during the week, *Shabbat* or Holidays, and depending on time, various configurations allow different *Zivugim* (unions), and therefore outflows of abundance of variable intensities.

שקר H
Sheker

Falsehood – Lie

The root of the *Sitra A'hra* (negative force) is in the lack, or absence of the *Kedushah.* Its existence was willed by the Creator to give man free will. With falsehood, it almost constantly tries to seduce him, and make him stumble.

See Sitra A'hra

Hebrew / Aramaic Phonetic	L	Dictionary

| שרעבי Shar'abi | | **Rabbi Shalom Shar'abi - The Rashash** |

Born in Shar'ab, Yemen in 1720, died in Jerusalem in 1777.

After leaving Yemen, he joined the *Yeshiva* of the *Mekubalim* "*Beth El*" in Jerusalem. He is known as the "Master of the *Kavanot*". His "*Siddur HaRashash*" is the *Siddur* (prayer book) used by some Kabbalists in their everyday prayers, and is based on the *Kavanot* of the Ari Z'al.

See Kavanot

Hebrew / Aramaic Phonetic	L	Dictionary

תא חזא A · **Come see (pay attention)**

Ta 'Haze · Expression frequently used in the *Zohar.*

תבונה א H · **Partsuf (Reason)**

Tevunah 1 · Sephira Malkhut of *Partsuf Imah* is sometimes an independent *Partsuf.*

See Partsufim Israel Saba and Tevunah

תבונה ב H · **Partsuf (Reason) 2**

Tevunah 2 · Sephira Malkhut of *Partsuf Tevunah* is sometimes an independent *Partsuf.*

See Partsufim Israel Saba and Tevunah

תגין A · **Crowns on the letters**

Tagin · From the lights that were invested inside of *Adam Kadmon* emerged numerous worlds in the way of his senses; which are called his branches. These "branches" are the lights that spread forth from *Adam Kadmon,* by way of its apertures in the head. They spread out from his eyes, ears, nose, mouth and forehead.

The *Ta'amim* (cantillation marks) are of the highest level and are subdivided in three: higher, middle and lower. The *Nekudot* (vowels) are second, also in three levels: higher, middle and lower. The *Tagin* (crowns) are third, and appear on top of some letters only. The *Autiot* (letters) are fourth.

The *Sephirot* that came out from the forehead of *Adam Kadmon* for the *Tikun* are of the aspect of the *Tagin* and of the name of *MaH (45).*

Hebrew / Aramaic *Phonetic*	L	Dictionary

The reading of the Torah is incomplete without the *Ta'amim, Nekudot, Tagin,* and *Autiot.* The *Autiot* are the expression of the *Ma'hshava* (thought). In combination with the *Ta'amim, Nekudot, Tagin,* or with other letters, they transform the higher lights into action.

תדיר H **Frequent – Regular**

Tadir There are regular emanations as the ones of everyday, and exceptions as the emanations of the Holidays and other special occasions.

תוך H *Inside*

Tokh See Levush

תולדה H **Consequence – Result**

Toladah All the outcomes of the higher emanations are a result of the different unions of the masculine and feminine lights. Each one of these reactions has numerous ramifications, with many details and outcomes and will result in illuminations of different intensities, for the guidance of the worlds.

תורה H *Torah*

Torah The Kabbalah is the mystical and esoteric explanation of the *Torah.* All the profound secrets explained in the Kabbalah, are alluded in the letters, words and different stories narrated in the *Torah.*

The *Torah* contains four levels of comprehension, of which the highest is the *Sod* (secret). At this level, we understand that our *Tefilot* and the accomplishment of

Hebrew / Aramaic Phonetic	L	Dictionary

each one of the *Mitsvot,* has a direct influence on the superior worlds and on their guidance.

The *Torah* has 248 positive and 365 negative commandments. Similarly, there are 613 veins and bones to man, 613 parts to the soul, and 613 lights in each *Sephira* or *Partsuf,* this number is not arbitrary, as there are important interrelations and interactions between them.

Through the knowledge of Kabbalah, we can get to a level of true understanding of the will of the Creator, and in a way "decode" the profound secrets of our holy *Torah.*

תחית
המתים
T'hiyat
HaMetim

H **Resurrection of the dead**

Final goal of the six thousand years.

After the *Shvirat HaKelim* (breaking of the vessels), 288 sparks of the lights came down as well to sustain the *Kelim* after they broke. A connection to their original lights was needed to keep them alive. The sparks correspond to the four *"A"V* of *ASMB,* 4 x 72 = 288. This fall of the *Kelim,* is also called their death.

It is important to understand that all that happens in our world, is similar to what occurred in this fall. The separation between *G"aR* (three first *Sephirot*), which are considered the *Mo'hin* (brains), and *Za"T* (the seven lower *Sephirot*), - the body, is like the death of a man, when his soul departs and goes up, while his body descends into the earth.

Hebrew / Aramaic Phonetic	L	Dictionary

The *Or* (light) that gives life to the *Keli* (recipient) is comparable to the soul that keeps the body alive. However, when a man dies and his soul separates from his body, the latter will remain with the "Habela *Degarmi*" (הבלא דגרמי), which like the 288 sparks, will allow the conservation of the body from the time the soul has left him, until the resurrection.

The goal of all the works, deeds and prayers of men in this existence, is to help and participate in the ascent of these sparks to their origin. At the completion of this *Tikun* (rectification) of unification between the fallen sparks and their *Kelim*, it will be the time of the resurrection of the dead and the arrival of *Moshia'h*.

See Gilgul, 'Ibur

תחת *Ta'hat*	H	***Under*** What is lower or subordinate.
תחתון *Ta'hton*	H	***Inferior – Lower*** What is under or subordinate.
תחתונים *Ta'htonim*	H	***Lower beings*** Separate beings – Angels, men etc.
תיכון *Tikhon*	H	***Middle*** *See Keli Tikhon*

Hebrew / Aramaic Phonetic	L	Dictionary

תיקון H **Rectification or action**

Tikun

In Hebrew, the word "*Tikun*" has different meanings. It can be understood as reparation or rectification but also as function, relation or action.

There are different types of *Tikunim*:

- *Tikunim* (reparations) that took place in the first emanations to repair the worlds.
- *Tikunim* (rectifications - relations) for the construction and inter-relations of the *Sephirot* and *Partsufim*.
- *Tikunim* (actions - functions) of certain *Partsufim* for the guidance of the world.
- *Tikunim* (rectifications) for the *Neshamot* (souls).

From the eyes of *Adam Kadmon* came out ten *Sephirot* of the feminine aspect of *BaN* (52), the three first *Sephirot* contained their lights but the seven lower *Sephirot* did not and broke. This caused an important damage called *Shvirat HaKelim* – the breaking of the vessels. The *Kelim* (recipients) of the seven *Sephirot* which did not contain their lights, fell to the lower worlds.

To sustain these *Kelim* after they broke, 288 sparks of their lights came down as well, because a connection to their original lights was needed to keep them alive. These sparks correspond to the four aspects of "*A"V* (72) of the names "*A"V* (72), *SaG* (63), *MaH* (45), *BaN* (52), 4 x 72 = 288.

Hebrew / Aramaic *Phonetic*	L	Dictionary

It is important to understand that all that happens in our world, is similar to what occurred in this fall. The *Tikun* is to help and participate in the ascent of the fallen 288 sparks to their origin. This can be done by accomplishing the *Mitsvot* and the *Tefilot*.

To repair the *Partsufim* after the *Shvirat HaKelim* (breaking of the vessels), the *Tikun* was the union of the *Sephirot* of *MaH* (45) and *BaN* (52) in complex arrangements, as to allow the feminine *BaN* to be repaired by the masculine *MaH,* and for the *Sephirot* to stand in the three-column arrangement for the guidance of kindness, rigor and mercy.

The *Tikunim* for the construction of the *Partsufim* (masculine and feminine) are achieved by way of *Zivug* (union), gestation and birth. The masculine corresponds to 'Hesed and MaH (45), the feminine to *Gevurah* and *BaN* (52).

At first, during the gestation, the lights of the aspect of *MaH* needed for the *Tikun* are drawn to the lights of *BaN*, and are kept in the upper *Nukvah* (the *Nukvah* above) to give birth to the *Partsuf.* Inside of *Nukvah*, it is arranged and completed until there is nothing more to add. When it is totally repaired, the *Partsuf* is revealed; this is the birth. There is afterwards a period of suckling, and then a first infancy and growth,

For the guidance, the *Tikunim* of the *Partsufim* are the actions, illuminations and inter-relations of the *Sephirot* and *Partsufim*, and their influence on the worlds. These *Tikunim* result in various illuminations of different

Hebrew / Aramaic Phonetic	L	Dictionary

intensities, depending on time and the actions of man.

The main *Tikunim* of the *Partsufim* are the ones of *Partsuf Arikh Anpin, Zeir Anpin* and *Nukvah*. These *Tikunim* are from the head, or the face of the *Partsufim*. The first *Tikun* is the one of the three heads of *Partsuf Arikh Anpin*:

1- *Gulgolta* - *Keter* of *Arikh Anpin*

2- *Avirah* - In the space between *Keter* and *'Hokhma* of *Arikh Anpin*, there is *Da'at* of *'Atik*

3- *Mo'ha* - *'Hokhma* of *Arikh Anpin*

These three heads are the roots of the direction of kindness, rigor and mercy. They emanate from *Arikh Anpin* to *Abah* and *Imah,* and from there, to the *Mo'hin* (brains) of *Z"A*.

The second *Tikun* is of the head of *Arikh Anpin*. It is achieved by the passing of the seven lower *Sephirot* of *'Atik* into the head of *Arikh Anpin,* before they are clothed in him.

The other *Tikunim* of *Arikh Anpin* are:

From his *Keter* - חיורתי ('*Hivarti*)

From *Avirah* (*Da'at* of *'Atik*; between *Keter* and *'Hokhma*) - נימין (*Nimin*)

From his *'Hokhma* called *'Hokhma Stimaah* - דיקנא (*Dikna*)

The hairs (lights) that come out from the face of *'Hokhma Stimaah,* and spread downward, divide in thirteen and are called the thirteen *Tikunim* of the *Dikna* of *Arikh Anpin*.

Hebrew / Aramaic Phonetic	L	Dictionary

The other *Tikunim* are lights needed for the attainment and abundance. However, the guidance itself is from the *Dikna*.

For *Partsuf Z"A* there are two *Tikunim*: the first *Tikun* is in his *Mo'hin* (brains), and is called his *Tselem* (צלם). The second *Tikun* of *Z"A* is expressed by the lights that come out of him, as the hair on his head, and on his face. These *Tikunim* are similar to the ones of *Arikh Anpin,* but with some differences. From *Arikh Anpin* all the hair come out from *'Hokhma Stimaah*, from *Z"A*; they come out from his *HBD* ('Hokhma, Binah, Da'at). The hairs of *Z"A* are black and intermingled; being more of the aspect of *Gevurah*, the hairs of *Arikh Anpin* are white, and express bounty.

The *Tikunim* of the *Dikna* (beard) of *Z"A*, are similar to the ones of *Arikh Anpin,* even if they are nine. However, with an illumination from *Arikh Anpin*, they become thirteen and act as a principle of kindness for the guidance of justice.

There are *Tikunim* realized by the interior lights of the *Partsuf,* and *Tikunim* or actions achieved by the lights on the exterior of the *Partsuf*, as the ones realized by his *Levush* (garment), his encircling lights (*Makifin*), and the *Hekhalot* (portals).

All these *Tikunim* are for the direction of the worlds.

For the soul, the *Tikun* is realized by the *Gilgul* (reincarnation), and by the *'Ibur* (attachment). By accomplishing what he did not accomplish of the 613 *Mitsvot*, man makes the necessary *Tikun* of his soul

Hebrew / Aramaic *Phonetic*	L	Dictionary

which can now elevate to the higher realms and rejoin its source.

The higher levels of the soul cannot be acquired at once. Most men only have the lower level of *Nefesh,* and if they merit, they will acquire the next levels - but one by one. To reach the next higher level of his soul, man must do the *Tikun* of the preceding level. If he needs to acquire the level of *Imah* of *'Asiah*, he must first do the *Tikun* of *Malkhut* of *'Asiah* and *Z"A* of *'Asiah,* and so on. To acquire his level of *Neshama*, he must do the *Tikun* of all the levels of the *Sephirot* and *Partsufim* of his *Nefesh* and *Rua'h.*

If man does not do the *Tikun* of the level of his soul for which he came, he comes back and reincarnates. As long as one undertakes the *Tikun* of his soul in three reincarnations, he will come back again as needed to complete his *Tikun*. However, if he maintains his wrong behavior, he will not come back after the third reincarnation.

Evil will disappear from this world and change to goodness, when the *Tikunim* will be completed. Consequently, these rigors will be appeased, and the *Sitra A'hra* (negative force) will not be able to attach to the higher lights anymore.

By giving man a role in the general *Tikun (Tikun 'Olam),* it is now up to him to restore and make the necessary reparations to the world. However, if man does not act accordingly, the *Tikun* will still be realized, but in the time set by the Creator.

Hebrew / Aramaic Phonetic	L	Dictionary
תיקונים *Tikunim*	H	***Rectifications or actions*** See Tikun
תכלית *Takhlit*	H	***Final goal*** The goal of all the complex inter-relations and possibilities of guidance have only one purpose: to allow man to merit by his own efforts, to get closer to his Creator and live the *Dvekut* – the adhesion with G-od. In this way, man will attain perfection and be directly involved in the ultimate goal of the creation, which is the revelation of G-od's sovereignty – *Giluy Ye'hudo.*
תכלת *Tkhelet*	H	***Azure*** Special color not found at present, which was used on the *Tsitsit* (fringes of the *Talit*). See Talit
תלת רישין *Telat Rishin*	A	***Three Heads*** The three heads of *Arikh Anpin* are the roots of the direction of kindness, rigor and mercy. They emanate from *Arikh Anpin* to *Abah* and *Imah,* and from there, to the *Mo'hin* (brains) of *Z"A*. These three heads are the first *Tikun* (action) of *Partsuf Arikh Anpin* they are: 1- *Gulgolta - Keter* of *Arikh Anpin* 2- *Avirah* - In the space between *Keter* and *'Hokhma* of *Arikh Anpin,* there is *Da'at* of *'Atik* 3- *Mo'ha - 'Hokhma* of *Arikh Anpin*

Hebrew / Aramaic *Phonetic*	L	Dictionary

In each one of the three heads, there are aspects of interiority and exteriority, as in all the lights. Each one of these aspects of interiority and exteriority subdivides in three more aspects: Interiority, encircling (*Makif*), and encircling of encircling (*Makif* of *Makif*).

The names of הוי"ה correspond to the aspect of interiority, the names of אהי"ה correspond to the aspect of exteriority. In each head, there are three הוי"ה, and three אהי"ה, the distinction for each one (of the הוי"ה and אהי"ה) is in the *Nekudim* it receives.

These three heads are the roots of the direction of kindness, rigor and mercy. They emanate from *Arikh Anpin* to *Abah* and *Imah,* and from there, to the *Mo'hin* of *Z"A*.

תמונה *Temunah*	H	***Image – Form***

Man is as the image of the higher lights, he has 248 limbs and 365 veins. Correspondingly, a *Sephira* or a *Partsuf* comprise of 613 main forces or lights, which afterward divide into many parts. This structure is also similar in the Torah, which has 248 positive and 365 negative commandments.

There is also a general image, or form, called the *Sephirotic* tree. As the Ram'hal explains, in order to learn the wisdom of *Kabbalah*, which is profuse with details, it is first necessary to have an image or a general idea of the *Sephirotic* tree. Once familiar with this general idea, one can start to study and

Hebrew / Aramaic Phonetic	L	Dictionary
		understand all the details that will further clarify this first image.
תמונות *Temunot*	H	***Images – Forms*** *See Temunah*
תניא *Tanya*	H	***Tanya*** *See Rabbi Shneur Zalman of Liadi*
תענוג *Ta'anug*	H	***Delight*** The utmost delight is to feel closeness to the Creator, by understanding His will and His ways.
תפארת *Tiferet*	H	***Sephira (beauty)*** Sixth of the *Sephirot*. Quality: kindness that makes the equilibrium between complete kindness and rigor. Column: Center – *Ra'hamim* (mercy) Position: Middle – center Other *Sephirot* on the same column: *Keter, Yesod, Malkhut* *Partsufim* made from this *Sephira:* One of the *Sephirot* that make the *Partsuf Z"A*. Corresponding name: *YHV-K* י-ה-ו-ה Corresponding *Miluy* of name: *MaH* (מה) 45 Corresponding vowel: *'Holam* Physical correspondence: Body Level of the soul: *Rua'h* *See Sephira, Partsuf*

Hebrew / Aramaic L Phonetic	Dictionary

תפילה H **Prayer**

Tefilah

The order of the *Tefilot* is based on the systems of ascension of the worlds, as explained in the Kabbalah. At this level, we understand that our *Tefilot* have a direct influence on the superior worlds, and on their guidance.

The Kabbalah teaches us that the world is guided by an extremely complex system of forces or lights, which through their interactions provoke chain reactions that impact directly on man and the worlds. Each one of these reactions has numerous ramifications with many details and results.

Starting from the first act in the morning of *Netilat Yadayim* (washing of the hands three times in alternation), until the end of the *Tefilah*, there is a constant elevation and adhesion of the worlds of *'Asiah* (action), *Yetsirah (formation)* and *Beriah (creation)* to the world of *Atsilut (emanation)*.

This is done by the *Hekhalot* (portals), they are the different levels of ascension of the *Tefilot* before reaching the *'Olam Atsilut* during the *'Amidah*. Their principal function is to allow the adhesion and attachment of these worlds in a precise order.

During the *Tefilot*, when one knows this system of ascension of the *Hekhalot*, he concentrates on the words or the names where are hinted the precise action of the *Hekhal (portal)*. He aims to help in the realization of the particular *Zivug* of the *Tefilah*.

To get from one world to the next a secret name

Hebrew / Aramaic *Phonetic*	L	Dictionary

called *MaV* (42) hinted during the *Kadish*, makes this ascension possible. This secret name of 42 letters is made with the four letters of the name י-ה-ו-ה , the *Miluy* (spelling) of each one of the four letters for a total of ten letters, and the *Miluy* of each one of theses ten letters for a total of twenty eight.

This name is hinted when we answer *Yehe Sheme* ..... until - *Be'alma*. The *Kadish* makes possible the ascent of each world to the next higher world, and the descent afterwards from the world of *Atsilut* to *'Asiah*.

The goal is to help prepare the different *Partsufim* of Z"A and *Nukvah* for their *Zivug (union)*.

For the abundance to come down to the world, *Partsuf Zeir Anpin* needs to unite with *Nukvah*. There can be abundance only when the masculine and the feminine are in harmony. Each day, according to the actions of man, the *Tefilot* during the week, *Shabbat* or Holidays, and depending on time, various configurations allow different *Zivugim* (unions), and therefore outflows of abundance of variable intensities.

Each new day, is of a new emanation that governs it. For each day, there are new *Zivugim* of different aspects of Z"A and *Nukvah*. A full day is divided in two; day and night, and each half is again divided in two (dawn and day, dusk and night).

Hebrew / Aramaic *Phonetic*	L	Dictionary

For each part, there is a *Tefilah*, for the two parts of day: *Sha'hrit* and *Min'ha*, for the two parts of nights: *'Arvit* and *Tikun 'Hatsot*.

Generally, the *Zivugim* are:
Sha'hrit - *Ya'acov* and *Ra'hel*
Min'ha – *Israel* and *Leah*
'Arvit – *Ya'acov* and *Leah* (from the chest up)
Tikun 'Hatsot – *Ya'acov* and *Leah* (from the chest down)
The *Zivug* of *Israel* and *Ra'hel* is realized during the *Tefilah* of *Musaf* on *Shabbat* and on other special occasions.

When one understands the systems and actions of the *Tefilot,* he realizes the importance of our rituals, because only man, by praying and the accomplishment of the *Mitsvot,* can influence these incredible forces.
See Kavanot, Hekhal (portal), Zivug, Kadish

תפילות *Tefilot*	H	**Prayers** See Tefilah
תפילין *Tefilin*	H	**Phylacteries**

The *Tefilin* represent the lights of the *Mo'hin* (brains) that break out from inside of *Partsuf Z"A* through his forehead. When these lights entered in him they were four (*Hokhma, Binah, 'Hasadim and Gevurot*), they became three (*'Hasadim and Gevurot* join) inside of him, and become four again when coming out; these

Hebrew / Aramaic Phonetic	L	Dictionary

are the four *Parashiot.*

Each one of these four lights also brings out an aspect of *Levush* (garment), which are the compartments for the *Parashiot.*

Since the *Mo'hin* comprise ten *Sephirot,* the *Tefilin* represent ten lights:

The compartment on the forehead are the *HBD* ('Hokhma, Binah, Da'at).

The two straps on the side of the head are *'Hesed* and *Gevurah*

The knot on the back is *Tiferet,* from there *Leah* comes out.

The two straps that come down on the sides are *Netsa'h* and *Hod; Netsa'h* until the chest, and *Hod* until the navel.

The *Tefilin* on the arm represent *Ra'hel.* The order of the *Parashiot* is the same as in the *Tefilin* on the head, but in only one parchment.

The *Yesod* of *Z"A* makes the ' *(Yud)* on the *Tefilin,* and from there (the arm of *Z"A),* the building of *Nukvah* starts.

The three wrappings on the biceps; correspond to the three first *Sephirot* of *Nukvah.* The seven wrappings on the forearm correspond to the seven lower *Sephirot* of *Nukvah.* The three wrappings on the finger correspond to the *NHY* (Netsa'h, Hod, Yesod) of *Z"A* which are the *Mo'hin* of *Nukvah.*

Hebrew / Aramaic Phonetic	L	Dictionary
		Since there are *Mo'hin* from *Abah,* and *Mo'hin* from *Imah,* there are two types of *Tefilin:*

Since there are *Mo'hin* from *Abah,* and *Mo'hin* from *Imah,* there are two types of *Tefilin:*
Tefilin of *Imah* – *Rashi*
Tefilin of *Abah* – *Rabenu Tam.*
The difference is in the order of the *Parashiot.*
See Tefilin, Tefilin of Rashi, Tefilin of Rabenu Tam

תפילין
דז"א
Tefilin
De Z"A

Tefilin of Z"A

The *Tefilin* on the head correspond to *Partsuf Z"A.*
As there are *Mo'hin* from *Abah,* and *Mo'hin* from *Imah,* there are two types of *Tefilin:*
Tefilin of *Imah* – *Rashi*
Tefilin of *Abah* – *Rabenu Tam.*
The difference is in the order of the *Parashiot:*
See Tefilin, Tefilin of Rashi, Tefilin of Rabenu Tam

תפילין
דיעקב
Tefilin
De
Ya'acov

H

Tefilin of Ya'acov

The *Tefilin* of *Rabenu Tam* on the arm correspond to *Ya'acov.*
At first, the four lights in *Yesod* of *Abah* come out with the lights in *Netsa'h* and *Hod* of *Z"A.* They go to *Ya'acov;* the lights of *Abah* make his *Mo'hin* – his *Tefilin,* and from him (*Ya'acov*) the lights of *Z"A* go to *Ra'hel,* who is behind him, to become her *Mo'hin* - her *Tefilin.*
The order of the *Parashiot* is:
1 - *'Hokhma* – קדש
2 - *Binah* - והיה כי יביאך
3 - *Gevurot* - והיה אם שמוע
4 - *'Hasadim* – שמע

337

Hebrew / Aramaic Phonetic	L	Dictionary
תפילין דרבנו תם *Tefilin De Rabenu Tam*	H	**Tefilin of Rabenu Tam** The *Mo'hin* from *Abah* make the *Tefilin* of *Rabenu Tam*. The order of the *Parashiot is*: *1 - 'Hokhma –* קדש *2 - Binah -* והיה כי יביאך *3 - Gevurot -* והיה אם שמוע *4 - 'Hasadim –* שמע
תפילין דרחל *Tefilin De Ra'hel*	H	**Tefilin of Ra'hel** The *Tefilin* of *Rashi* on the arm correspond to *Ra'hel*. The *Nukvah* (*Ra'hel*) also has an aspect of *Tefilin*, and attaches on the left arm (*Gevurah*) of *Z"A*. She (*Nukvah*) has four *Parashiot* in her *Tefilin*, and receives her *Mo'hin* (brains) through *Netsa'h* and *Hod* of *Z"A*. The *Yesod* of *Z"A* makes the ׳ *(Yud)* on the side of the *Tefilin* of *Ra'hel*, and from there (the arm of *Z"A*), the building of *Nukvah* starts. The three wrappings on the biceps; correspond to the three first *Sephirot* (*G"aR* of *Nukvah*). The seven on the forearm correspond to the seven lower *Sephirot* (*Za"T* of *Nukvah*). The three wrappings on the finger correspond to the *NHY* (Netsa'h, Hod, Yesod) of *Z"A* which are the *Mo'hin* of *Nukvah*. See Tefilin, Tefilin of Rashi.
תפילין דרשי *Tefilin De Rashi*	H	**Tefilin of Rashi** The *Mo'hin* from *Imah* make the *Tefilin* of *Rashi*. The order of the *Parashiot is*: *1 - 'Hokhma –* קדש

Hebrew / Aramaic Phonetic	L	Dictionary
		2 - *Binah* - וְהָיָה כִּי יְבִיאֲךָ 3 - *'Hasadim* – שמע 4 - *Gevurot* - וְהָיָה אִם שָׁמוֹעַ *See Tefilin, Tefilin of Rashi, Tefilin of Rabenu Tam*
תקיף *Takif*	H	**Hardness** Associated to rigor and *Gevurot*.
תקיפים *Takifim*	H	**Strong – Hard** *See Takif*
תרדמה *Tardema*	H	**Sleep – Somnolence** At first *Partsuf Z"A* is in a state of *Tardema* (somnolence), to act it needs to get his *Mo'hin* (brains) from *Partsuf ISOT* or *Partsuf Abah* and *Imah*, and to get to a stage of growth. Inside of *Imah*, *Partsuf Z"A* goes through a period of gestation, followed by a first period of infancy and a first growth. In the first growth his *Mo'hin* are from *NHY* (Netsa'h, Hod, Yesod) of *Tevunah*. During the time of the gestation, *Z"A* is not really acting as it is being built, at the time of suckling it starts to act, and at the growth it is ready to act.
תרי"ג *Taryag*	H	**613** There are 613 veins and bones to man, similarly, there are 613 *Mitsvot,* 613 parts to the soul, and 613 lights in each *Sephira* or *Partsuf*, this number is not arbitrary, as there are important interrelations and interactions between them.

Dictionary

English –
Hebrew / Aramaic

English	L	Phonetic	Hebrew / Aramaic
288 (numeric value)	H	*Rapa'h*	רפ"ח
288 sparks	A	*Rapa'h Nitsutsot*	רפ"ח נצוצות
32 Paths of wisdom	H	*Lamed Bet Netivot 'Hokhma*	ל"ב נתיבות חכמה
613	H	*Taryag*	תרי"ג
A virtuous woman is a crown of her husband	H	*Eshet Hail Ateret Ba'ala*	אשת-חיל עטרת בעלה
Abdomen	H	*Beten*	בטן
Abundance	H	*Shefa'*	שפע
Action	H	*Pe'ulah*	פעולה
Actions	H	*Pe'ulot*	פעולות
Adhesion – Adherence	H	*Dvekut*	דבקות
Adulthood – Growth	H	*Gadlut*	גדלות
Air – Space	H	*Avir*	אויר
Allegory	H	*Mashal*	משל
Amulet	H	*Kmia'h*	קמיע
Angel	H	*Malakh*	מלאך

English	L	Phonetic	Hebrew / Aramaic
Angels	H	Malakhim	מלאכים
Aspect - Feature – Quality	H	Be'hinah	בחינה
Aspects - Features – Qualities	H	Be'hinot	בחינות
Assembly of Israel	H	Knesset Israel	כנסת ישראל
Atsilut, Beriah, Yetsirah and Asiah	H	ABYA	אבי"ע
Attached - Joined to	H	Davuk	דבוק
Attachment	H	'Hibur	חיבור
Attachment - Relation - Similitude	H	Kesher	קשר
Attainment - Comprehension	H	Hasagah	השגה
Attracts – Draws	H	Moshekh	מושך
Attribute (quality) of judgment	H	Midat HaDin	מדת הדין
Attribute - Quality – Measure	H	Mida	מדה
Attribute (quality) of bounty	H	Midat Ha'Hesed	מדת החסד

English	L	Phonetic	Hebrew / Aramaic
Attribute (quality) of Mercy	H	Midat HaRa'hamim	מדת הרחמים
Attributes - Qualities – Measures	H	Midot	מידות
Authority – Domain	A	Reshuta	רשותא
Authority – Domain	H	Reshut	רשות
Awakening	A	Mit'arin	מתערין
Awakening from above	A	Eta'aruta de La'ila	אתערותא דלעילא
Awakening from below	A	Eta'aruta de Letata	אתערותא דלתתא
Axis	H	Tsir	ציר
Azure	H	Tkhelet	תכלת

English	L	Phonetic	Hebrew / Aramaic
Back of the neck	H	'Oref	עורף
Back to Back	H	A'hor Be A'hor	אחור באחור
Back to Face	H	A'hor B Panim	אחור בפנים
Backside – Behind	H	A'hor	אחור
Blessed is He	H	Barukh Hu	ברוך הוא
Blessed is He - Initials	H	B'H	ב"ה
Beard	H	Zakan	זקן
Beard (illuminations of the face)	A	Dikna	דיקנא
Beginning – First	H	Reshit	ראשית
Bestowal	H	Hashpa'ah	השפעה
Big – Adult	H	Gadol	גדול
Birth	H	Leida	לידה
Blessing	H	Berakha	ברכה
Blood	H	Dam	דם
Body	H	Guf	גוף
Bones	H	'Atsamot	עצמות
Bound - Tied	H	'Akudim	עקודים

English	L	Phonetic	Hebrew / Aramaic
Bound – Tied	H	'Akud	עקוד
Boundary – Limit	H	Gevul	גבול
Bounty	H	'Hesed	חסד
Brain	A	Moa'h	מוח
Brains	A	Mo'hin	מוחין
Brains of growth	A	Mo'hin de Gadlut	מוחין דגדלות
Brains of infancy	A	Mo'hin de Katnut	מוחין דקתנות
Branch	H	'Anaf	ענף
Branches	H	'Anafim	ענפים
Branches of A"K	H	'Anafe A"K	ענפי א"ק
Breaking	H	Shvira	שבירה
Breaking of the vessels	H	Shvirat HaKelim	שבירת הכלים
Breath – Vapor	H	Hevel	הבל
Bride	H	Kalah	כלה

English	L	Phonetic	Hebrew / Aramaic
Cantillation notes	H	Ta'amim	טעמים
Cantillation signs, vowels, crowns and letters.	H	Ta'amim, Nekudot, Tagin, and Autiot.	טעמים, נקודות, תגין, אותיות
Carving	H	'Hakika	חקיקה
Celestial mentor	H	Maggid	מגיד
Change – Difference	H	Shinuy	שינוי
Chest	H	'Hazeh	חזה
Child - Infant – Fetus	H	Valad	ולד
Choice	H	Be'hira	בחירה
Circle - Circular	H	'Igul	עיגול
Circles - Circulars	H	'Igulim	עיגולים
Cleaving	H	Beki'a	בקיעה
Clothe	H	Malbush	מלבוש
Clothes	H	Malbushim	מלבושים
Clouds of Glory	H	'Anane Kavod	ענני כבוד
Coarse	H	Gass	גס
Colliding	H	Hakaah	הכאה

English	L	Phonetic	Hebrew / Aramaic
Come see (pay attention)	A	Ta 'Haze	תא חזא
Commandment	H	Mitsva	מצווה
Commandments	H	Mitsvot	מצוות
Complete	H	Shalem	שלם
Complete - Finish	H	Gamur - Gmurah	גמור-ה
Completeness	H	Shelemut	שלמות
Concealed - Hidden	H	Ganuz	גנוז
Conduit	H	Tsinor	צינור
Conduits	H	Tsinorot	צינורות
Consequence – Result	H	Tolada	תולדה
Contraction or retraction	H	Tsimtsum	צמצום
Corporeality	H	Gashmiut	גשמיות
Counting of the 'Omer	H	'Omer	עמר
Covenant – Circumcision	H	Berit	ברית
Covered – Concealed	H	Mekhusim	מכוסים
Creation from nothing	H	Yesh Meein	יש מאין

English	L	Phonetic	Hebrew / Aramaic
Creator	H	*Yotser*	יוצר
Creator	H	*Boreh*	בורא
Creature	H	*Briah*	ברייה
Crowns on the letters	A	*Tagin*	תגין
Curtain	A	*Parsa*	פרסא
Curtain	H	*Pargod*	פרגוד
Cutting	H	*'Hatach*	חתך
Cutting – Separation	H	*Nesirah*	נסירה

English	L	Phonetic	Hebrew / Aramaic
Darkness	H	'Hoshekh	חושך
Darkness	A	Kardinuta	קרדינותא
Days	H	Yamim	ימים
Day	H	Yom	יום
Death	H	Mitah	מיתה
Decrease – Diminution	H	Mi'ut	מיעוט
Decree - Edict	H	Gezera	גזרה
Delight	H	Ta'anug	תענוג
Descent	H	Yeridah	ירידה
Desire – Will	A	Ra'ava	רעוא
Desire to receive	H	Ratson Lekabel	רצון לקבל
Deterioration – Damage	H	Kilkul	קלקול
Diagonal	H	Alakhson	אלכסון
Difference – Change	H	Hevdel	הבדל
Digging – Deepening	H	'Hafirah	חפירה
Direct – Straight –	H	Yashar	ישר
Disqualified	H	Pasul	פסול

351

English	L	Phonetic	Hebrew / Aramaic
Disqualified	H	*Pesulim*	פסולים
Distancing	H	*Har'haka*	הרחקה
Distant – Far	H	*Ra'hok*	רחוק
Distinction – Insight	H	*Av'hana*	אבחנה
Disturbance	H	*Hafra'ot*	הפרעות
Divine presence	A	*Shkhinteh*	שכינתיה
Divine presence	H	*Shekhina*	שכינה
Drawing – Extension	H	*Hamshakha*	המשכה
Drawn	H	*Nimshakh*	נמשך
Dress	H	*Mitlabesh*	מתלבש
Drop	H	*Tipah*	טיפה

English	L	Phonetic	Hebrew / Aramaic
Ear	H	Ozen	אוזן
Ears	A	Udnin	אודנין
Ears, nose, mouth	H	Ozen, 'Hotem, Pe	אח"פ
Earth	H	Adamah	אדמה
Edge or side of the face	H	Peah	פאה
Edges – Ends	H	Ktsavot	קצוות
Elevation – Ascent	H	'Aliyah	עליה
Emanator	H	Maatsil	מאציל
Embrace	H	'Hibuk	חיבוק
Embryo - Fetus	H	'Ubar	עובר
Emenated being	H	Neetsal	נאצל
Emenated beings	H	Neetsalim	נאצלים
Encircling	H	Makif	מקיף
Encircling	H	Makifin	מקיפין
Encircling	H	Mesavev	מסבב
Encircling Brains	H	Mo'hin Makifin	מוחין מקיפין
Encircling light	H	Or Makif	אור מקיף

353

English	L	Phonetic	Hebrew / Aramaic
Encircling Sephirot	H	Sephirot 'Igulim	ספירות העיגולים
End – Extremity	H	Sof	סוף
End – Extremity	H	Siyum	סיום
Entrance	H	Kenisah	כניסה
Equivalence	H	Hashavah	השוואה
Essence	H	Mahut	מהות
Essence – Nature	H	'Atsmut	עצמות
Essential	A	'Ikar	עיקר
Evil – Bad	H	Ra'	רע
Evolution - Chain of events	H	Hishtalshelut	השתלשלות
Explanation	H	Bi'ur	ביאור
Exterior	H	'Hitson	חיצון
Exterior Keli	H	Keli 'Hitson	כלי חיצון
Exteriority (The)	H	'Hitsoniut	חיצוניות
Extremities of the hairs on the head	A	Nimin	נימין
Extremity of the Yud	H	Kots shel Yud	קוץ של יוד
Eyes	H	'Enayim	עיניים

English	L	Phonetic	Hebrew / Aramaic
Face or Front	H	*Panim*	פנים
Face to back	H	*Panim B A'hor*	פנים באחור
Face to Face	H	*Panin B Panim*	פנים בפנים
Fall	H	*Nefilah*	נפילה
Fallen – Falling	H	*Noflim*	נופלים
Falling	H	*Nofel*	נופל
Falsehood – Lie	H	*Sheker*	שקר
Female – Feminine	H	*Nekevah*	נקבה
Feminine waters	A	*Mayin Nukvin*	מיין נוקבין
Feminine. Sephira Malkhut –Ra'hel, Leah	A	*Nukvah*	נוקבא
Fifth level of the soul	H	*Ye'hidah*	יחידה
Fifth of seven Tikunim of Arikh Anpin	A	*'Amer Naki*	עמר נקי
Filth – Foulness	A	*Zuhama*	זוהמא
Final goal	H	*Takhlit*	תכלית
Fire	H	*Esh*	אש
First growth of Z"A	A	*Gadlut rishon shel Z"A*	גדלות ראשון של ז"א

English	L	Phonetic	Hebrew / Aramaic
First infancy of Z"A	A	Katnut rishon shel Z"A	קטנות ראשון של ז"א
First intercourse	A	Bia Kadma'a	ביאה קדמאה
First man	H	Adam ha Rishon	אדם הראשון
First Nine	H	Tet Rishonot	ט' ראשונות
First of the three heads of Arikh Anpin	A	Gulgolta	גלגלתא
First rate – Important	H	Meshuba'h	משובח
Fixed – Unchanging	H	Kvu'im	קבועים
Flesh	H	Bassar	בשר
Folding of the legs of Arikh Anpin	H	Kipul Reglaim shel Arikh Anpin	קיפול רגלים של אריך אנפין
Food – Subsistence	H	Mazon	מזון
Force – Strength	H	Koa'h	כח
Forehead	A	Mits'ha	מצחא
Forehead	H	Metsa'h	מצח
Forehead of mercy	H	Metsa'h HaRatson	מצח הרצון
Foreskin	H	'Orla	ערלה

English	L	Phonetic	Hebrew / Aramaic
Form	H	*Tsura*	צורה
Fourth level of the soul	H	*'Hayah*	חיה
Fourth of the seven Tikunim of the head of Arikh Anpin	A	*Ra'ava Demits'ha*	רעוא דמצחא
Frequent – Regular	H	*Tadir*	תדיר
Fringe	H	*Tsitsit*	ציצית
Full	H	*Maleh*	מלא
Future	H	*'Atid*	עתיד

G

English	L	Phonetic	Hebrew / Aramaic
Garden of Eden	H	Gan 'Eden	גן עדן
Garment	H	Levush	לבוש
Garments	H	Levushim	לבושים
Gate – Portal	H	Sha'ar	שער
Gestation – Attachment	H	'Ibur	עיבור
Girl	H	Na'arah	נערה
Giving birth	H	Olada	הולדה
Guarantors - Mutual responsibility	H	'Arevim	ערבים
Guidance	H	Hanhagah	הנהגה
Gulgolta Levanah	A	Gulgolta Levanah	גלגלתא לבנה

English	L	Phonetic	Hebrew / Aramaic
Hairs	H	Se'arot	שערות
Hair	H	Se'ar	שער
Hard	A	Kashin	קשין
Hardness	H	Kashiut	קשיות
Hardness	H	Takif	תקיף
Head	A	Reisha	רישא
Head	H	Rosh	ראש
Hearing	H	Shemi'ah	שמיעה
Heart	H	Lev	לב
Heavenly chariot	A	Merkavah	מרקבה
Firmament	H	Raki'a	רקיע
Heavy	H	Kaved	כבד
Heel	H	'Ekev	עקב
Higher (ה) Hey	A	Hey Ela'a	ה' תתאה
Hidden 'Hasadim	H	'Hasadim Mekhusim	חסדים מכוסים
Higher – Superior	H	'Elyon	עליון
Higher – Superior (s)	H	'Elyonim	עליונים

English	L	Phonetic	Hebrew / Aramaic
'Hirik – Vowel I	H	*'Hirik*	חיריק
His unicity	H	*Yi'hudo*	יחודו
'Hokhma, Binah and Da'at	H	*HaBaD*	חבד
'Holam – Vowel O	H	*'Holam*	חולם
Hole	H	*Nekev*	נקב
Holly – Saintly	H	*Kadosh*	קדוש
Holiest	H	*Kodesh Kodashim*	קדש קדשים
House	H	*Bayit*	בית
Husk – Glow	H	*Klipa Nogah*	קליפה נוגה
Husk (negative force)	H	*Klipa*	קליפה
Husks (negative forces)	H	*Klipot*	קליפות

English	L	Phonetic	Hebrew / Aramaic
Illuminate – Explain	A	*Lehair*	להאיר
Illumination	H	*Hearah*	הארה
Images – Forms	H	*Temunot*	תמונות
Image – Form	H	*Temunah*	תמונה
Importance	H	*'Hashivut*	חשיבות
Important	H	*'Hashuv*	חשוב
Imprint – trace	H	*Reshimu*	רשימו
Imprint –seal	H	*Roshem*	רושם
Impure	H	*Tameh*	טמא
Impure (plur)	H	*Tmeim*	טמאים
In the form of	H	*Betziur*	בציור
Inanimate	H	*Domem*	דומם
Incense	H	*Ketoret*	קטורת
Increase	H	*Hakhpala*	הכפלה
Inferior – Lower	H	*Ta'hton*	תחתון
Influencer	H	*Mashpia'h*	משפיע
Initials of the main destructive Angel	H	*S"M*	ס"מ

English	L	Phonetic	Hebrew / Aramaic
Inner – Internal	H	*Pnimi*	פנימי
Inner Light	H	*Or Pnimi*	אור פנימי
Innovation	H	*'Hidush*	חידוש
*Insemination – Receptio*ı	H	*Klitah*	קליטה
Inside	H	*Tokh*	תוך
Instinct – Impulse	H	*Yetser*	יצר
Intention – Concentration	H	*Kavanah - Kavanot*	כוונה
Interior Brains	H	*Mo'hin Penimin*	מוחין פנימין
Interior Keli	H	*Keli Pnimi*	כלי פנימי
Intermediate Keli	H	*Keli Tikhon*	כלי תיכון
Intermittently	H	*Lifrakim*	לפרקים
Internality	H	*Pnimiut*	פנימיות

English	L	Phonetic	Hebrew / Aramaic
Jerusalem	H	*Yerushalaim*	ירושלים
Joseph	H	*Yosef*	יוסף
Kabbalist	H	*Mekubal*	מקובל
Kamatz – Vowel A	H	*Kamatz*	קמץ
Kindnesses	H	*'Hasadim*	חסדים
King	H	*Melekh*	מלך
Kings	H	*Melakhim*	מלכים
Kings of Edom	A	*Malkin Kadmain*	מלכין קדמאין
Kiss	A	*Neshikin*	נשיקין
Knowledge	H	*Da'at*	דעת
Knowledge of the truth	H	*'Hokhma HaEmet*	חכמת האמת
Kodesh Kodashim	H	*Kodesh Kodashim*	קדש קדשים
Kubutz - Vowel U	H	*Kubutz*	קובוץ

English	L	Phonetic	Hebrew / Aramaic
Lack – deficiency	H	'Hissaron	חסרון
Leah - Partsuf Nukvah	H	Leah	לאה
Legend	H	Agadah	אגדה
Legs	A	Raglin	רגלין
Legs	H	Reglayim	רגליים
Legs of Arikh Anpin	A	Ragle Arikh Anpin	רגלי אריך אנפין
Letters	H	Autiot	אותיות
Level	H	Madrega	מדרגה
Levels	H	Madregot	מדרגות
Light	A	Butsina	בוצינא
Light	H	Or	אור
Lights	H	Orot	אורות
Lights of the ears	H	Orot HaOzen	אורות האוזן
Lights of the eyes	H	Orot Ha'Enayim	אורות העינים
Lights of the forehead	H	Orot HaMetsa'h	אורות המצח
Lights of the mouth	H	Orot HaPeh	אורות הפה
Lights of the Nose	H	Orot Ha'Hotem	אורות החוטם

English	L	Phonetic	Hebrew / Aramaic
Livelihood	H	'Hayut	חיות
Long	H	Arokh	ארוך
Looking	H	Habtah	הבטה
Looking – Observation	H	Histaklut	הסתכלות
Lord	H	Adon	אדן
Love (name of a portal)	H	Ahavah	אהבה
Lower	H	Matah	מטה
Lower (ה) Hey	A	Hey Tataa	ה' אלעה
Lower beings	H	Ta'htonim	תחתונים
Lower Garden of Eden	H	Gan' Eden Takhton	גן עדן תחתון
Lower Nekudot	H	Nekudot Ta'htonot	נקודות תחתונות
Luck - Destiny - Constellation	H	Mazal	מזל

English	L	Phonetic	Hebrew / Aramaic
Make round	H	'Agol	עגל
Man – Human	H	Adam	אדם
Masculine	H	Zakhar	זכר
Masculine	A	Dukhrin	דוכרין
Masculine and feminine	A	Dukhrin Ve Nukvin	דוכרין ונוקבין
Masculine waters	A	Mayin Dukhrin	מיין דוכרין
Material – Physical	H	'Homer	חומר
Measurement	H	Amah	אמה
Measurement	H	Shi'ur	שיעור
Mercy	H	Ra'hamim	רחמים
Middle	H	Emtsa'h	אמצע
Middle	H	Tikhon	תיכון
Middle Nekudot	H	Nekudot Atsma'iot	נקודות אמצעות
Miluy (spelling) of the name ה-ו-ה-י *with a total of 45*	H	MaH	מ"ה

English	L	Phonetic	Hebrew / Aramaic
Miluy (spelling) of the name י-ה-ו-ה with a total of 63	H	*SaG*	ס"ג
Mineral, vegetal, animal and the spoken	H	*Domem, Tsomeakh, 'Hay, Medaber*	דומם, צומח, חי, מדבר
Mitigation – Sweetening	H	*Hamtakah*	המתקה
Mixed	H	*Me'orav*	מעורב
Mixed multitude	H	*'Erev Rav*	ערב רב
Mixture	H	*'Iruv*	עירוב
Mo'hin of Z"A	H	*Tselem*	צל"ם
Moment of bounty	H	*'Et Ratson*	עת רצון
Months of pregnancy	H	*Yar'hei 'Ibur*	ירחי עיבור
Moon	A	*Sihara*	סיהרא
Moon	H	*Sahar*	סהר
Moral	H	*Nimshal*	נמשל
Mouth	H	*Peh*	פה

English	L	Phonetic	Hebrew / Aramaic
Name of a Levush	H	'Hashmal	חשמל
Names	H	Shemot	שמות
Navel	H	Tabur	טבור
Negative force	A	Sitra A'hra	סיטרא אחרא
Nekudot (Punctuation) of SAG	H	Nekudot de SAG	נקודות דס"ג
Non luminous mirror	A	Aspaklaria de lo Nehara	אספקלריא דלא נהרא
Nose	H	'Hotem	חוטם
Nullification	H	Bitul	ביטול
Numerical values of the letters	H	Gematria	גימטריה

English	L	Phonetic	Hebrew / Aramaic
Of the letter ' (yud)	M	Yudin	יודין
Of ה (H)	M	HaHin	ההין
On – On top of	H	'Al	על
One – Unique	H	E'had	אחד
One and Unique	H	Ya'hid u Meyu'had	יחיד ומיוחד
One of the names of G-od	H	Elokim	אלוקים
One of the names of the Creator	A	EHY' H de Alephin	אהי"ה דאלפין
One of the names of the Creator	H	EHY' H	אהי"ה
Opening – Entrance	H	Peta'h	פתח
Order	H	Seder	סדר
Organ – Limb	H	Ever	אבר
Organs – Limbs	H	Evarim	אברים
Other	H	A'her	אחר
Outside	H	'Huts	חוץ

English	L	Phonetic	Hebrew / Aramaic
Parapet (railing)	H	*Ma'akeh*	מעקה
Part of the beard under the lower lip	H	*Shibolet ha Zakan*	שבולת הזקן
Parts	A	*Prakin*	פרקין
Partsuf – Ancient	A	*'Atik Yomin*	עתיק יומין
Partsuf – Long countenance	A	*Arikh Anpin*	אריך אנפין
Partsuf Abah	H	*Abah*	אבא
Partsuf Arikh Anpin	A	*'Atika*	עתיקא
Partsuf Imah	H	*Imah*	אמא
Partsuf Israel Saba	H	*Israel Saba 1*	ישראל סבא א
Partsuf Israel Saba 2	H	*Israel Saba 2*	ישראל סבא ב
Partsuf Nukvah	A	*Partsuf Nukvah*	פרצוף נוקבא
Partsuf Ra'hel	H	*Ra'hel*	רחל
Partsuf Zeir Anpin (Small countenance)	A	*Zeir Anpin*	זעיר אנפין
Partsufim Abah and Imah	H	*Abah ve Imah*	אבא ואמא

English	L	Phonetic	Hebrew / Aramaic
Partsufim Israel Saba and Tevunah	H	*Israel Saba and Tevunah*	ישראל סבא ותבונה
Passing	H	*'Over (im)*	עובר(ים)
Past	H	*'Avar*	עבר
Pata'h – Vowel A	H	*Pata'h*	פתח
Phylacteries	H	*Tefilin*	תפילין
Place – space	H	*Makom*	מקום
Pleasure – Delight	A	*Inug*	עינוג
Plural of Miluy	H	*Miluyim*	מילוים
Plural of Partsuf	H	*Partsufim*	פרצופים
Plural of Sephira	H	*Sephirot*	ספירות
Plural of the letter Aleph	A	*Alphin*	אלפין
Plural of Yesod	H	*Yesodot*	יסודות
Point	H	*Nekud*	נקוד
Point – Dot	H	*Nekudah*	נקודה
Points	H	*Nekudim*	נקודים
Portal – Level	H	*Hekhal*	היכל

English	L	Phonetic	Hebrew / Aramaic
Portals – Levels	H	Hekhalot	היכלות
Practical Kabbalah	H	Kabbalah Ma'asit	קבלה מעשית
Prayer	H	Tefilah	תפילה
Prayers	H	Tefilot	תפילות
Praying shawl	H	Talit	טלית
Pregnancy- Gestation	H	Herayon	הריון
Preparation	H	Hakhana	הכנה
Primordial man	H	Adam Kadmon	אדם קדמון
Prophet	H	Navi	נביא
Prophets	H	Neviim	נביאים
Punctuation - Point	H	Nikud	נקוד
Punctuation – Vowels – Points	H	Nekudot	נקודות
Punishment	H	'Onesh	עונש
Pure – Clean	A	Dakhya	דכיא
Purity	H	Zakhut	זכות

English	L	Phonetic	Hebrew / Aramaic
Rabbi Its'hak Luria Ashkenazi	H	Ari Z'al	ארי ז"ל
Radiance, illumination	H	Ziv	זיו
Ratson (portal)	H	Ratson	רצון
Ray – Line	H	Kav	קו
Rears	H	A'horaim	אחוריים
Reason – Cause	H	Sibah	סיבה
Reasons – Causes	H	Sibot	סיבות
Receiver	H	Mekabel	מקבל
Receptacle –Container	H	Beit Kibul	בית קבול
Recipient –Vessel	H	Keli	כלי
Recipients – Vessels	H	Kelim	כלים
Refined	H	Mezukak	מזוקק
Reincarnation	H	Gilgul	גלגול
Rejects - To push	H	Do'heh	דוחה
Remedy – Protection	H	Segulah	סגולה
Rectifications or actions	H	Tikunim	תיקונים

English	L	Phonetic	Hebrew / Aramaic
Rectification or action	H	Tikun	תיקון
Resemblance – Image	H	Demut	דמות
Resurrection of the dead	H	T'hiyat ha Metim	תחית המתים
Returning	H	'Hozer	חוזר
Returning light	H	Or 'Hozer	אור חוזר
Revelation – Clarity	H	Giluy	גילוי
Revelation of his unity	H	Giluy Yi'hudo	גילוי יחודו
Reward	H	Sakhar	שכר
Rib	H	Tsela'	צלע
Righteous	H	Tsadikim	צדיקים
Righteous	H	Tsadik	צדיק
Rigor	H	Gevurah	גבורה
Rigor – Judgment	H	Din	דין
Rigors	H	Gevurot	גבורות
River – Stream	H	Nahar	נהר
Roof	H	Gag	גג
Root	H	Shoresh	שורש

English	L	Phonetic	Hebrew / Aramaic
Saintly and Blessed He is	A	Kudsha Berikh Hu	קודשא בריך הוא
Saintly and Blessed He is	H	Kadosh Barukh Hu	קדוש ברוך הוא
Sanctity – Holiness	H	Kedushah	קדושה
Scepter of Elokim	H	Mateh Elokim	מטה האלהים
Scepter of Moshe	H	Mateh Moshe	מטה משה
Screen	H	Masakh	מסך
Seal	H	'Hotam	חותם
Sealed – Imprinted	H	Ne'htam	נחתם
Second growth of Z"A	H	Gadlut sheni shel Z"A	גדלות שני של ז"א
Second infancy of Z"A	H	Katnut sheni shel Z"A	קטנות שני של ז"א
Second of the seven Tikunim of the head of Arikh Anpin	A	Tela Debadul'ha	טלא דבדולחא
Second of the three heads of Arikh Anpin	A	Avirah	אוירא
Secret	H	Sod	סוד
Secret	A	Raza	רזא

English	L	Phonetic	Hebrew / Aramaic
Secrets	H	Sodot	סודות
Seeing	H	Reiya	ראיה
Segol – Vowel E	H	Segol	סגול
Selection or clarification	H	Birur	בירור
Separation	H	Prishut	פרישות
Sephira	H	Sephira	ספירה
Sephira Foundation	H	Yesod	יסוד
Sephira Royalty	H	Malkhut	מלכות
Sephira – Crown	H	Keter	כתר
Sephira – Glory	H	Hod	הוד
Sephira – Wisdom	H	'Hokhma	חכמה
Sephira Beauty	H	Tiferet	תפארת
Sephira Bounty	H	'Hesed	חסד
Sephira Knowledge	H	Da'at	דעת
Sephira Rigor	H	Gevurah	גבורה
Sephira Splendor	H	Netsa'h	נצח
Sephira	H	Binah	בינה

English	L	Phonetic	Hebrew / Aramaic
Understanding			
Sephirot - Crowns	H	*Ketarim*	כתרים
Sephirot of BaN (52)	H	*Sephirot Shl BaN*	ספירות של ב"ן
Sephirot of MaH (45)	H	*Sephirot Shel MaH*	ספירות של מ"ה
Service – Duty	H	*'Avodah*	עבודה
Seven kings	M	*Zayin Melakhim*	ז' מלכים
Seven kings	A	*Shev'at Malkin*	שבעת מלכין
Seven lower	H	*Zayin Ta'htonot*	זין תחתונות
Seventh of seven Tikunim of the head of Arikh Anpin	A	*'Hotma*	חותמא
Shabbat, 7th day	H	*Shabbat*	שבת
Shevah – Silent vowel	H	*Shevah*	שוא
Shoulders	A	*Ktafin*	כתפין
Shuruk– Vowel U	H	*Shuruk*	שורוק
Sign (s)	H	*Ot (ot)*	אות (ות)
Simple	H	*Pashut*	פשוט

English	L	Phonetic	Hebrew / Aramaic
Sinews	H	*Gidim*	גידים
Six edges	H	*Vav Ktsavot*	ו' קצוות
Sixth of the seven Tikunim of the head of Arikh Anpin	A	*Peki'hu De'inin*	פקיחו דעינין
Skin	H	*'Or*	עור
Sleep – Somnolence	A	*Dormita*	דורמיטא
Sleep – Somnolence	H	*Tardema*	תרדמה
Smallness – Infancy	H	*Katnut*	קטנות
Smelling	H	*Reya'h*	ריח
Soil – Dust	H	*'Afar*	עפר
Soul - First level of the soul	H	*Nefesh*	נפש
Soul - Second level of the soul	H	*Rua'h*	רוח
Soul - Third level of the soul	H	*Neshama*	נשמה
Souls	H	*Neshamot*	נשמות
Souls (first level)	H	*Nefashot*	נפשות
Source – Origin	H	*Makor*	מקור

English	L	Phonetic	Hebrew / Aramaic
Space – Vacuum	H	'Hallal	חלל
Spark	H	Nitsuts	ניצוץ
Sparks	H	Nitsutsot	ניצוצות
Speaking	H	Medaber	מדבר
Speech	H	Dibur	דיבור
Spelling	H	Miluy	מילוי
Spellings	H	Miluyim	מילוים
Spelling (interior) of the name of 'A"V	H	Miluy shel 'A"V	מילוי של ע"ב
Spelling (interior) of the name of MaH	H	Miluy shel MaH	מילוי של מ"ה
Spelling (interior) of the name of SaG	H	Miluy shel SaG	מילוי של ס"ג
Spiritual	H	Ru'hani	רוחני
Spirituality	H	Ru'haniut	רוחניות
Spreading	H	Hitpashtut	התפשטות
Stone of stone	H	Even Avanim	אבן אבנים
Straight Sephirot	H	Sephirot Yashar	ספירות הישר

English	L	Phonetic	Hebrew / Aramaic
Straight, linear light	H	Or Yashar	אור ישר
Straightness	H	Yosher	יושר
Strong – Hard	H	Takifim	תקיפים
Subordinate	H	Taffel	טפל
Suckling	H	Yenikah	יניקה
Surround	H	Sovev	סובב
Sustenance	H	Mezonot	מזונות
Sweetening	H	Mituk	מיתוק

English	L	Phonetic	Hebrew / Aramaic
Temple	H	*Beit ha Mikdash*	בית המקדש
Three first Sephirot	H	*G' Rishonot*	ג' ראשונות
Three first Sephirot	H	*G"aR*	ג"ר
Tree of Knowledge of Good and Bad	H	*'Ets Hada'at Tov ve Ra'*	עץ הדעת טוב ורע
Ta'amim, Nekudot, Tagin, and Autiot.	H	*TaNTA*	טנת"א
Tefilin of Rabenu Tam	H	*Tefilin De Rabenu Tam*	תפילין דרבנו תם
Tefilin of Ra'hel	H	*Tefilin De Ra'hel*	תפילין דרחל
Tefilin of Rashi	H	*Tefilin De Rashi*	תפילין דרשי
Tefilin of Ya'acov	H	*Tefilin De Ya'acov*	תפילין דיעקב
Tefilin of Z"A	H	*Tefilin De Z"A*	תפילין דז"א
Ten	H	*'Eser*	עשר
Ten plagues	H	*'Eser Makot*	עשר מכות
Tenuous - Refined	H	*Zakh*	זך
There is	H	*Yesh*	יש
Thick	H	*'Avey*	עבה
Thick – Coarse	H	*'Av*	עב

381

English	L	Phonetic	Hebrew / Aramaic
Thickening	H	Ita'but	התעבות
Thickening	H	'Ibuy	עיבוי
Thickness – Coarseness	H	'Aviyut	עביות
Thin - Fine – Tenuous	H	Dak	דק
Third of seven Tikunim of the head of Arikh Anpin	A	Kroma Deavirah	קרומא דאוירא
Third of the three heads of Arikh Anpin	A	Mo'ha Stimaah	מוחא סתימאה
Thirty nine	H	Tal	טל
Thoughts	H	Ma'Hashavot	מחשבות
Thought	H	Ma'Hashavah	מחשבה
Three Heads	A	Telat Rishin	תלת רישין
Three on three	H	Gimel Be Gimel	גימל בגימל
Throat	H	Garon	גרון
Throne	H	Kisey	כיסא
Throne of glory	H	Kisey HaKavod	כיסא הכבוד
Throne of rigor	H	Kisey HaDin	כיסא הדין

English	L	Phonetic	Hebrew / Aramaic
Throne of mercy	H	*Kisey Ra'hamim*	כיסא הרחמים
Times	H	*Zmanim*	זמנים
Time	H	*Zman*	זמן
Time – Moment	H	*'Et*	עת
To allow	H	*LeHatir*	להתיר
To be more stringent	H	*LeHa'hmir*	להחמיר
To decree	H	*Gazar*	גזר
To guide	H	*LeHanhig*	להנהיג
To higher	H	*Lema'la*	למעלה
To hold – Attach	H	*A'hizah*	אחיזה
To live – Sustain	H	*LeHa'hayot*	להחיות
To lower	H	*Lemata*	למטה
To receive	H	*Lekabel*	לקבל
Tree	A	*Ilan*	אילן
Tree of life	H	*'Ets Ha'Haim*	עץ החיים
Troops - Army	H	*Tsevaot*	צבאות
Tsere – Vowel E	H	*Tsere*	צירה

English	L	Phonetic	Hebrew / Aramaic
Under	H	Ta'hat	תחת
Unification – Union	H	Yi'hud	יחוד
Unifications – Unions	H	Yi'hudim	יחודים
Union	H	Zivug	זיווג
Union of the kisses	A	Zivug shel Neshikin	זווג דנשיקין
Union of the Yesodot	H	Zivug shel Yesodot	זווג של יסודות
Unions	H	Zivugim	זיווגים
Unique	H	Meyu'had	מיוחד
Unique – Singular	H	Ya'hid	יחיד
Unknown head	A	Radl'a	רישא דלא אתידע
Upper	A	'Ilaa	עלאה
Upper Garden of Eden	H	Gan 'Eden 'Elyon	גן עדן עליון
Upper light	H	Or 'Elyon	אור עליון
Upper Nekudot	H	Nekudot Elyonot	נקודות עליונות
Upright	H	Zakuf	זקוף

English	L	Phonetic	Hebrew / Aramaic
Vacant	H	*Panuy*	פנוי
Vegetal	H	*Tsomea'h*	צומח
Voice	H	*Kol*	קול
Void	H	*Bohu*	בוהו
Water	A	*Mayin*	מיין
Water	H	*Mayim*	מים
Way	H	*Derekh*	דרך
Well	A	*Bira*	בירא
Well	H	*Beer*	באר
Wheel	H	*Galgal*	גלגל
Wicked –Sinner	H	*Rasha'*	רשע
Will – Desire	H	*Ratson*	רצון
Will to bestow	H	*Ratson Lehashpia*	רצון להשפיע
Window	H	*'Halon*	חלון
Wisdom – Intelligence –	H	*'Hokhma*	חכמה
Without - Nothing	H	*Ein*	אין
Works of creation	H	*Ma'ase Bereshit*	מעשה בראשית

English	L	Phonetic	Hebrew / Aramaic
Works or acts of the Heavenly Chariot	H	*Ma'ase Hamerkava*	מעשה המרקבה
World	A	*'Alma*	עלמא
World	H	*'Olam*	עולם
World of action – of man	H	*'Asiah*	עשיה
World of creation – of the souls	H	*Beriah*	בריאה
World of Emanation	H	*Atsilut*	אצילות
World of formation – of the angels	H	*Yetsirah*	יצירה
World of points	M	*Olam HaNikudim*	עולם הנקודים
World of reparation	H	*Olam HaBerudim*	עולם הברודים
World of the attached	H	*'Olam Ha'Akudim*	עולם העקודים
Worlds	H	*'Olamot*	עולמות
Zeir Anpin	A	*Z"A*	ז"א
Zeir Anpin and Nukvah	A	*Z"uN*	זו"ן
Zohar (splendor)	A	*Zohar*	זוהר

Tables

Different levels of the souls

Soul / World	'Asiah	Yetsirah	Beriah	Atsilut	Atsilut
Nefesh	Nukvah	Nukvah	Nukvah	Nukvah	Nukvah
Nefesh	Zeir	Zeir	Zeir	Zeir	Zeir
Nefesh	Imah	Imah	Imah	Imah	Imah
Nefesh	Abah	Abah	Abah	Abah	Abah
Nefesh	Arikh	Arikh	Arikh	Arikh	Arikh
Rua'h	Nukvah	Nukvah	Nukvah	Nukvah	Nukvah
Rua'h	Zeir	Zeir	Zeir	Zeir	Zeir
Rua'h	Imah	Imah	Imah	Imah	Imah
Rua'h	Abah	Abah	Abah	Abah	Abah
Rua'h	Arikh	Arikh	Arikh	Arikh	Arikh
Neshama	Nukvah	Nukvah	Nukvah	Nukvah	Nukvah
Neshama	Zeir	Zeir	Zeir	Zeir	Zeir
Neshama	Imah	Imah	Imah	Imah	Imah
Neshama	Abah	Abah	Abah	Abah	Abah
Neshama	Arikh	Arikh	Arikh	Arikh	Arikh
'Hayah	Nukvah	Nukvah	Nukvah	Nukvah	Nukvah
'Hayah	Zeir	Zeir	Zeir	Zeir	Zeir
'Hayah	Imah	Imah	Imah	Imah	Imah
'Hayah	Abah	Abah	Abah	Abah	Abah
'Hayah	Arikh	Arikh	Arikh	Arikh	Arikh
Ye'hidah	Nukvah	Nukvah	Nukvah	Nukvah	Nukvah
Ye'hidah	Zeir	Zeir	Zeir	Zeir	Zeir
Ye'hidah	Imah	Imah	Imah	Imah	Imah
Ye'hidah	Abah	Abah	Abah	Abah	Abah
Ye'hidah	Arikh	Arikh	Arikh	Arikh	Arikh

Hekhalot (portals)

	Hekhal / Portal	**Corresponding to**
First	לבנת הספיר (*Livnat Hasapir*)	*Yesod* and *Malkhut*
Second	עצם השמים (*Etsem Hashamayim*)	*Hod*
Third	נוגה (*Nogah*)	*Netsa'h*
Fourth	זכות (*Zekhut*)	*Gevurah*
Fifth	אהבה (*Ahavah*)	*'Hesed*
Sixth	רצון (*Ratson*)	*Tiferet*
Seventh	קדש קדשים (*Kodesh Kodashim*)	*Keter, 'Hokhma,* *Binah*

Sephirot

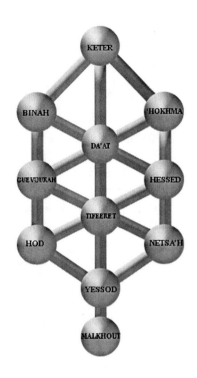

Rigor	Mercy	Kindness
	Keter Crown	
Binah Understanding		**'Hokhma** Wisdom
	Da'at *Knowledge*	
Gevurah Rigor		**'Hesed** Bounty
	Tiferet Beauty	
Hod Splendor		**Netsa'h** Glory
	Yesod Foundation	
	Malkhut Kingship	

389

Vowels

Sephira	Vowel
Keter	Kamatz
'Hokhma	Pata'h
Binah	Tsere
'Hesed	Segol
Gevurah	Shevah
Tiferet	'Holam
Netsa'h	'Hirik
Hod	Kubutz
Yesod	Shuruk
Malkhut	No vowel

The seven main planets correspond to seven Sephirot

Sephira	Planet	
'Hesed	Moon	לבנה
Gevurah	Mars	מאדים
Tiferet	Sun	חמה
Netsa'h	Venus	נוגה
Hod	Mercury	כוכב
Yesod	Saturn	שבתאי
Malkhut	Jupiter	צדק

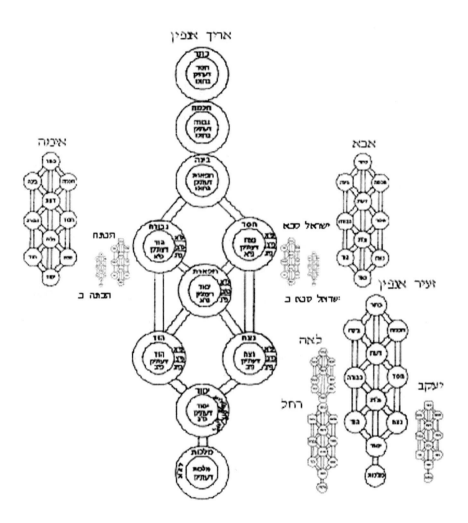

LaVergne, TN USA
29 December 2010
210509LV00009B/43/P